fP

Also by Sara M. Evans

Personal Politics
Born For Liberty

History says, Don't hope
On this side of the grave.
But then, once in a lifetime
The longed-for tidal wave
Of justice can rise up,
And hope and history rhyme.

—Seamus Heaney, from *The Cure at Troy*

TIDAL WAVE

CHAPTER 1

The Way We Were;
The Way We Are

THE "FIRST WAVE" of women's rights activism in the United States built slowly from its beginnings in the middle of the nineteenth century, finally cresting in 1920 with the passage of the nineteenth Amendment to the U.S. Constitution guaranteeing women the most fundamental right of citizenship, the vote. It swelled slowly and steadily, riding this single, symbolic issue. By contrast, a "second wave" of women's rights activism in the last half of the century arose almost instantly in a fast-moving and unruly storm, massive from the very outset. This driving storm, with shifting winds and crosscurrents, never focused on a single issue and sometimes seemed to be at war as much within itself as with patriarchy. Yet that storm, with all its internal conflicts, produced a tidal wave of feminism that washed over the United States and changed it forever.

It is startling to realize that in the early 1960s married women could not borrow money in their own names, professional and graduate schools regularly imposed quotas of 5–10 percent or even less on the numbers of women they would admit, union contracts frequently had separate seniority lists for women and men, and sexual harassment did not exist as a legal concept. It was perfectly legal to pay women and men differently for exactly the same job and to advertise jobs separately: "Help Wanted—Men" and "Help Wanted—Women."

Feminism, the broad banner under which the second wave named itself, not only shattered a set of legal structures that upheld inequalities between women and men but also challenged prevailing "common-

1

sense" everyday practices built on the assumption that women were naturally docile, domestic, and subordinate. Should a corporate secretary also be an "office wife" who serves coffee and buys birthday presents for the boss's wife? Should etiquette demand that men hold open doors for women but not the reverse? Must women change their names upon marriage? Can men tolerate having a female boss? Can women operate heavy machinery or wield surgical knives with meticulous precision? Must women always be the ones to make and serve coffee? Would successful businessmen take legal advice from female lawyers? Can language accommodate the possibility that firemen, policemen, and chairmen might, in fact, be women? Are women's incomes, in fact, secondary? Is a woman working outside the home by definition a "bad mother"? Is a man whose income cannot support his family by definition a failure at manhood? Can rape occur within a marriage?

Many of these issues remain unresolved decades later. Certainly, ongoing inequalities and injustices, such as sexual harassment, unequal pay, job discrimination, female poverty, and restrictions on reproductive rights, are easy to document while the cultural debate on "women's place" continues apace. In many ways the legal structure has changed, but the vision of equality that undergirds those changes continues to be illusive. Women's opportunities for work and for equal compensation remain systematically limited. The structure of work outside the home and the continued expectation that women have primary responsibility for child care and housework still force mothers into impossible choices between the demands of work and of family. And in the United States, as throughout the world, women continue to face unconscionable levels of violence and harassment.

The democratic mobilization of women to challenge inequality and to claim their civic right to be full participants in making changes and solving the problems of the twenty-first century will be essential for the foreseeable future. Indeed, it has always been needed. I use the word *feminism* to name that mobilization and the egalitarian ideas that inspire it. The term "feminism" came into being in late nineteenth century France and was adopted by a segment of the U.S. movement for woman suffrage (the vote) in the 1910s. Those early feminists sought cultural as well as legal change. In the early 1970s, women's rights activists adopted feminism as a common label, bridging enormous ideological and strategic differences. Should women work inside existing institutions, such as the political party system, universities, and corporations, or should they create new ones? Should they prioritize economic rights, reproductive rights, or cultural change? Should they seek alliances with men? Can they work simultaneously on the problems of race, poverty, and militarism while maintaining a focus on sexual equality? The differences among feminists are so deep that some regularly challenge others' credentials as feminists. Yet the energy of the storm that drives them all comes from their shared challenge to deeply rooted inequalities based on gender.

For the purposes of this book, it makes no sense to insist on a more precise definition of the term "feminist": my focus is on the movement itself in all its diversity of ideas, constituencies, strategies, and organizations. There are, however, some distinctive characteristics of that movement as it has ebbed and flowed between the mid-1960s and the beginning of the twenty-first century. Perhaps its most distinctive characteristic has been the challenge to the boundary between the "personal" and the "political" captured in an early slogan, "The Personal Is Political." Under this banner, the movement politicized issues that had long been deemed outside the purview of "politics," including sexuality, domestic violence, and the exercise of authority within the family. It also confronted the ancient association of men and maleness with public life (politics and power) and women and femaleness with domesticity (personal life and subordination). The result was a far more radical challenge (in the sense of *fundamental*, going to the roots) than efforts simply to gain admission for women into the public world of civic and economic rights. It raised questions about the nature of politics and about our very understanding of maleness and femaleness with all it implies for personal relationships, sexuality, and the family, and in so doing, it questioned one of the most fundamental and intimate forms of hierarchy, one that has been used in myriad contexts to explain, justify, and naturalize other forms of subordination. The result of this feminist challenge has been a political, legal, and cultural maelstrom that continues to this day.

I argue here that the brilliant creativity and the longevity of feminism in the late twentieth century is grounded in the breathtaking claim that the personal is political. At the same time, this confluence of personal-private and public-political contained the seed of the movement's repeated episodes of fragmentation and self-destruction. On the one hand, "the personal is political" empowered both individuals and groups to challenge inequities that the culture defined as natural. Women sued corporations and unions; invented new institutions, such as havens for battered women; created journals, day care centers, and coffeehouses; ran for public office; and wrote new laws and lobbied them through. On the other hand, the linkage of personal and political led some to a search for purity, for "true" feminism in the realm of ideas and the formula for a perfectly realized feminist life. The pursuit of perfection made it difficult to entertain complexity, sliding easily into dogmatism. Differences of opinion and lifestyle betrayed the "true faith" and could not be tolerated. Thus, this is a history rife with contradiction: growth and fragmentation, innovation and internal conflict. One cannot understand it without exploring the interplay of these contradictory tendencies, because they are inextricably linked both to the movement's capacity to reinvent itself and to the necessity to do so. Repeatedly pronounced "dead," feminism in the late twentieth century has again and again risen phoenix-like in new and unexpected contexts, unnoticed by those who attended the funeral.

The origins of this deep contradiction can be located historically in the nature of women's subordination in the United States after World War II and in the political context of racial conflict and identity politics at the time of the feminist rebirth in the late 1960s and early 1970s. The creative side of the movement has flourished despite political repression, and indeed often in response to it. Fragmentation and self-destruction have also been driven at different times by economic downturns and government surveillance and infiltration and in the 1980s by a governmentally sanctioned backlash. Yet feminism is still alive and well at the beginning of the twenty-first century. Having accomplished, at least partially, many of its goals, there are many aspects of feminism that have become so much part of the mainstream (language, laws, labor force, and access to professional education) we take them for granted. In addition, current forms of feminist activism are not particularly oriented toward visibility in the sense of large public demonstrations. It is less discernible than it has been in recent decades. Such an eclipse is dangerous, however, as the history of feminist activism represents a heritage new generations need if they are to re-create it yet again.

One of the motives behind the writing of this book is my own awareness that the loss of historical memory would have far-reaching consequences. It would force future generations to invent feminism as if they had no shoulders on which to stand, repeating the unfortunate experience of many in the 1960s. It took some time for the emerging feminist movement to recover its own roots and realize that this was not the first time such issues had been raised and fought for. For example, the so-called "first wave," the fight for woman suffrage, had waxed and waned over the course of a century and in the 1910s it had blossomed into a many-sided movement that mobilized the energies of hundreds of thousands of women. In those years, women's rights gave birth to feminism's rebellious cultural criticism, although it never responded to the demands of African-American women for full inclusion. By the end of the 1930s, however, "feminism" had been marginalized into a narrow, single-issue movement for the Equal Rights Amendment (ERA).[1] In the 1950s, as the generation that would initiate the "second wave" was coming of age, feminism, as either a set of ideas or a social movement, was virtually invisible. Perhaps this explains why such a large number of activists became professional historians. Certainly I am not the only historian who wishes to spare the next generation the rage we experienced about having been cut off from our own history in all its complexity.

The loss of historical memory between the great suffrage victory in 1920 and the post-World War II era has sobering parallels to the late twentieth century. The 1920s, like the late 1980s and 1990s, were a time when individualism flowered among women. In both these eras of flashy wealth, blotting out the continuing reality of desperate poverty, middle-class women gained new access to education and to a broader range of paid jobs and young women engaged in sexual experimentation and lifestyles that offered consumption as a primary form of self-expression. Women's battles, they believed, had been won. "Feminism" was a label that restricted their individuality when all they had to do was go ahead and live out their equality. As Dorothy Dunbar Bromley wrote in *Harper's Magazine* in 1927:

> "Feminism" has become a term of opprobrium to the modern young woman. For the word suggests either the old school of fighting feminists who wore flat heels and had very little feminine charm, or the current species who antagonize men with their constant clamor about maiden names, equal rights, woman's place in the world, and many another cause . . . ad infinitum.[2]

In the 1920s, the white women's movement split in two. It was rent by the conflicting goals of social reformers, on the one hand, for whom women's suffrage was part of a broader agenda that ultimately shaped key aspects of the New Deal and the emerging welfare state, and the National Women's Party, on the other, which focused single-mindedly on passage of the Equal Rights Amendment to complete the process of establishing legal, constitutional equality for women. As that battle erupted again and again in the 1920s, 1930s, and into the 1940s, "women's rights" and "feminism" took on increasingly narrow and distant connotations, feeding popular images of feminists as shrill, elitist, "mannish," and antifamily. Younger women were not recruited, and by the 1950s feminism was so thoroughly marginalized that most young women were entirely unaware of it.

There are significant differences between the interwar era (1920–1940) and the last 20 years, but the similarities are striking nonetheless. The conservative attack on the women's movement has trumpeted the same themes for more than a century, warning against "mannish" women and the endangered patriarchal family. In the 1970s, aroused conservatives like Phyllis Schlafley attacked feminists as "anti-family, anti-children, and pro-abortion." She went on to characterize the new journal, *Ms.*, as "a series of sharptongued, high-pitched, whining complaints by unmarried women. They view the home as a prison, and the wife and mother as a slave."[3]

The Republican ascendancy led by Ronald Reagan in the 1980s endowed antifeminists like Schlafley with intellectual authority and placed people who agreed with her in major administrative posts. Writers like George Gilder, who had insisted since the early 1970s that "women's place *is* in the home," became intellectual insiders, blaming feminists (most of whom in his view were single mothers, lesbians, or simply unmarried) for destroying the moral fabric of America with demands for day care.[4] Despite the Republican embrace of the traditional patriarchal family, the 1980s were also an era of rampant individualism and high consumption. Like the twenties, they were a time when educated women could experiment with newly available opportunities—for careers as well as sexual encounters. As early as 1982, Susan Bolotin wrote in the *New York Times* that women then in their twenties were a "postfeminist" generation. Typically they told her, "I don't label myself a feminist. Not for me, but for the guy next door that would mean that I'm a lesbian and that I hate men." A conservative young woman, Rachel Flick, contended feminism had become "an exclusively radical, separatist, bitter movement." Young women just out of college, confident in their ability to find well-paying jobs and to make it on their own, saw feminists as shrill, bitter, ugly, and lacking a "sense of style."[5] By 1991, Paula Kammen lamented the resulting loss to her generation, which came of age in the 1980s when "young feminists didn't seem to exist." With no access to consciousness-raising experiences or other links to prior generations, they were defenseless against the stigma of feminism. All they knew were the stereotypes: "The twisted, all-too-common logic about feminists goes like this: If you stand up for women, you must hate men. Therefore, you must be angry. Thus, you must be ugly and can't get a man anyway. Hence, you must be a dyke."[6]

The attacks on feminism, however, were far more intense in the 1980s and 1990s than in the 1920s and 1930s. Radio talk shows, for example, fill the airwaves with venomous attacks on "femininazis" (a term coined by conservative talk show host Rush Limbaugh) and use feminism as a foil for expressions of discontent about an enormous range of issues. As an indicator of the major difference between these eras, this suggests that feminism in the late twentieth century, in contrast to the

1920s and 1930s, had continued to be a powerful and ever-changing force in American life, generating new organizations, new issues, and new ideas. It would be a mistake, then, to take the critics at face value. Rather, one must read their venom as a response to something they perceive to be very powerful, and there lies a clue to the story that must now be told.

In this chapter, I describe the necessity of this history, my own argument about the nature and the trajectory of the movement from the mid-1960s to today, and my relationship to the project as both participant and historian. Chapter 2 summarizes the origins of the Second Wave, the dual vision of founders from two generations focused respectively on equality and liberation and the new political terrain created by the process of consciousness-raising. Chapter 3 explores the creative innovations of the "golden years" during which this new movement generated massive changes in laws, revived the battle for the ERA, and founded a vast array of new organizations and institutions. Chapter 4 wrestles with the realities of internal conflict and fragmentation that coexisted with the generative excitement of those early years. It argues that there are historically specific reasons that conflict intensified in the middle 1970s. Chapter 5 analyzes new aspects of the movement in the middle to late 1970s, often emerging out of conflict. The paradox of feminism becomes clearer as we analyze its continuing process of transformation and rebirth. The demise of early women's liberation produced socialist and cultural feminism and a multitude of new institutions ranging from health clinics and shelters to women's studies programs and journals. At the same time, activists in the policy arena consolidated many gains with their connections to the Carter administration (1967–1980) and shared the international ferment generated by the United Nations International Women's Year conferences. Chapter 6 challenges the story of decline in the 1980s, recognizing on the one hand the reality of backlash but on the other the revival of feminism in new forms (e.g., Emily's list) and within mainstream institutions, such as schools and churches. Chapter 7 finds feminism in the early 1990s becoming stronger as a new generation rearticulates the necessity of feminism in a world already fundamentally changed by the women's movement. Backlash against feminism, framed as an attack on "political correctness," had become an obsession for political conservatives. Feminism grew stronger in the aftermath of the Clarence Thomas-Anita Hill hearings, however, and it also drew strength from the massive growth of global women's rights activism in the developing world.

IN THE SUMMER of 1992 at a cabin on a small lake in Ontario, I joined five other women for the second reunion of a women's liberation group that had met between 1968 and 1970 in Chapel Hill, North Carolina. I had just begun to think about the project that evolved into this book, so I asked permission to tape a discussion about the meaning of our shared experience both at the time and in our subsequent lives. Very quickly it became clear that Group 22 (as we called ourselves back then) had been a transforming experience even for those who participated only for a year. The spirit of Group 22 captures some of the excitement of the feminist revival in the late 1960s and was typical of many others. We believed we were changing the world and that what we did could make a difference. The group offered a new freedom from marginalization for women with aspirations for both meaningful work and motherhood. We experimented and created institutions, read about and corresponded with other groups, and in many ways changed our lives permanently.

Group 22 convened in the summer of 1968 when Paula Goldsmid and I both moved to North Carolina from Chicago, where we had met in another consciousness-raising group. I was returning to North Carolina after 9 months of immersion in the newborn women's liberation movement. Previously, as an undergraduate at Duke, I had been active in civil rights, union support, and antiwar work. It was sheer luck that I happened to be in Chicago in 1967–1968, where I stumbled into one of the founding women's liberation groups known as the West Side Group. A neophyte in these national movement networks, I remember myself as one of the silent ones in a group of powerful, brilliant women. I was a sponge, thrilled by the effortless way the movement seemed to grow as group members reported new start-ups every month and travelers from New York, Washington, Ann Arbor, Toronto, Seattle, Berkeley, and Los Angeles came through town with tales of newly forming women's liberation groups. That year in Chicago I must have joined four or five different groups as they emerged, each of which dove into the debates: Just what was the problem for women? Why were they subordinate? What kinds of activism should we initiate to bring about change? While we talked about grand strategies, we experimented with tactics: skits in laundromats and at subway stops (known as guerrilla theater), leaflets, caucuses within community organizations and unions, and special women's workshops at meetings related to the antiwar movement or civil rights. For the moment it seemed that everything worked. The response was electric. As it dawned on us that a new movement was coming into being, we had a thrilling sense that we could, in fact, make history. Women's liberation provided a space where our yen to make the world a better place felt like it had no bounds. I returned to North Carolina in the summer of 1968 with missionary fervor to build the movement. As soon as Paula arrived, we called a meeting.

When Group 22 sputtered into being in 1968, it was the first women's liberation group in North Carolina. We had no name at first, but as new groups quickly spun off or formed independently, such labels as the "single women's group" or the "older women's group" seemed clumsy. So we decided to number ourselves—not hierarchically but randomly, choosing numbers that pleased us: 22 was Paula's favorite number. By early 1970 Group 22 had transformed itself into a children's book writing and publishing collective called Lollipop Power. As Lollipop Power, Inc., it persisted until the mid-1980s, long after most originators moved away.

The early members of Group 22 were in many ways homogeneous, brought together through friendship, school, and work networks: white, college-educated, some of us veterans of the civil rights and student movements. During 1968–1969, many came only once or twice. Those of us who stayed found something there that changed our lives in ways we had been yearning for. Like my Chicago groups, and every other consciousness-raising (CR) group around the country, we searched for ways to ask, and answer, the "big questions." Why are women's choices so limited? How do they internalize a stereotyped view of themselves? Is it biology? How can we raise children without imposing limiting stereotypes? Is it possible to redefine relationships between women and men—marriage, sexuality, parenthood?

Some of these questions prompted action related to what quickly became a central theme of the group: how do we create new ways to raise children, for ourselves and for society? Three of us, who were pregnant when we met in the fall of 1968, planned and executed a child care cooperative in which six parents, mothers and fathers alike, took turns caring for three infants between 8:30 and 5:30 every weekday. It lasted only 1 year, but that cooperative made it possible for me to begin graduate school in the fall of 1969. Several younger women split off to form their own CR group because they found our focus on childhood socialization not "relevant" to their immediate interests. For Group 22, however, partly because most of us had, or were about to have, children, and partly because we had a high concentration of sociologists, the ways that children "learn" to be female or male became the focus. In many other consciousness-raising groups, women talked about and thought through their own socializations. Instead, we were determined to find ways to *do* it differently and to make it possible to liberate children from the constraints of cultural prescription. Ultimately, the need to turn that concern into action led to the creation of Lollipop Power.

Before the first meeting, all of us had already embarked on life choices very different from those of our mothers' generation. Yet more than 20 years later, participants remembered feeling that they were clueless about how to *live* those lives and how to deal with the internal and external criticism that seemed ubiquitous. Several described walking into their first meeting and feeling "at home" immediately. They talked about relief at experiencing social support for their efforts to combine mothering with careers. Even more important, I suspect, was that their strong-minded, outspoken, quirky individualism received affirmation in Group 22 rather than placing them on the margins. Two women, both already mothers, immediately changed their married names back to their birth names. The rest of us did not, but we cheered Linda when she created quite a fuss by refusing to register at the Chapel Hill hospital where she had gone for surgery until they agreed to list her records under her own name rather than her husband's.[7]

Group 22 was downright evangelical. Eager to spread the movement, we helped organize new groups, organized a newsletter so that multiplying groups could stay in touch, and participated in regional gatherings and workshops. We wanted answers (imagining naively that they existed), and we plugged through a mixture of turgid sociological "sex role" literature and angry mimeographed pamphlets that circulated from group to group around the country. In the days before the internet, the inexpensive mimeograph made it easy to disseminate ideas and essays. When we read them, we joined a national conversation about just what this movement was, what kind of change it should advocate, and possible strategies for getting there. Like our sisters across the country, we wanted to change things both in our own lives (renegotiating housework and child care with male partners was a big item) and in the world. In true countercultural style, we looked for gaps where we could create counterinstitutions. Disappointed with the children's literature we knew, we started Lollipop Power and set out to write, edit, and publish our own. Three of us wrote the first three books, and we all vividly remembered that late night at the University of North Carolina campus Y when we and many friends and supporters printed, collated, and stapled our first book. The next year we waged a campaign to force the University of North Carolina to provide day care for employees and students. When that failed (despite a "baby-in" in the administration building), we founded the Community School for People Under Six, still in operation after three decades.

A look at the subjects of the first three Lollipop Power books reveals that our feminism was not markedly different from that of any liberal feminist group, though most of us thought of ourselves as radicals.[8] In simple picture-book stories, we scrambled sex roles—female heroines, moms who study, fathers who nurture—and conveyed a broad sense that girls (and boys) could do anything they choose. *Jenny's Secret Place*, which I wrote, featured a 5-year-old girl who used her mother's study desk as a secret place to dream about freedom, whose father baked her birthday cake, and who shared her secret with her little brother once she fulfilled her dream of learning to ride a two-wheel bicycle. *Did You Ever* showed, in rhymed couplets, that whether you were a girl or a boy "you can do everything." *Martin's Father* described a single-parent family: a boy whose dad cooks, tucks him into bed, and takes him to day care. At first we had no prescriptions beyond our opposition to traditional sex roles.

We also knew that our experiences were not the same as those of all women, though we inevitably fell into language that presumed such commonality. Probably our greatest intolerance was toward the women we felt most judged by, those in earlier generations who, we believed, would accuse us of maternal failure for not choosing a life of total devotion to husband and children. Class difference was a major topic of discussion. We read Lee Rainwater and Mirra Komarovsky on the plight of poor and working-class housewives and told each other stories from our own backgrounds (which were considerably more varied than our current statuses, ranging from working-class ethnic immigrant to professional middle class).[9] There were many perspectives, in fact, that we had few ways to imagine.[10] When the Community School for People Under Six opened its doors in the fall of 1970 in the basement of a black church, the issue of race also became increasingly salient, though, to be honest, in those Black Power years we were mostly waiting for black women to tell us what to think about them. Not surprisingly, by the second or third year, Lollipop Power stories had begun deliberately to challenge the stereotypes of race and class.

Group 22 left a mark on the lives of all of its members. One founded the women's caucus of the American Statistical Association and co-founded the women's caucus of the American Public Health Association; another is a leading feminist scholar and activist in Canada; a third went on to direct the women's studies program at Oberlin and moved from there into collegiate administration; a fourth built her career founding and running day care centers. Several find little direct linkage between their feminism and their current work lives except that they treasure their own independence and believe in their right to meaningful work. Some later came out as lesbians (a topic Group 22 never got around to discussing, although its successor groups certainly did).

In our group, those of us with children thought long and hard about how to raise a new, and different, generation. We realized we were doing this without a compass. Sharing our stories two decades later, we acknowledged that we had all been humbled by the overwhelming power of culture. We asked each other sheepishly, Did your daughters get into Barbies? Did your sons play with guns? How did you get through the teen years? The answers were all over the map. It isn't that we thought we'd be doing this in a vacuum but that we simply had no inkling about how to think. Frankly, the stories we told were not so different from stories about anybody else's kids raised with a strong emphasis on tolerance and respect for others. With a sobered recognition of the role of sheer good luck, we took pleasure in describing the good people our kids have become and comfort in sharing the hard bumps along the way.

At least one member of Group 22 spoke with some bitterness about the impact of feminism on her life. She plunged into professional school, convinced that she could "do anything," but the professional path she tried did not work out successfully. She finds herself now doing work that she does not love and finding pleasure in the details of private life. Our naive search for perfection became, for her, not only "you can" but "you should" and set a standard of expectation that was, finally, undermining. For most of us, however, the legacy of this group, as of thousands of others, is one of greater freedom and new possibility.

For me, the experience in Chicago followed by Group 22 and its successor groups became a springboard into my career as a historian. The questions raised in women's groups about the origins of female subordination and the links between women's liberation and other social movements around labor, peace, and civil rights led me to challenge the knowledge I had received as an undergraduate history major and a graduate student in political science. I recalled the single class in which women were acknowledged to have some historical agency: Anne Firor Scott drew on her research on southern white women to tell us about the importance of women in Progressive Era politics and their utter invisibility in existing historical accounts. At the time I had been too busy fighting other battles to think much about the implications, but several years later that experience endowed me with an unshakable belief that we could recover the stories of women in the past. Although there were no women teaching American history at the University of North Carolina in 1969 and no courses on women's history, several other students arrived with similar questions and we discovered that self-education was entirely possible simply by writing papers on women in connection with virtually any course. Little did we know that we were part of a cohort of several thousand across the country, collectively inventing women's history as a major field of historical inquiry and women's studies as a discipline. The first Berkshire Conference on the History of Women in 1972 drew 800 participants, to the astonishment of its organizers; 2 years later more than 1,500 scholars showed up for a second Berkshire Conference.

Having worked briefly as an organizer, and inspired by the organizers I had known in Chicago, my driving questions had to do with the origins and nature of collective action for change. How is it, I wondered, that those with less power find it possible to initiate change and to act together? How do women come to see themselves as a group with the capacity to make history? I looked at bread riots and strikes, but I also studied women in the Socialist Party in the late nineteenth and early twentieth century, a rather transparent search for foremothers of the movement with which I identified. That led me to the subject of the dissertation I eventually wrote, *Personal Politics: The Roots of Women's Liberation in the Civil Rights Movement and the New Left.*[11] By the time I embarked on that project in 1972, the women's movement had become a massive and highly complex phenomenon. Its history, however, was already being told in ways I knew to be incorrect. The founding of the National Organization for Women could be recounted with ease, but the origins of the groups that called themselves women's liberation were little understood and frequently described as something like an offshoot of NOW. Among feminist radicals, anger at men on the left framed a story in which women in the student movements of the sixties were so victimized that they were virtually driven to form a separate movement.[12] I knew that women's liberation was not an offshoot of NOW, and from my Chicago and North Carolina experiences I knew that most early feminist activists saw women's liberation as deeply rooted in their experiences in the civil rights movement and the New Left.

In *Personal Politics* I argued that parts of the southern civil rights

movement (especially the Student Non-violent Coordinating Committee, SNCC) and the community organizing projects of the Students for
a Democratic Society (SDS) provided unique opportunities for young
women to learn the skills of movement building as well as a set of democratic ideas and ideals (the "beloved community" in the civil rights
movement; "participatory democracy" in SDS) that enabled them to
challenge the sexism they experienced in the movement and in society.
Those movements, in the early years at least, were certainly less sexist
than American society as a whole. And the leadership of black women in
the southern movement, women like Fannie Lou Hamer, Ella Baker,
and many others, provided white women reared in the domestic culture
of the fifties with powerful role models. By the late sixties, however,
both the civil rights and antiwar movements had adopted strongly masculine, even militaristic, language and methods of mass protest that
eclipsed existing female leadership. The stage was set. Armed with
hard-won skills, self-confidence, and the ideals acquired in civil rights
work, groups of women began to turn these assets to their own use, frequently in response to those sparking moments when male arrogance
tried to put them in their place. The parallels to the role of the abolition
movement as a training ground for the first women's rights movement
in the United States were extremely strong. In both cases, also, despite
the intimate link between the movements for racial justice and for
women's rights, the issues affecting women of color were treated as
anomalies and frequently ignored. As feminism evolved in the late
twentieth century, this would become both a central dilemma and a
powerful theoretical concern.

Tidal Wave is in some sense a sequel to *Personal Politics*, although the
scope is substantially different. The first book analyzed the origins of
one branch of the feminist movement that exploded into being in the
late 1960s; this one traces the trajectory of that broader movement
across the succeeding decades with an eye to understanding the shared
dynamics that underlay its immense and complex diversity. The journey
toward this book has been by turns inspiring and painful. It is a history
that I, and many of my readers, have lived, yet from any particular vantage point the larger picture is difficult if not impossible to imagine. My

hope is to contribute to an ongoing conversation about the meanings of that larger picture,[13] as well as to affirm for future generations that they do indeed have a history, by turns glorious and distressing, on which they can build. With this heritage, there is no question that the women's movement will continue to reinvent itself. History cannot predict when, or where, or how. It is simply a legacy, prickly and uneven and only partially understood, but nonetheless proof that women have already changed the world and that they will continue to do so.

CHAPTER 2

Personal Politics

Revolutionary Survival: Lesson One

More women
Should throw
More dishes
At more walls
More often

—Unsigned, November 1970[1]

In the mid-1960s, most Americans hardly knew there was such a thing as feminism. The postwar era's emphasis on suburban domesticity, early marriage, consumerism, and high fertility produced a generation of women only vaguely aware that there were issues worthy of discussion regarding the place of women in society.[2] Yet the terrain on which they lived their lives was changing at a remarkable pace, pulling their experiences increasingly out of line with the words and concepts available to describe them. The pressure that built up in this disjuncture explains much of the explosive force of the women's movement in the late sixties and early seventies, and that energy, like a tsunami that carries the force of an ocean floor earthquake, seemed to flow in all directions at once.

In 1963 Betty Friedan in *The Feminine Mystique* described an aspect of this dilemma as "the problem that has no name." Virtually every powerful cultural institution—magazines, television, advice books, schools, and religious leaders—prescribed a middle-class ideal for women: they were to be wives and mothers, nothing more, nothing less. Friedan called this ideology the "feminine mystique" and went on to describe the isolation of suburban life for highly educated women whose child-rearing years were largely over by their mid-thirties. They enjoyed a life filled with "labor saving conveniences" but also isolated from what many thought of as the "real world." Suburbs gave a new, geographic twist to the old split between private and public, family and work, personal and political. The work suburban women actually did, inventing new forms of creative motherhood and elaborating networks of volunteer institutions, was not seen as, well, *real* work. Invisibility, lack of definition, and barriers to entry into the (male) public world left millions of women to cope with a nameless private anguish.[3]

The privatized definition of the suburban housewife also operated as an all-pervasive force limiting the possibilities and aspirations of additional thousands whose lives no longer conformed to the tenets of the feminine mystique. The dramatic expansion of education and service industries in the aftermath of World War II created millions of jobs for women. Married women entered the labor force faster than any other group in the population through the fifties and sixties, earning incomes that made it possible for their families to enter the middle-class world of home ownership, automobiles, televisions, and higher education for children. They met open exclusion, however, both from higher paying blue-collar jobs and from managerial and professional occupations. Female-dominated jobs, such as clerical work, were ghettos that offered less pay and fewer opportunities for advancement. Until 1963 it was perfectly legal, and very common, to pay women less than men for exactly the same work on the presumption that only men were breadwinners.

The silence imposed on women was a source of pain and confusion in many women's lives but most acutely in the lives of educated women, who received contradictory and ultimately unresolvable messages about their lives. The small but growing minority of professional women in the 1950s faced a lonely struggle. Maria Iandolo New, Chief of Pediatrics at Cornell University Medical College, remembered decades later the chastising words of a medical school dean in 1950 in response to her plea that her application be judged on its merits and not dismissed because she had married. "You are an impertinent young lady, and I am more sure than ever that we do not want you in our medical school." Major law firms routinely rejected female applicants like Ellen Peters, first in her class at Yale Law School in 1954, and Ruth Bader Ginsburg, first at Columbia in 1959 and later a Supreme Court Justice. In 1957, Madeline Kunin, a student at Columbia University Graduate School of Journalism, applied for a newsroom job at the *New York Times*. She was offered a job in the cafeteria. Kunin later served three terms as Governor of Vermont and was President Clinton's Deputy Secretary of Education. While these women persevered, many dropped out when professors announced that "women don't belong in graduate school." Those who persisted hid their pregnancies and paid careful attention to dress and demeanor. Male colleagues encountered in professional settings routinely assumed that the white women present were secretaries, and black women, domestics.[4]

A new generation, raised in postwar affluence, flooded colleges and universities in the 1960s. Many recalled bitterly that they had no idea what their work should be or how to imagine themselves as adults. Their lives were rife with mixed messages. Certainly they knew they were supposed to marry, have children, age gracefully, and enjoy grandchildren, but their actual life choices included college, graduate school, and professional expectations. "In my generation," as philosopher Sara Ruddick put it, "women's work histories were so buried in our life histories as to be barely visible." Unable to write her dissertation while her husband pursued his first academic job, she wrestled with an indescribable "pain of worklessness." "I had learned to think of life as a matter of personal relations, to think about myself as a daughter, wife, friend, and lover. I knew more about myself as a mother, more about babies even before I ever had children, than I knew about myself as a worker."[5]

In June 1967, Marilyn Young, a recent Ph.D. in history, confided to her diary, "How ineffective. I shall live out the rest of my life as if it weren't really happening and then die surprised . . . I have no proper work, and for me that is hard. And I grow lazier, mentally, by the hour." She remembers her life then as happy for the most part, caring for small children and playing the role of faculty wife. Her own Ph.D. in history was just "money in the bank," insurance. "Much later, in a women's consciousness-raising group, I spoke the bitterness of those years. But I . . . I wasn't angry *then*."[6] For such women there was " . . . an invisible, almost amorphous weight of guilt and apology for interests and ambitions that should have been a source of pride," a sense of an unvalidated life.[7]

Women with graduate degrees were still a small minority, but it is easy to detect broad changes in behavior that show millions of women, and men, making choices that no longer conformed to dominant cultural values. The trend toward younger marriage reversed; by the mid-1960s people married later and more of them not at all. The introduction of the birth control pill, which had weakened the link between sex and marriage, also helped accelerate the falling fertility rates as the "baby boom" vanished precipitously. Married women and women with children continued to enter the labor force in massive numbers. Those who dropped out to bear and raise children devoted fewer and fewer years to child care as an exclusive occupation. The flood of young women into colleges and universities was matched by a rising tide of older women returning to continue and complete educations suspended in the 1950s. Millions, then, knew that something was amiss, that they should have more than just a private life, but few could give it a name or link individual experiences to give form to their collective grievance.

When women's consciousness-raising groups began to spring up everywhere, these were the women who walked in the door and immediately felt at home. In later years they talked about the "click," that moment of naming after which the world looked and sounded and felt different—crystal clear and infuriating.[8] In thousands of ways they immediately set out to *do something*, and their actions surged through the landscapes of American daily life.

THE SPECIFIC ORIGINS of the second wave of feminism in the United States lay in the experiences of two cohorts of women, predominantly middle-class, who came to feminist activity with different but complementary perspectives. The older group were professionals involved in the networks surrounding federal and state commissions on the status of women. The younger branch of feminism grew among activists in the civil rights and student movements of the 1960s.[9] Both groups were deeply inspired by the civil rights movement that from the mid-1950s had offered a model of people consigned to the margins of American society, who nonetheless laid claim to their full rights as citizens and in the process enriched and redefined the meaning of American democracy. Each had also learned the skills of public life and developed a belief in gender equality in the sixties through their involvements in government commissions on the status of women and the civil rights movement itself.[10] Then, having discovered their own capacity for public action as women, each found the remaining power of patriarchal structures and mores intolerable. Together they moved to create a new wave of feminist activism.

The founders of NOW came together through a network of government commissions on the status of women. When President Kennedy appointed a national commission in December 1961 and state governors followed suit in subsequent years, they unwittingly facilitated an organized revolt.[11] Professional women on such commissions, or commission staffs, explored and documented the broad patterns of discrimination each had experienced in her own career. Empowered to think about and recommend policy changes, they enjoyed a period of community building and political consciousness-raising, only to discover that as insiders they could do little without organized pressure from the grass roots.

Similarly, young women in the civil rights and student movements engaged in passionate, and sometimes courageous, action in the name of egalitarian ideals. Breaking the middle-class rules of female decorum as they organized for voter registration, taught in freedom schools, and joined demonstrations likely to land them in jail, they discovered themselves as political actors, acquiring the necessary skills as they went along. In the civil rights movement they were immersed in a community long bowed down by racism and grinding poverty but that vibrated with a new sense of rights and collective power. The eloquence and raw courage of southern black leaders, many of them women, contributed to the sense that the vision of a "beloved community" of black and white together was worth risking one's life. Every community, for example, had its "mamas." One SNCC worker wrote that "there is always a 'mama.' She is usually a militant woman in the community, out-spoken, understanding, and willing to catch hell, having already caught her share." He gave the example of 70-year-old "Mama Dolly" in Lee County, "who can pick more cotton, 'slop more pigs,' plow more ground, chop more wood, and do a hundred more things better than the best farmer in the area." These were the same women who risked their lives to register to vote, who mobilized their friends and neighbors to do the same, and who housed and fed white civil rights volunteers at great cost and danger to themselves.[12] The movement was infused with the conviction that the beloved community was more than a distant ideal, it was already visible in the ways they lived their daily lives. When it came to relationships between women and men, however, such egalitarian ideals did not always hold. Too often women found themselves expected to perform the "housework" of the movement, to assume clerical tasks, and to remain outside the limelight. In that contradiction, they found a new voice, claiming for themselves as women the ideals of radical egalitarianism.

THE FEMINIST CHALLENGE owed much of its subsequent shape and character to the broader political climate surrounding its birth. The late 1960s was a time when many saw themselves as "making history" in apocalyptic ways. Popular cultural images of "the sixties" often draw from these years when despair and utopianism fed on each other. The civil rights movement had taken a black nationalist turn, expressing the rage of urban black youth by indicating a willingness to use violence in self-defense and emphasizing racial solidarity. The horrors of the Vietnam War dominated the national news as they reshaped both radical and mainstream politics, even bringing down a president when Lyndon Johnson announced he would not run for reelection in 1968. The assassinations of Martin Luther King, Jr. and Robert Kennedy shook the nation. By 1969–1970, the student movement, never particularly well organized, began to implode, turning against its own national organizations (Students for a Democratic Society, University Christian Movement, and even the student YMCA) amid hypermasculine revolutionary and militaristic rhetoric: "shut down the Pentagon," "stop the war machine," "days of rage."[13]

At the same time, however, assassinations, the inhumanity of war on nightly television, and urban riots contrasted with hippie gatherings, called be-ins or gentle Thursdays, and images of long-haired youth placing flowers on the bayonets of National Guardsmen. Young men as well as women playfully resisted the constraints of gender in hair, dress, lifestyle, and nonmarital sexual expression. That those same young men also referred to women as "chicks," relegated them to housekeeping tasks, and accorded them status based on relationships with male leaders only fueled the rage those women were so shocked and empowered to discover within themselves.[14]

"Equality" and "liberation" were the demands that launched the second wave of women's rights activism. Both slogans challenged the ways women had been differentiated from, and subordinated to, men, but the first drew on the liberal discourse of equal rights and the second proposed a cultural and ideological transformation in which sex roles would be eliminated. "Equality" made a reasonable, liberal request for legal and economic equity; "liberation" raised a set of radical demands about culture and subjective identity.[15]

EQUALITY . . .

WHEN THE FOUNDERS of NOW huddled over lunch at the closing session of a Conference of State Commissions on the Status of Women in 1966, they determined to found a grassroots civil rights lobby for women whose goal would be "to take action to bring women into full participation in the mainstream of American society now, assuming all the privileges and responsibilities thereof in truly equal partnership with men."[16] The NOW statement represented in some ways a modernized version of the first declaration of women's rights in Seneca Falls, New York in 1848 by reclaiming for women the republican ideals of equal participation and individual rights. The founders of NOW included author Betty Friedan, Dr. Kathryn Clarenbach, head of the Wisconsin Status of Women Commission, Caroline Davis and Dorothy

Haener from the Women's Department of the United Auto Workers (UAW), and African-American lawyer Pauli Murray, coauthor of a landmark article on legal discrimination, "Jane Crow and the Law." Mary Eastwood, Murray's coauthor, and Catherine East were critical players behind the scenes who had linked Betty Friedan with key people across the country and pressed her to assume public leadership of what would become NOW. These women's experiences on both state and national commissions had made them experts on legal obstacles and other forms of public discrimination against women. Soon NOW mounted campaigns for strengthening and enforcing federal antidiscrimination laws: picketing against the continued existence of sex-segregated want ads; pressuring the administration to include sex on the list of discriminations prohibited for federal contractors and for enforcement of Executive Order 11375; and insisting that the Equal Employment Opportunity Commission (EEOC) enforce Title VII of the 1964 Civil Rights Act, which prohibited employment discrimination on the basis of sex as well as race, religion, and national origin.[17]

Despite this shared agenda, there were differences of emphasis among early NOW members. When NOW endorsed the Equal Rights Amendment (ERA) in November 1967, founding members from the United Auto Workers had to resign and withdraw the use of union offices and mailing facilities until they could successfully change their union's anti-ERA position (which they did in 1970). Another group left in 1968 when NOW formally endorsed legalized abortion, fearing such a position would interfere with their primary interest in employment and education discrimination. That group founded the Women's Equity Action League (WEAL). NOW leaders worried that the two organizations would compete, but one of the founders of WEAL, attorney Elizabeth Boyer, assured NOW that her organization would not compete for members but would draw in new, somewhat more conservative constituencies so that the two organizations could continue to work as allies.[18]

The spreading networks of overlapping memberships, which sustained NOW, WEAL, and in 1971 the National Women's Political Caucus, included from the outset a significant number of African-

American women in leadership positions. These were professional women who had long worked with white women on such issues as civil rights, poverty, and labor union activism. They could rely on the mutual respect that grew from shared work. Aileen Hernandez, for example, was the only woman appointed to the first Equal Employment Opportunity Commission (created by the 1964 Civil Rights Act to handle complaints of discrimination), where she became convinced that the Commission could not enforce the law against sex discrimination without pressure from the grass roots. She was elected president of NOW in 1970. An even more flamboyant figure was Florence (Flo) Kennedy, who had been a feminist at least since Columbia Law School rejected her application in the late 1940s on the grounds of sex. She gained admission by threatening to sue on the grounds of racial discrimination using what she referred to as the "testicular approach," applying "the right kind of pressure to the appropriate sensitive area."[19] Active in NOW and then in more radical groups and a founder of the National Black Feminist Organization in 1973, Flo Kennedy was beloved by the movement and the media for her colorful and outspoken feminism.

These African-American women and others, such as Pauli Murray, Elizabeth Koonz, Director of the Women's Bureau of the Department of Labor in the Nixon Administration, Addie Wyatt of the Amalgamated Meatcutters Union, Ruth Weyand, Associate Counsel of the International Union of Electrical Workers (IUE), and Dorothy Nevels, a founder of Federally Employed Women in 1968, had come of age in the 1940s and 1950s when professional women of any race were highly unusual. They had battled first for access to credentials and again for the most minimal forms of opportunity and recognition. They knew firsthand the realities of both racial and sexual discrimination, and it does not appear to have occurred to them that they should choose one over the other to fight.

. . . AND LIBERATION

IN CONTRAST TO the NOW and WEAL focus on equality in public life, the radical branch of the women's movement placed private life at the center. The women's liberation movement, as it quickly became known, had little use for formal politics or detailed policy discussions in the first year or two. Its founders saw themselves as revolutionaries. Their model was black separatism, and their driving passion was fury at cultural definitions of women as secondary, inferior sexual objects. Like the feminist foremothers in the 1910s, they mounted a sweeping challenge to cultural definitions of womanhood and femininity. Their first skirmish, in fact, was with an older generation of activists in Women's Strike for Peace (WSP), who opposed war in the name of motherhood.

WSP had represented a revival of the maternal feminism of the suffrage generation and a link to progressive activism from the thirties and forties. An organization of middle-class housewives with progressive, activist leanings, Women's Strike for Peace was founded in 1961 at the height of the Cold War. Proclaiming their concern for peace in the name of mother love, their actions were harbingers of women's reentry into political action in the name of womanhood, but their categories clashed headlong with the passionate proclamations of younger activists. In January 1968, under the banner of the Jeanette Rankin Brigade, named in honor of the first woman in Congress and the only Congressperson to vote against American entry into both world wars, WSP organized an antiwar demonstration of several thousand women in Washington, D.C.[20]

"Radical women," the term "women's liberation" would soon follow, began to meet in small groups in Chicago and New York in the fall of 1967. At a planning meeting for the Brigade held in Chicago by WSP, members of the newly formed West Side Group showed up to express their disagreement with any claim that women's authority derived from their roles as "wives and mothers." The president of WSP, Dagmar Wilson, was on the whole very supportive of the new feminism and hoped that the younger radicals would join their march. The gulf in rhetoric was insurmountable, however. Longtime peace activists simply could not understand the fierceness of women's liberation's rejection of traditional roles. Younger women were utterly unmoved by their point of view, considering it merely another capitulation to societally designated roles. The only self-respecting position from which one could oppose the war, they insisted, was that of citizen or person.[21] The Chicago and New York groups decided to attend the Jeanette Rankin Brigade demonstration to proclaim their opposition to any representation of women that depended on their relations with men and to invite other radical women to join them in their new endeavor. New York women came with props (a coffin and banners) to announce the "burial of traditional womanhood." Kathie Sarachild (note the newly created matrilineal name) offered an oration in which she argued that it was necessary to bury the traditional woman because

> . . . [W]e cannot hope to move toward a better world or even a truly democratic society at home until we begin to solve our own problems. . . .
>
> Yes, sisters, we have a problem as women alright, a problem which renders us powerless and ineffective over the issues of war and peace, as well as over our own lives. And although our problem is Traditional Manhood as much as Traditional Womanhood, we women must begin on the solution.
>
> We must see that we can only solve our problem together, that we cannot solve it individually as earlier Feminist generations attempted to do.[22]

A contingent of about 500 then broke away from the march to discuss this new movement and immediately fell into harsh debate, a harbinger of discord that marked one facet of this turbulent movement from the outset.[23]

In the places where New Left activism remained strong, radical women clashed over their yet undefined goals and methods. Were radical women organizing themselves within a broader coalition of students and antiwar activists, or were they in the process of breaking away to create something utterly separate? Who would be their primary constituency? At what level did they expect changes to occur, and how would they bring these about? The bitter arguments that raged into the early seventies reflected the pain many felt as they faced open hostility and ridicule from men they had associated with, as well as well as growing desperation and internal self-destruction of the New Left itself.

Some women felt they had little to lose in breaking away. Others believed that their identities (as well as personal relationships) were at stake. Ellen Willis put it bitterly: "We were laughed at, patronized, called frigid, emotionally disturbed man-haters and—worst of all on the left!—apolitical."[24] Those who were clearest about breaking completely with what they called the "male-dominated left" called themselves radical feminists and labeled their opponents "politicos." The latter was an unfair designation and the "politico-feminist split" was less a split than a debate in most places. A different theoretical and organizing perspective ultimately evolved from the politico side of this discussion, calling itself socialist feminism.*

The growth of the women's movement thus depended less on specific ideas than on the ability of women to tell each other their own stories, to claim them as the basis of political action. By 1968 the women's liberation movement was clearly separate from the antiwar movement and such discussions had been named "consciousness-raising." They began as a spontaneous occurrence among activists with experience in either civil rights or the student New Left. Women with roots in those movements understood that to act politically against injustice involved personal transformation, and they believed that any movement for change should exemplify the values it sought to bring to the society as a whole. In civil rights this vision was embodied in the idea of "the beloved community" of black and white together; in Students for a Democratic Society it was the ideal of "participatory democracy" and, finally, in the rebellious counterculture, the goal devolved into a more anarchistic response to the impositions of societal authorities: "do your own thing."

Women who met initially to discuss the problems they were having as women within the student movement poured out their own stories and listened in amazement as others described the same patterns. The anger and energy this storytelling unleashed created an opportunity to redefine the world using their own lives as a template. Pam Allen, a member of an early San Francisco group, described women's liberation

---

*See the extended discussion of socialist feminism in Chapter 5.

groups as a "free space" where women could "think independently of male-supremacist values." Early members of New York Radical Women (Kathy Sarachild, Anne Forer, Carol Hanisch, Elizabeth Sutherland Martinez, and Rosalyn Baxandall) christened the procedure "consciousness-raising." True to their New Left heritage, they were inspired by stories of women in the Chinese Revolution who "spoke bitterness" to develop collective support for change.[25] As one radical feminist group (Redstockings) put it in their manifesto,

> We regard our personal experience, and our feelings about that experience, as the basis of an analysis of our common situation. We cannot rely on existing ideologies as they are all products of male supremacist culture. We question every generalization and accept none that are not confirmed by our experience.
>
> Our chief task at present is to develop female class consciousness through sharing experience and publicly exposing the sexist foundation of all our institutions.[26]

Remarkably similar processes can be found in groups that were less eager than Redstockings to discard *all* received wisdom, seeing themselves rather in the context of a broader left and drawing on the Marxist-feminist theories then emerging in Europe. In Bread and Roses, for example, a Boston women's liberation group that formed in 1969 (about the same time as Redstockings in New York), founders recalled,

> When our group started, . . . it was a wonderful time to be in the women's movement. It may have been a unique moment. It felt then almost as though whatever stood in our way would be swept away overnight, with the power of our ideas, our simplicity, our unanswerable truth.[27]

Consciousness-raising was an intense form of collective self-education. "It seems impossible that adults have ever learned so much so fast as we did then. We taught each other sexual politics, emotional politics, the politics of the family, the politics of the SDS meeting."[28] Another

Bread and Roses member, Jane Mansbridge, said: "We had the feeling that we were, like Columbus, sailing at the edge of the world. Everything was new and intense."[19]

Throughout 1968 and 1969 the women's liberation movement grew at an accelerating rate. The belief among movement founders that they were starting a revolutionary process was confirmed by the overwhelming response they met at every turn. It was not necessary to have well-developed organizing skills: just to say the words "women's liberation" seemed to be enough. No one was keeping a list—and many groups existed without the knowledge of others nearby—but the experience in city after city was that groups would form and multiply almost effortlessly. In some places, like New York City, where the movement tended to be highly ideological, multiplication often looked like sectarian hairsplitting. Alice Echols and others have described how New York Radical Women spawned WITCH (Women's International Terrorist Conspiracy from Hell) and Redstockings, which in turn spawned the Feminists. What was really "radical?" Were women's rights, outside a broader left coalition, necessarily "bourgeois" and "reformist?" Or was the left itself a captive of patriarchal thinking? If "women's liberation" was the only truly revolutionary movement, what defined its radicalism? How could it escape hierarchy? Were sexual relationships with men a form of consorting with the enemy? The solutions were not clear, but it was the energy of the debate and the passion with which participants engaged these new ideas that spilled out into dozens of mimeographed articles, manifestos, newsletters, and, by 1970, journals, including *Notes from the First Year* (New York), *Up from Under* (New York), *No More Fun and Games* (Boston), *Women: A Journal of Liberation* (Baltimore), *Voice of the Women's Liberation Movement* (Chicago), *Ain't I a Woman?* (Iowa City), *The Voice of the Women's Liberation Front* (Chicago), *It Ain't Me Babe* (Berkeley) and its spin-off paper, *The Women's Page, Everywoman* (Los Angeles), *Tooth and Nail* (Bay Area), *Sister* (Los Angeles), and *And Ain't I a Woman?* (Seattle).

From the outset, this movement was led by young women in their twenties, veterans of sixties activism. Women's liberation groups appeared on virtually every large campus, to be sure, but they were equally represented off campus. Numbers are difficult to come by, but without question by 1970, women's liberation was on the tip of everyone's tongue and the initiators were in a mad struggle to find the head of the parade! At this explosive stage, however, cracks appeared between radical activists of color and white activists. Many women's liberation groups, for example, emulated the rhetoric of black nationalism, a politics of identity that emphasized separatism, familial analogies ("sisterhood"), personal storytelling, and sameness. They were oblivious to what Shirley Lim calls their "social capital," the shared networks, language, and experience that made calling a meeting easy and intimacy among strangers almost immediate.[30] They also believed, with some reason, that militant black women were not interested. Like others in the white New Left, many women's liberation groups supported the Black Panther Party, oblivious to its virulent sexism, which was only recently described by women in the party, such as Elaine Brown and Kathleen Cleaver.[31] Thus it is ironic, but not really surprising, that radical feminist groups were overwhelmingly white—even more so than their liberal counterparts.

In the summer of 1968, when radical women met to plan a national gathering for the fall, they debated a proposal to invite the participation of black women by contacting Kathleen Cleaver of the Black Panther Party. Yet, one participant argued successfully against such an overture by drawing on her own experience in welfare organizations, where militant black women "set the tone and they manage to completely cow white women. . . . I understand the problem. But they hold the cards on oppression . . . and they let white women know it. I don't want to go to a conference and hear a black militant woman tell me she is more oppressed and what am I going to do about it."[32] In fact, radical white women could not imagine a way to reach out to feminists in racial minority groups because of their own definitions of "militancy" and the authority they accorded separatist black leaders. They were oblivious to the existence, for example, of a group of black women in Mount Vernon and New Rochelle, New York, who by 1969 were actively engaged in an analysis of the problems facing black women in the economy, in the family, and in the movement. In a series of passionate papers they announced that "It is time for the black woman to take a look at herself, not just individually and collectively, but historically," rejecting their "black brothers['] . . . continual cautioning that we must not move on our own or we will divide the movement. . . . [B]lack revolutionary women are going to be able to smash the last myths and illusions on which all the jive-male oppressive power depends."[33]

Most militant black women were also oblivious to the existence of black women's liberation groups, and they quickly perceived the women's liberation movement as white. Fearing co-optation, subordination of the goals of black liberation, and division between women and men in the black movement, many black women expressed disdain: "I don't think any of them are real people involved in anything real. . . . God only knows what their goals are. To me, maybe a lot of publicity for White women to say aren't we great." That many militant black women also expressed a level of empathy, identification, and support for the specific goals of economic equity and elimination of sex discrimination in employment was obscured, however, by their overwhelming emphasis on racial solidarity.[34]

Indeed, given the strong focus on racial group identity in the late sixties and early seventies, it is not surprising that activist women of color began to challenge the men in their organizations at about this same time, but their organizing rarely reached across racial lines, even to other women of color. Within the Chicano movement, for example, women began to hold workshops at least by 1969, but feminists were immediately stigmatized. "Women's lib" and "women's libbers" became epithets used to characterize Chicana feministas "as man-haters, frustrated women, and 'aggringadas,' Anglo-cized."[35] In 1969 at a Chicano Youth Conference in Denver, the workshop on women reported its consensus that "the Chicana does not want to be liberated." Nonetheless, pressure to address women's issues continued to grow. In 1970, a women's workshop at the Mexican American National Issues Conference in Sacramento voted to create the Comision Feminil Mexicana, an independent organization. Their founding resolution stated that "the effort of Chicana/Mexican women in the Chicano movement is generally obscured because women are not accepted as community leaders either by the Chicano movement or by the Anglo establishment."[36] They immediately set out to work on such issues as child care (both legislation and establishing centers), abortion, establishing communication with government agencies to give voice to Chicana concerns, and setting up opportunities for leadership training. Like other small groups, "it has also infused more humor into [members'] work. Now, they can laugh as well as cry about personal problems. A means to discuss anxieties, fears, ask questions that could never be asked of others is available through members of the organization."[37]

Through 1970, Chicanas organized women's workshops and caucuses at numerous conferences and Chicano journals planned special issues on women, despite continuing criticism.[38] When Jennie Chavez wrote an article about Mexican-American women's liberation in the University of New Mexico student newspaper, she "caught more shit than I knew existed from both males and females in the movement." Nevertheless, she organized a women's group, Las Chicanas, that grew strong despite ridicule.[39] This ferment culminated at the first national conference of Chicana activists in Houston, May 1971, when 600 women gathered, eager to discuss their roles in the movement and to create an agenda for Latinas. About a third of those attending, however, defined themselves as "loyalists" not "feminists." One participant recalled that " . . . the fears of being associated with non-movement activities hung over the conference like a confusing and disorganizing paranoia" until the loyalists finally walked out, protesting a resolution declaring that "traditional roles are, for Chicanas, no longer acceptable or applicable."[40]

Similarly Asian-American women and American Indian women began to analyze the problems facing women in their own groups and to organize despite accusations that to do so was divisive. Asian-American students who met in an Asian studies seminar at Berkeley started a group "to critically examine and discuss our roles as Asian women. Significantly, our efforts have been met with enthusiasm, hostility, curiosity, understanding, caution, relief, anger, joy and always—controversy." Out of their discussions came a journal, *Asian Women*.[41] Specific historical realities, however, made it difficult to identify broadly with all women. Not only were most minority women attuned to racial solidarity, but also their responses to specific issues, such as the family or abortion, had a different resonance in each group. The writings of Asian-American feminists, for example, articulate the difficulty they faced in overcoming their own socialization in a culture that overtly devalued women and inculcated values of obedience and filial piety. The daughters and granddaughters of immigrants whose parents remembered internment camps during World War II and lives of harsh and menial labor, they also resented the economic privileges of most women.[41] Native American women, by contrast, spoke about their heritage of ancient traditions of female power, which had been eroded by the imposition of white forms of government; families that had never been small and nuclear; and issues regarding land, education, health, and sheer survival. Their women's organizations in the 1970s defined their mission in relation to the Indian community as a whole.[43]

Thus, although within 2–3 years there were women's caucuses, workshops, journals, and/or organizations in virtually every racially identified group, the women's liberation movement continued to be perceived as predominantly white. In contrast to racial minorities, white women, as members of a racial majority, were the norm, rarely thinking of themselves in racial terms, and they felt no pressure to sustain a political connection based on shared oppression with white men. As a result they found it easy to identify themselves with "all women" and to assume that their analyses and ideas could and should apply to all. "Intimacy and mutuality," as Shirley Lim has pointed out, was premised on "exclusivity."[44] In such a situation the difficulties facing any interracial coalition of women were profound, and they shaped the subsequent evolution of the women's movement. Those who made a serious effort to work on issues of common concern usually stumbled.

Barbara Grizzuti Harrison described an attempt to work across racial lines among parents at a school in Brooklyn in 1971, who organized a "sex roles" committee to press for curricular change: "When black women attended Sex Roles Committee meetings, those meetings were occasions for bewilderment, acrimony, anger, and pain. We wanted a feeling of solidarity with black women, both because it was an emotional necessity for us, and because we deemed it a tactical necessity to present a united front to the school. But the differences between black women and white women were so profound that goodwill, kindness, and intelligence were not always enough." White women idealized black women, imagining them to be united and strong. Black women were not really all that united, but they did share a deep anger toward white women, whose solicitude seemed condescending and who didn't really see racism as the most important issue. Interactions were difficult. In the face of black women's anger, white women remained silent, acquiescent. Vulnerable to the criticism that the women's movement was white and middle class, "we needed the black women . . . to assuage our guilt and to disarm òur critics."[45]

When Harrison interviewed several black women at length, she discovered some of the issues and realities that undergirded their anger: "My mother took care of rich white kids." "I didn't think they were oppressed; I thought they were cowards."[46] Another woman pointed out that white women's capitulation was part of a useless rhetorical dance: " . . . you people got sucked in every time. Why did you fall all over yourselves when guilt was laid on you? . . . When black women are doing their thing by showing off and whites do their thing by accepting guilt, we're nowhere."[47]

Feminists of color had to wage a lonely struggle to find a feminist voice of their own in these first years. Fran Beal founded the Women's Liberation Committee of SNCC in 1968. She recalled shivering in a Harlem doorway in the winter of 1970, gathering courage to give an invited speech to " . . . a group of nationalists who preached that the demand for women's rights was a white plot to divide the black Liberation Movement, that abortion was genocide, and that women should be supporting the men's new-found 'manhood' by walking ten steps behind. I was the designated hitter and felt as if I was about to become the main attraction at a metaphorical lynching party." She gave her talk, and "[w]hile no one called for my head, no one stood and supported our views. As I exited the room, however, two young women whispered to me, 'Right on, sister.' I never forgot those quiet expressions of support. . . ."[48]

Among college and university students in the late 1960s, however, the YWCA offered a space for unity of black and white women primarily around issues of race. Renetia Martin was a student at Berkeley in the late 1960s. The black student movement she found there discouraged women's leadership. The student YWCA, however, was a women's organization that linked her to an older generation of black female leaders and the possibility of interracial discussion. Black women in the YWCA, under the leadership of Dorothy Height and Valerie Russell, were already wrestling with the meaning of black power, and they organized a separate meeting before the YWCA National Convention in Houston in April 1970. Young women (17–35) also held a separate meeting, and Renetia, Chair of the National Student YWCA and therefore a leader in both, became a pivotal figure in pushing adult blacks toward militancy while winning the active support of young women of all colors. When the formal conference opened, 2,700 women, "all kinds, all ages, all shapes, all sizes," met in a hall hung with banners "for peace, for justice, for freedom, for dignity." Young women declared their activism and their discomfort with religious labels, naming themselves Young Women Committed to Action. All 500 black delegates stood as their report was read, demanding that the fight against racism become the singular focus of the YWCA. In response, the convention adopted the One Imperative: "To thrust our collective power toward the elimination of racism wherever it exists and by any means necessary." Everyone present still remembers slender, militant young Renetia Martin pronouncing her benediction: "In the name of Malcolm, Martin and Jesus—Power to the struggle."[49]

Following the convention, Renetia returned to Berkeley where, through the auspices of the campus YWCA, she began to organize personal support groups for black women. The demand for such groups was huge, and the women who came were filled with pain. These were, in fact, consciousness-raising groups, but they did not go by that name and they remained primarily focused on personal support rather than political action.[50] Black nationalists had made the reclamation of "manhood" a centerpiece of the black movement by the early seventies.[51] They were perhaps the most vociferous, but similar attitudes also prevailed in the Chicano movement, the militant American Indian Movement (AIM), and Asian-American civil rights movements as well. Black feminism had no room to breathe. Consciousness-raising was about all that could be done.

THE ENERGY OF INTERNAL conflict was the flip side of an immense creativity unleashed by the women's movement between 1967 and 1975. In these heady days, the women's movement was decentralized in the extreme. Unaware of historical precedents, they replicated the brilliant "Do Everything" policy of Frances Willard in the 1880s. As President of the Women's Christian Temperance Union, Willard announced that local chapters would choose their own focus. Unconstrained by national priorities that were either too radical or too restrictive for their own taste, the WCTU chapters rapidly became a major force for progressive reform, stretching their opposition to alcohol and immoral male behavior to include activism in behalf of children (founding kindergartens and the PTA), working women, female prisoners, and even suffrage.[52]

Similarly, NOW's structure encouraged the creation of "task forces" at the local and national levels on virtually any topic. These, in turn, issued a string of reports—on sexism in education, legal discrimination, or violence against women—with recommendations for action. Eleanor Smeal recalled that "We were not real philosophical in those days [the early 1970s in Pittsburgh]. We became instant experts on everything. On child care. Started our own nursery school. We worked on employment cases. . . . First we started organizing local NOW chapters. Then we organized the state. I went to every village and town, organizing; if you have just one or two people, you can get a chapter going. I organized housewives. Because that's where I was. You have to do what you know. It never occurred to me that we weren't going to get housewives, and we did. We have."[53]

Women's liberation, with its antistructure, antileadership, "do your own thing" ethos, spawned thousands of projects and institutions. Most of those actions will probably never be recorded precisely because they were so spontaneous and ubiquitous. Jan Schakowsky, for example, was aware of the women's movement in 1968 and 1969, but as a suburban housewife she had no idea how to get involved. With two kids in diapers, "I felt totally trapped." But she found time to read about feminism between diaper changes and at naptime. "By the time my husband walked in the door all hell would break loose. He was responsible for all the evils of the world and especially responsible for keeping me trapped. What kind of person was he? Didn't he understand?" She felt supported by "all those unseen people" she was reading about. "I knew that if I ever met Gloria Steinem we would be best friends." Her first consciousness-raising group was a consumer action group she and her neighbors formed in the early 1970s. They initiated a meat boycott to protest inflationary prices and spent their meetings discussing their problems as women "and the kinds of changes as women that we had to go through in order to face those things."[54]

The accelerating spread of the women's movement finally caught the national media's attention in 1968 and 1969. Between January and March 1970, substantial stories on the movement appeared in virtually every major journal and broadcast network.[55] Media attention tended to be condescending if not hostile, but the powerful message overrode its medium. Indeed, the zeal of feminists was fed in equal parts by their optimism that an egalitarian world was possible and by the hostility and derision they met at every turn. They may have felt, initially at least, that they were simply claiming a birthright, the opportunity to pursue their own dreams and to participate as equals in public and private life. But leftists shouted at feminist speakers, "Take her off the stage and fuck her!" and on ABC News a senator called women's liberation a bunch of "braless bubble heads."[56] *Time* took note of the new movement with the claim that "the radical women have opened a Pandora's box. But that of course is their birthright. They are her direct descendant." *Time* announced 4 months later that " . . . last week the movement scaled new *piques*. . . ."[57] When the U.S. House of Representatives passed the Equal Rights Amendment in August 1970, the *New York Times* editorialized on "The Henpecked House," and James J. Kilpatrick described the ERA as "the contrivance of a gang of professional harpies. . . . [M]en who voted for this resolution had but one purpose in mind, to get these furies off their backs."[58] In general, media coverage sensationalized and mocked women's liberation with nicknames like "women's lib" and "libbers."[59] One editor was known to have instructed a journalist to "get the bra-burning and karate up front."[60]

No bras were burned at least in the early years, when the "bra-burner" epithet appeared, although one of the organizers of a demonstration against the Miss America Pageant in August 1968 suggested ahead of time to a journalist that they might be.[61] Instead, participants tossed "objects of female torture" (girdles, bras, curlers, issues of the *Ladies Home Journal*, and so on) into a "freedom trash can," auctioned off an effigy of Miss America ("Gentlemen, I offer you the 1969 model. She's better every year. She walks. She talks. She smiles on cue. *And* she does housework."), and crowned a live sheep.[62]

Only 2 years later, proliferating groups and media coverage had made the new feminism a major topic of national debate. Many mainstream institutions faced feminist insurgencies from within as well. Sheila Collins described herself "as one of those odd birds, an aroused woman, and also as a former seminary student now a minister's wife and the mother of two preschool-age children. . . ." In 1969, she and several other women in the New York Conference of the United Methodist Church "formed a task force to discuss the 'woman' issue and to influence our church to take some kind of action in regard to women's liberation." Their concern, like that of numerous other small groups interested in sex role socialization, was to analyze and to challenge the images of girls and boys that dominated their denomination's Sunday school curricula. "The church must repudiate once and for all the unchristian formula of male superiority-female inferiority. . . . [It] can begin to join the revolutionary age by taking a second look at its own literature."[63] Soon after that the national magazine of the Methodist Student Movement, *motive*, published one of the earliest collections of women's liberation writings in a special issue edited by Charlotte Bunch and Joanne Cook.[64]

When NOW called for a "women's strike" on August 26, 1970 in commemoration of the fiftieth anniversary of the passage of the 19th Amendment to the Constitution granting women the right to vote, the national scope of this new movement became visible to activists and observers alike. Its insistence on the politics of personal life were likewise on display as women took action under the slogan: "Don't Iron While the Strike is Hot." *Life* magazine reported that

> . . . in Rochester, NY, women shattered teacups. In Syracuse they dumped 50 children in the city hall. In New York City, Boston and Washington thousands marched and rallied and hundreds more held teach-ins and speech-ins in dozens of other cities. Women's liberation is the liveliest conversational topic in the land, and last week, all across it, the new feminists took their argument for sexual equality into the streets. . . .[65]

In New York City between 20,000 and 50,000 women staged the largest women's rights rally since the suffrage movement, blocking Fifth Avenue during rush hour. Theatrical and humorous actions abounded: a guerrilla theater group in Indianapolis portrayed the middle-class female life cycle from "sugar and spice" to "Queen for a Day"; Boston women chained themselves to a huge typewriter; women in Berkeley marched with pots and pans on their backs; New Orleans reporters ran engagement announcements under photos of future grooms; stewardesses carried posters challenging discriminatory airline rules (about which they did, in fact, successfully sue): "Storks Fly—Why Can't Mothers?"[66]

THE CONTAGION OF FEMINISM lay in its ability to touch women at a deeply personal level, politicizing matters that were previously taken for granted as "the way things are." When *Newsweek* published a cover story on the women's movement it hired a freelance writer, having rejected versions by the few females in the ranks of reporters and editors. The day the cover story reached the newsstands, however, a group of women on the staff called a press conference to announce that they had filed a sex discrimination complaint with EEOC. At that time all but one of the *Newsweek* research staff were women; all but one of its fifty-two writers were men.[67]

Sophy Burnham laughed when she received an assignment from *Redbook* to do a story on the women's movement. "A lunatic fringe," she thought. But "within a week I was so upset, I could hardly focus my ideas." In 4 months of listening to women's anger, pain, and quest for identity, "chords were struck that I had thought long dead. . . . I thought I had come to terms with my life; but every relationship—husband, child, father, mother—was brought into question." By the end she was a convert: "I am now offended by things that would never have bothered me before. I am now a feminist. I am infused with pride—in my sisters, in myself, in my womanhood."[68]

The wide spectrum of feminist activism that existed by 1969–1971 in many cities attracted a broad range of women. NOW and WEAL chapters (and in 1971 the National Women's Political Caucus) attracted middle-class professional and semiprofessional women who had experienced discrimination in employment and in the political arena. These were women who were ready to jump in and work systematically both in the courts and in the legal system. Radical groups, in contrast, drew first on a constituency of New Left activists. Consciousness-raising also drew in women who were attracted to the idea of a women's movement but who came with many questions about whether women were really oppressed and in what ways. These two modes of organizing soon overlapped.

For example, Iowa feminist Bev Mitchell recalled, "I became a feminist in 1971 when I went to Chicago for a weekend with my someday-to-become-ex-husband. We were just two Nebraskans gawking at the big buildings. There was a women's liberation rally in Grant Park. It was just about the most exciting thing I had ever been to. It was also scary. I remember one woman dressed in nothing but the American flag. Her fingernails were three inches long and she had a sparkly top hat. It was fabulous. It was the first time I had ever been to a speech or a political rally where I agreed with every single point, or it was something I had never thought of before and in the next twenty minutes I mulled it over, and said, 'Yes, that is true.'"

Back in Cedar Rapids, Iowa, she joined several other women she had met in graduate school in Cedar Rapids to form a women's liberation group. When they learned another group had met the same week, the two joined forces. The second group had been convened by the (then) wife of a major industrialist in Cedar Rapids. The combined group included prominent, powerful women and countercultural leftists alike.

When they learned that the Cedar Rapids civil rights code omitted women altogether,

> Sally Madden and the other important women went on a rampage. They just said, 'You will do this.' They were supported by the scary, hippie women, . . . women dripping with beads. Remember that the eleventh commandment of waspdom is, 'Thou shalt not make a scene.' We used this as a tool. The men on the [civil rights] commission were not used to seeing blue-collar women. They were scared to death that between their wives, who were capable of incredible fury, and these hippies, God knows what would happen. So protection for women was put in the code.[69]

This group went on to desegregate lunchrooms with sit-ins and set up child care, self-defense, and women's medical self-help classes; they "made honest men of the media by having a Summer Camp Bra-Burn, two weeks of tent/trailer lakeside encampment for women and children. . . . Every morning we raised a bra on an improvised flagpole while a member . . . played 'God Bless America' on her kazoo." After the passage of Title IX, a member of the school board sent a carefully marked copy of the Cedar Rapids school system budget anonymously. With compelling evidence of disparate expenditures on sports for girls and boys in hand, they filed a successful Title IX complaint. In 1973 the group agreed to affiliate with NOW, primarily to prevent an anti-ERA woman from forming a chapter there, but they kept their original name, Cedar Rapids Woman's Caucus.[70]

Music and the visual and performing arts were also part and parcel of the women's liberation movement from the outset and a major form of consciousness-raising outreach. Women's liberation rock bands emerged in Chicago, New Haven, and Austin determined to "take the sexism out" by writing new words and tunes and by doing everything (playing instruments, serving as sound technicians, and moving equipment) rather than being only vocalists.[71] Women artists responded to the movement with a new sense of their work and their audience. In 1969, painter and sculptor Judy Chicago began to describe her own work as using explicitly female imagery "to show that the subject matter of my work is my identity as a woman." She and other artists felt released by the women's movement from striving for neutrality (or at least avoiding work that could be viewed as "feminine"). "Until the Women's Movement came along, I felt unable to say that my work was not about plastic or color but about my investigation of my vagina as a metaphysical question."[72] In 1970, Chicago announced an exhibition at California State University Fullerton and her legal name change (from a married name that she never actually used) with a photo of herself as a prizefighter, lolling in her corner of the ring with brazen arrogance. The announcement read: "Judy Chicago: a name change and an across-the-board feminist challenge."[73]

For many feminists, art became one way of building the movement, and the focus of women's art was intensely personal and self-reflective: consciousness-raising in another medium.[74] At their show in New York entitled "Women's Art" in 1971, Vivian and Emily Kline focused on daily, domestic objects: a clothesline, bridge cards, a lace tablecloth, chocolate candy, a mop, pink curlers, Tampax, a corsage, a bridal veil. They made them gigantic—a 12 foot mop, a 6 foot Tampax—as conceptual art. Dozens of other artists took up the themes of personal exploration, using images of childbirth to represent women's oppression as well as women's creativity. The result, for observers, was a participatory experience "of doing instead of just being, . . . [of looking] at ourselves with sympathy, not shame. . . ."[75] By 1975, Lucy Lippard could argue that conceptual art as a whole had been redirected by women. "The turn of Conceptual Art toward behaviorism and narrative about 1970 coincided with the entrance of more women into its ranks and with the turn of women's minds toward questions of identity raised by the feminist movement."[76] Playing with identity, an artist like Martha Wilson photographed herself as a man and then as a man dressed as a woman. "Art-making is an identity-making process . . . I could generate a new self out of the absence that was left when my boyfriend's ideas, my teachers' and my parents' ideas were subtracted."[77]

CONSCIOUSNESS-RAISING WAS most powerful in the first 5 years of the women's movement. With CR groups, women discovered that their experiences were not unique but part of larger patterns, and they discovered female community. They named themselves a sisterhood, a familial metaphor for an emerging social and political identity that captured the key qualities of egalitarianism, love, and mutual responsibility. Because the groups had little or no structure, they could be formed anywhere, from offices to churches to neighborhoods. At meetings, women discovered that the personal issues of daily life—housework, child rearing, sexuality, etiquette, and even language—could be political issues susceptible to collective action and change. Nothing was beyond discussion.

This spreading debate soon infected informal female networks, such as office and neighborhood friendships, religious groups, and other voluntary associations. The new feminism necessitated extensive redefinition of roles, attitudes, and values because the traditional definitions of women and men were so at odds with women's actual experience. Feminists argued vehemently about whether the division between public and private was universal or particular to American society in recent times and whether women were essentially different from or the same as men. The heat of their debate opened new windows on women's lives as individuals and as citizens and marked the difficulty of devising new categories for their changing reality.

At first, whatever anyone tried, the movement grew. The liberal desire to battle discrimination in the legal arena, the radical feminist insistence on awakening a female "class consciousness," and the socialist-feminist attraction to community organizing—all "worked," and each reshaped the other. NOW task forces on working women, for example, by the early seventies found ready allies among women in emerging socialist-feminist groups interested in organizing clerical workers.[78] Similarly, NOW task forces on health and education paralleled and sometimes joined forces with such efforts as rape crisis hot lines or curriculum reform generated by women's liberation groups.

Yet the radical feminist experiments with extreme forms of democracy, some of them quite rigid, created problems that pervaded all branches. Any activist who received media attention, for example, was likely to be dubbed a "star" and urged to step aside so that other women could share the limelight. Some groups sought to equalize participation in discussion by passing out tokens. When anyone spoke she used one of her tokens, and once the tokens were gone she had no more access to the floor. Similarly, groups that insisted that they would have no leaders quickly succumbed to what Jo Freeman (founder of the West Side Group in Chicago) later called the "tyranny of structurelessness," in which leaders denied their own roles and groups found themselves incapable of holding anyone accountable.[79]

Nonetheless, as women analyzed and politicized the embodied experience of being female and the supposedly "natural" familial roles of wife, mother, and daughter, they also invented new institutions and modes of public action. The range of these actions illustrates their energetic belief that anyone could take action and could make history. Feminists politicized issues relating to the body (rape, violence, abortion, and sexuality) and to the family (marriage and child care) simply by following through on intuitions and patterns discovered in the process of consciousness-raising. Little could they know in these early years that cultural issues like abortion, "family values," and sexual preference would etch deep and lasting fault lines in the American body politic.

The Politics of the Body

From the beginning, feminists focused on highly intimate subjects. Groups analyzed childhood experiences for clues to the origins of women's oppression, they discussed relations with men, marriage, and motherhood, and they talked about sex. Frequently, discussion led to action, and action on one topic led to another. For example, in an early meeting of New York Radical Women, several women described their experiences with illegal abortion. For most it was the first time they had told anyone beyond a close friend or two. A group of women, subsequent founders of Redstockings, then decided to disrupt a legislative hearing scheduled to hear testimony from fourteen men and one woman (a nun). Claiming that women who had experienced abortion were the "real experts," they demanded to testify. When the legislative committee refused to hear them, they held a public "speak-out" on March 21, 1969, drawing an audience of 300.[80] Thousands of women,

hearing about such speakouts, joined in. Journalist Gloria Steinem recalled that "For the first time, I understood that the abortion I had kept
so shamefully quiet about for years was an experience I had probably
shared with at least one out of four American women of every race and
group."[81]

Women's liberation groups thus made themselves the "shock troops"
of abortion rights, joining an already active abortion law reform movement.[82] For the most part they offered public education alongside services and assistance to women rather than lobbying for reform.
Numerous groups, for example, began to assist women seeking illegal
abortions to find competent doctors. Word of mouth usually resulted in
a flood of requests. In Chicago, members of the Chicago Women's Liberation Union began offering counseling and referrals in 1969, continuing work done by Heather Booth with help from some members of the
West Side Group. Calling themselves Jane, they began to shift in late
1970 from making referrals to doing the abortions themselves. By the
time they disbanded in 1973, abortion collective members estimate that
they had performed over 11,000 illegal abortions with a safety record
that matched that of doctor-performed legal abortions.[83]

At about the same time that "Jane" arose, a consciousness-raising
group made up primarily of graduate students and writers for an underground newspaper in Austin, Texas also shifted its focus to abortion referral. They built an alliance with local members of the Clergy
Consultation Service on Abortion who maintained close contacts with
doctors to ensure high-quality services, and by 1973 they referred more
than 6,000 women. In September 1969, sitting around at a garage sale
to raise money for the group, Sarah Weddington, a recent law school
graduate, discussed with another group member the legal risks of their
activities and volunteered to do some legal research. That research revealed that outside of Texas, where the law forbade abortion even in
cases of rape and incest, judicial and legislative precedents offered reason for hope. Thus began the process that resulted in the landmark
Supreme Court case, *Roe v. Wade*, in which Sarah Weddington argued
her first case at the age of 25.[84]

Sarah Weddington's small group had initially formed in the fall of

1969 to discuss a pamphlet entitled "Women and Their Bodies" by a women's health collective in Boston. The collective had formed as a result of a series of discussions about female sexuality within Bread and Roses. Inspired to gather information about women's health, they named themselves the "doctor's project." They first created a recommended list of female gynecologists, then moved on to teach a course and to write the pamphlet that found its way to Austin. Even after the demise of Bread and Roses, this group continued as the Boston Women's Health Book Collective and formally published a revised edition of their pamphlet as a book, *Our Bodies, Ourselves*. Still in print, the book demystifies medical expertise by giving women direct information through personal stories and narratives stressing women's sexual self-determination.[85] Similarly, Anne Koedt's paper, "The Myth of the Vaginal Orgasm," and the enthusiasm elicited in early workshops on sexuality, made understanding orgasm and learning to masturbate regular items at consciousness-raising sessions. One of the most common memories of such groups revolves around the moment when one woman confesses that she had faked orgasm; one after another would acknowledge the same.[86]

Efforts to increase women's sexual autonomy frequently sparked concerns about the problem of sexual violence as well. Cell 16 in Boston made headlines with its advocacy of female celibacy (which never really caught on) and karate for self-defense (which did). One of the classic realizations in CR groups had to do with the sexual objectification and vulnerability of women in public. Meredith Tax, a founder of Bread and Roses, described the daily experience of young women:

> A young woman is walking down a city street. She is excruciatingly aware of her appearance and of the reaction to it (imaginary or real) of every person she meets. She walks through a group of construction workers who are eating lunch in a line along the pavement. Her stomach tightens with terror and revulsion; her face becomes contorted into a grimace of self-control and fake unawareness. . . . What they will do is impinge on her. They will demand that her thoughts be focused on them. They will use her body with their

eyes. They will evaluate her market price. They will comment on her defects, or compare them to those of other passers-by. . . . They will make her feel ridiculous, or grotesquely sexual, or hideously ugly. Above all, they will make her feel like a *thing*.[87]

Susan Griffin took this a step further in a pathbreaking article on rape in 1971: "I HAVE NEVER BEEN FREE OF THE FEAR OF RAPE," she wrote. "RAPE IS AN ACT OF AGGRESSION in which the victim is denied her self-determination. It is an act of violence, which . . . always carries with it the threat of death. And finally, rape is a form of mass terrorism. . . ."[88]

The first rape crisis hot line was established in Washington, D.C. in 1972, and rape crisis centers quickly emerged across the country, founded by women's liberation groups and NOW chapters alike. By the mid-1970s, NOW chapters had formed more than 300 local and state rape task forces. Rape crisis centers provided counsel and advice to rape victims, assisted them in dealing with police and medical personnel, set up speaker's bureaus, offered self-defense courses and training for health care professionals and police, and created support groups for victims.[89]

The movement to create shelters for battered women grew from a similar impulse. The first such shelter, Women's Advocates in St. Paul, Minnesota, grew from a consciousness-raising group in 1971. They soon wrote a handbook on divorce and set up a telephone service to provide legal information. In response they were flooded with requests for emergency housing. They collected pledges to support the rent on a small apartment and a telephone answering service in 1973, but the demand was so great that members began taking women into their own homes. By 1974, when Women's Advocates opened the first shelter, the collective already had 18 months experience working with battered women. Other shelters grew out of rape crisis hot lines and coalitions between battered women and feminist activists.[90]

THUS, CONSCIOUSNESS-RAISING groups were the seedbeds for what grew into diverse movements around women's health, abortion, and violence against women. Sexual politics took a different direction, however, when an overtly lesbian feminism was articulated in the late sixties and early seventies. Anne Koedt's pathbreaking article, "The Myth of the Vaginal Orgasm"—passed from hand to hand throughout the country before publication in *Notes from the First Year*—was a rousing call to sexual autonomy for women. She challenged the subordination of women's desire to a model of sexuality codified in Freud's assertion that there were two kinds of female orgasms, the immature "clitoral" orgasm and the mature "vaginal" orgasm. Koedt cited recent research by sexologists Masters and Johnson proving that all female orgasms were centered in the clitoris, which has many times more nerve endings than the relatively insensitive vagina.[91] For heterosexuals, this suggested that women learn more about their own bodies, perhaps by reading *Our Bodies, Ourselves* or discussing orgasm and techniques of masturbation in a CR group and using that information to claim an equal right to sexual pleasure in relations with men. On the other hand, Koedt's suggestion that the penis was irrelevant to female sexual response led some to advocate celibacy and others to argue the superiority of lesbian relations.

Lesbianism, however, was still a strong social taboo. The many lesbians active in the various branches of the emerging women's movement were generally silent about their own sexuality. The personal bent of feminist discourse made that silence increasingly painful and rankling, as did the emergence of gay liberation in late 1969. Sidney Abbott and Barbara Love described their experience this way:

> For lesbians, Women's Liberation is not an intellectual or emotional luxury but a personal imperative. . . . In the beginning, the highest aspiration of most lesbians in the women's movement was just that—to be included. For the first two years of the second wave of feminism, this desire to be included was the perspective from which lesbians viewed the women's movement. In the midst of gathering for Women's Liberation, they continued to submit to oppression by hiding so that they could be included, or worse, defensively trying to prove the obvious—that they were also "real" women.
>
> Then came Gay Liberation.[92]

Soon, sharp debates and confrontations broke out across the country as lesbians announced their presence and demanded attention, validation, and action based on *their* experience.

In NOW chapters the debates were more structural: they had to do with who elected officers were and what issues could be the focus of task forces. The New York chapter underwent at least two "purges," which removed vociferous lesbian leaders such as Rita Mae Brown from offices and positions of authority.[93] Betty Friedan steadfastly opposed what she saw as a diversion into "sexual politics" that would alienate most American women. Her fears of the "lavender herring" were partially allayed, however, as she came to realize how many feminist veterans whose commitment had been the backbone of the movement in the early, lean years were, in fact, lesbians.[94] After 3 years of conflict, in the fall of 1971 the national NOW convention finally passed a resolution ending

BE IT RESOLVED THAT N.O.W. RECOGNIZES THE DOUBLE OP-
PRESSION OF LESBIANS;

BE IT RESOLVED THAT A WOMAN'S RIGHT TO HER OWN PER-
SON INCLUDES THE RIGHT TO DEFINE AND EXPRESS HER OWN
SEXUALITY AND TO CHOOSE HER OWN LIFE-STYLE AND

BE IT RESOLVED THAT N.O.W. ACKNOWLEDGES THE OPPRES-
SION OF LESBIANS AS A LEGITIMATE CONCERN OF FEMINISM.[95]

At least within NOW, the issue ceased to be a source of extreme division from that point on.

Among younger women in a generation marked by sexual experimentation and challenges to traditional sexual mores, the issue of lesbianism erupted as yet another form of personal politics. At the Second Congress to Unite Women on May 1, 1970, a meeting of a wide spectrum of feminist groups initially called by NOW, a group wearing "Lavender Menace" T-shirts and calling themselves Radicalesbians disrupted the proceedings on opening night to challenge the movement's prejudices by reading a paper entitled "The Woman-Identified Woman."

What is a lesbian? A lesbian is the rage of all women condensed to the point of explosion. . . . Lesbian is the word, the label, the condition that holds women in line. . . . Lesbian is a label invented by the man to throw at any woman who dares to be his equal. . . . Affixing the label lesbian not only to a woman who aspires to be a person but also to any situation of real love, real solidarity, real primacy among women is a primary form of divisiveness among women."[96]

By the time Radicalesbians staged this protest, the gay liberation movement was already more than a year old. Many lesbians found themselves caught between the male-dominated gay rights movement (in which people like Karla Jay and Rita Mae Brown, based on their own experience in Redstockings, fought for the creation of lesbian consciousness-raising groups) and the homophobia of the women's movement. For Jay, "the Lavender Menace zap action . . . remains . . . the single most important action organized by lesbians who wanted the women's movement to acknowledge our presence and our needs."[97]

Throughout the country the intense experiences of consciousness-raising groups evoked sexual tensions. The intimacy of such groups, the emotions they unleashed, felt to many like a kind of falling in love. A member of Bread and Roses described how

much of the energy that had heretofore gone into sexual relationships and especially couples was now being directed towards women friends and the women's community in general. This accounted for much of the strength and intensity of these new ties. Even women who remained in traditional heterosexual couples report 'getting high' from the energy level.[98]

Since most participants were, and remained, heterosexual, when some of this energy was expressed in directly sexual terms many responded with fear and anxiety. A letter read aloud at a 1970 Bread and Roses Retreat, and later widely published, challenged "my sisters" not to " . . . see me with strange eyes." "Why when I love my sisters wholly do I make you uneasy? Why, if I talk of my feelings, do you look away? . . . The irony of it all is that I probably would never have discovered my homosexuality without women's liberation."[99] Susan Griffin realized in retrospect that she had been a lesbian before she was married and that she had slipped into a kind of "numbness, a loss of an old self. . . . All it took was a weekend away from home at a women's conference and the experience of a few moments of what it is like to be supported by and to support other women, and I began to come alive again."[100]

The hostile labeling of all feminists as lesbians was a common experience. It reached the national media in December 1970, when *Time* exposed Kate Millett's bisexuality with the comment that "her disclosure is bound to discredit her as a spokeswoman for her cause, cast further doubt on her theories and reinforce the views of those skeptics who routinely dismiss all liberationists as lesbians."[101] By that time, whatever divisions existed over the political meanings of lesbianism, both gay and straight feminists understood that such a charge could not be allowed to stand. A group of highly visible feminist leaders in New York (including journalists Gloria Steinem and Susan Brownmiller, African-American lawyer Flo Kennedy, and founder of the Feminists Ti-Grace Atkinson) called a press conference to assert the common ground between women's liberation and gay liberation. They read statements of support from Aileen Hernandez and Wilma Scott Heide, national leaders of NOW, and from Congresswoman Bella Abzug and appear to have diffused the issue at least in the national press.[102] The issues that had been raised, however, continued to be a focal point for divisions within the women's movement, and as in the case of abortion, they evolved from a forbidden and private matter into one of the most prominent and divisive topics in mainstream politics.

THE POLITICS OF THE FAMILY

Most consciousness-raising groups probably talked as much or more about the politics of the family as they did about the rape, abortion, or health issues. From the first report of the Presidential Commission on the Status of Women in 1973, issues of family policy would take a prominent place (at least rhetorically) on the agenda of policy-oriented activists. Consciousness-raising groups, however, came to the question of family first as a result of their quest for the origins of women's oppression and their reexamination of the workings of power in intimate relations. Both groups relied heavily on "sex role socialization" theory to explain how women internalized traditional passive definitions of femininity.[103]

Pat Mainardi's early paper, "The Politics of Housework," was a particularly effective consciousness-raising tool. Reading it produced that familiar "click" of recognition. In it she explained the texts and subtexts of household arguments trotted out by men:

"I've got nothing against sharing the housework, but you can't make me do it on your schedule." MEANING: Passive resistance. I'll do it when I damned well please, if at all. . . .

"I hate it more than you. You don't mind it so much." MEANING: Housework is garbage work. It's the worst crap I've ever done. It's degrading and humiliating for someone of my intelligence to do it. But for someone of your intelligence. . . .

"Women's liberation isn't really a political movement." MEANING: The Revolution is coming too close to home.[104]

When Anita Shreve interviewed women about their experiences in consciousness-raising groups, she found that women, incensed at the inequities of household labor, would storm home from their women's liberation meetings to demand "that their husbands or lovers participate in shit-work [housework]." They would return with tales "of subterfuge in the most willing of husbands."[105] Across the country, similar interactions recurred thousands and thousands of times.

Meanwhile feminists also hotly debated the links between women's oppression and the nuclear family. In this instance, the drive for theoretical explanation ultimately reflected the very specific experiences of young, white, mostly unmarried women and built real barriers to the very women they hoped to reach. Although younger feminist radicals were divided on the issue of marriage, most indicted it and the nuclear family as key sources of women's oppression, claiming that women were "kept in their place" and prevented from developing autonomous identities through their roles as wives, mothers, and daughters. Historian and Bread and Roses member Anne Popkin argued that this analysis led to "a vehement (though in retrospect not well thought out) rhetorical crusade against the nuclear family."[106] Young women in consciousness-raising groups across the country critiqued their own upbringing and their mothers' restricted roles. The vast majority of them were well-educated and white.[107] Their conversations were, as Popkin notes, "highly charged" by the fact that they themselves were at or approaching "the age when they were 'expected' to start families of their own, yet the prospect made them anxious."[108] Single mother Alice Kessler-Harris recalled that her group was notably unsympathetic to her dilemmas as a working mother. In fact, they refused to meet at her home on the grounds that she needed to be "separated" from her daughter.[109] Some groups went so far as to restrict the numbers of married women who could belong in the belief that their perspective would be biased by their commitment. The most famous and influential example of this was the Feminists, founded by Ti-Grace Atkinson in a break from the New York City chapter of NOW, which announced that no more than one-third of its voting members could be "in either a formal (with legal contract) or informal (e.g., living with a man) instance of the institution of marriage" on the grounds that "the identification of each woman's interests with those of a man prevents her from uniting with other women and seeing herself as a member of the class of women."[110]

Younger feminists' critique of the family and of motherhood as an identity—and the demographic reality that their generation was delaying childbirth and curtailing fertility to an astounding degree—meshed with the weariness of older feminists whose child care needs were behind them.[111] Florence Falk-Dickler, then head of the National NOW Task Force on Child Care, complained that women in her own NOW chapter were more interested in employment issues than in child care. Betty Friedan recalled that although there was a national task force on day care she was unable to develop a strong constituency on this issue in any way comparable to the energy that emerged on such issues as abortion or employment discrimination. " . . . [T]he women who started NOW had had their fill of child care, or they were young professional women who had no children."[112]

The few who did pursue the issue at a policy level, however, discovered that child care was an issue that touched a deep public anxiety about the changing roles of women. Activists in the Chicago Women's Liberation Union's Action Committee for Decent Child Care were shocked by the depth of resistance and hostility they met in the community when they tried to organize around the issue. Project organizer Day Piercy recalled that she had "never been in a situation where people started with an issue and then went for the entire person. It made the women I was working with really feel as though they were bad mothers and there was something seriously wrong with them."[113] When Congress passed a landmark day care funding bill in 1971, it was vetoed by President Nixon on the grounds that it "would commit the vast moral authority of the national government to the side of communal approaches to child rearing [instead of] the family-centered approach."[114]

Instead of legislative solutions, concerns about "sex role socialization" led to the creation of dozens of "liberated" day care centers and a variety of other projects designed to intervene in the socialization of girls and young women. For example, Group 22 in Chapel Hill, North Carolina, read the existing sociological literature on sex roles and decided to create a child care center and to write and publish children's books—hence the birth of the Children's School for People Under Six and Lollipop Power. The book publishing group forming Lollipop Power learned through the feminist grapevine that there were others with similar ideas. At a meeting in 1970, the founders of Lollipop Power and the founders of the Feminist Press decided to avoid duplication of labor in the publication of books for children. Lollipop Power would produce preschool picture books and the Feminist Press would publish books for young readers.[115]

A different approach, pioneered by a group in Minnesota, illustrated the blending of NOW liberalism with women's liberation-radicalism. Cheri Register of Twin Cities Female Liberation and Gerri Helterline of NOW met in a crush of demonstrators outside the men-only Oak Grill on the twelfth floor of Dayton's Department Store in Minneapolis on August 26, 1970. Frustrated that they would probably never be able to get inside, Register and Helterline, with several others, decided to head over to Powers Department Store (which had a similar males-only dining room) and "desexegrate" that one. Register had thought of NOW women as somewhat suspect, not really radical, but she was surprised to discover in the course of the day that "Gerri was just like me." Both of them had from time to time spoken to high school classes— Helterline as a member of the NOW speaker's bureau, Register as a representative of Female Liberation—and both were feeling frustrated. Piecemeal efforts were not enough. "We were not sure how to make contacts, but we wanted an onslaught in the schools."[116]

So, they each brought a couple of like-minded friends from their respective associations and constituted themselves as the Emma Willard Task·Force, named for an early nineteenth century pioneer in women's education. As word of their availability spread, invitations to speak in classrooms snowballed, and that, too, began to be frustrating. It was time consuming, repetitive, unpaid work; they worried that they were just "the freak of the week" or the "Friday Special." In talking to teachers they also began to learn more about the obstacles teachers faced even when they wanted to change the curriculum. "We needed to move up in the hierarchy. Not knowing what to do—we just went right to the top, to the Commissioner of Education." They sent a letter to the Commissioner in April 1971 demanding a meeting.[117]

Over the next few months Emma Willard Task Force members met frequently with an official in the Department of Education, Don Hatfield, and became regular participants in a network of human relations training programs mandated by the state. "Our name was on the wire as people who could be called in to talk about sexism. It was a kind of 'advanced freak of the week': the black person, the Indian, the Chicano, and then us." They also put together a packet of curriculum materials, later a book that sold many thousands of copies through the workshops they conducted over several years. Emma Willard burned out after a few years, however. They did this work for little or no money, setting aside their own career goals (Register's dissertation, for example, was delayed by more than a year) and realizing only late in the day that there was a whole industry of consultants on race and human relations who were well paid for similar work.[118] Nonetheless, Emma Willard left a mark on the schools of Minnesota, which today require that all districts offer "multicultural, gender-fair" curricula. The work of the Emma Willard Task Force paralleled the efforts of other feminist investigations into educational practices, books, and textbooks.[119]

Near the end of the Emma Willard Task Force Packet from 1972 was a two-page mimeographed paper entitled "High School Women: The Suburban Scene." One of the readings for a ninth grade "Women's Liberation Mini Course" offered in Bloomington, Minnesota, offers evidence of the rapid spread of ideas and action as well as a glimpse of how personal politics spread beyond the boundaries of the organized movement.

The paper was by eighth grader Connie Dvorkin, who described herself as "a pacifist and a vegetarian since October 1968." She had learned of the women's liberation movement on radio station WBAI while at home in a conservative New York suburb. She wrote off for information and immersed herself in the literature that arrived.

> Ironically the very night I was reading it I was baby-sitting and watching TV. The show, "I Love Lucy," was an episode where the two women were to be equal to the men for one night . . . and they couldn't do it. They had to depend on their husbands. . . . The kids I was sitting for laughed their asses off, and I realized that I would have, too, five months earlier.
>
> Now, with awakened eyes, I could see all the brainwashing of my sisters that goes on at school.

Hearing that a court had struck down dress codes that required skirts for girls, she began to wear pants and found that she felt "more equal with boys." Then, with her mother's support, she waged a successful fight to take shop instead of home economics.[120]

Hundreds of schools faced similarly rebellious young women, frequently backed by supportive parents and the organized force of local feminists. Radio shows similar to WBAI's had sprung up across the country. Whereas talk shows welcomed the controversy surrounding women's liberation but were not necessarily sympathetic forums, alternative radio stations, many based on campuses, provided opportunities for feminists to create their own radio shows.[121] Girls like Connie Dvorkin were listening, and the networks (and mimeograph machines) were in place to spread responses like hers quickly.

CONSCIOUSNESS-RAISING presaged a broader societal trend toward the personal in the 1970s. Its success rested at least in part on its congruence with an emerging national mood. The "human potential movement" encompassing transcendental meditation, "T-groups," and encounter groups brought therapeutic activities into many public settings in the late sixties. Educational institutions at all levels, as well as business and civic organizations throughout the country, used "encounter groups" to build morale and increase productivity. The emphasis on emotional openness and honesty—even among total strangers—could be unsettling. A *Time* reporter who attended a seminar at Esalen Institute said, "Every aspect of so-called proper behavior is discarded. Every emotion is out in the open—everybody's property." Nudity was not uncommon—for example at the hot sulfur springs at Esalen—as participants sought to remove public personae and "strip down" to some personal essence.[122]

In contrast to the inward turn of the human potential movement, however, the energy released in this early phase of the Second Wave drew on a fusion of private life and political action that allowed women to make *public* claims based on personal experience, to challenge the "naturalness" of women's secondary status in public settings, and to point out that power operates even at the most intimate levels, that the personal is political. This assault on the status quo was coupled with a utopian optimism about future possibilities. Nothing would be taken for granted. Perfection was possible. The critical guide to the diagnosis of problems and to proposing changes was personal experience. This was both the brilliance and the deepest flaw of women's liberation.

For several years, however, personal politics unleashed a phenomenally diverse burst of creativity. It created a political agenda and a political constituency, and it fostered myriad institutional innovations as women sought to create new avenues for action on issues previously considered private. Ultimately it reshaped the political terrain of the United States as a whole.

CHAPTER 3

The Golden Years

We intend to settle for nothing less than equal representation
in all levels of political power.

—CONGRESSWOMAN BELLA ABZUG, JULY 1971

IT WAS AN "odd-lot coalition of activists from Congress and the women's liberation movement" from the outset,[1] but when 300 women gathered in Washington, D.C. in July 1971 to form the National Women's Political Caucus (NWPC), they heralded a new force on the national political landscape. The speakers were nationally prominent political activists whose lineages linked the new feminism to other struggles for justice, past and present: Fannie Lou Hamer, a Mississippi civil rights leader, knew firsthand the importance of electoral politics, having endured eviction and severe physical brutality for insisting on her right to vote; Bella Abzug, an activist from the forties and fifties, a member of Women's Strike for Peace, a Congresswoman from 1970 to 1976, known for her loud, brassy, and eccentric ways, Bella's trademark big-brim hats could be spotted at a distance; Gloria Steinem, professional journalist, founder of *Ms.* magazine; Betty Friedan, labor activist in the fifties, journalist, and founder of NOW; and Shirley Chisholm, the first black woman elected to Congress. The Caucus leadership was middle-class and well-connected, but they had recruited to this meeting younger activists of many races, creating a mix that was, in the words of *Newsweek's* reporter, "rowdy" and "kinetic as group therapy." Reportedly, accounts and photographs of the meeting reached President Nixon at his home in San Clemente where he and his aides bantered about how it looked "like a burlesque." "Obviously," retorted Bella Abzug, "the president and his advisers are accustomed to viewing women only in terms of flesh shows." Despite their characteristic unruliness and wrangling, the newly formed NWPC set strategic goals to increase women's representation in the political parties and in Congress, and they pledged to end "racism, sexism, institutional violence and poverty through the election and appointment of women to public office, party reform, and the support of women's issues and feminist candidates across party lines."[1]

Organizations and projects proliferated after 1970 as the dynamism of the movement spread to different constituencies—political insiders and outsiders, civil rights groups, working women, professional and academic disciplines, publishing. . . . The founding meeting of NWPC is a microcosm of the unruliness, creativity, and power unleashed by feminism. Each time women acted collectively, in turn, offers a glimpse of stirrings at the grass roots, where debates on "woman's place" had become the stuff of everyday life, and women suddenly found themselves empowered to challenge and change situations as small as a word or as large as the structure of their lives. The success of so many organized efforts, indeed, rested on the coiled energy of individual women, newly aware of previously unspoken injustices and ready to spring into action (or at least to speak loudly) on the issues that touched them most. It took some time for the backlash they provoked to gather support, so for a few years, wherever they could sustain a focus on shared goals, it seemed that nothing could stop this wave of change.

Washington insiders named the early years of the Second Wave the "golden years" because they achieved an unprecedented amount of legislation designed to correct gender inequities. Feminism emerged at the same time that women (in 1968) voted in equal numbers with men for the first time. In recent decades, women had not been perceived to be a coherent interest group. Suddenly they were a potential majority with a mind of its own. With feminist radicalism in the background, challenging gender roles across the board and politicizing disturbing new issues about the body and the family, issues framed as "equal opportunity" seemed simple, obvious, and mild.[3] So, for a few years, from about 1968 to 1975, the U.S. Congress seemed hell-bent on figuring out just what women wanted and giving it to them. Hearings, votes, and legislative victories came with breathtaking speed, and Congress passed more legislation in behalf of women's rights than it had considered seriously for decades. Courts, too, responded to the changed environment and the meticulously argued briefs of feminist lawyers, issuing a string of rulings that enlarged women's rights and opportunities.

Victories were never simple, however. Each had its own behind-the-scenes story about the combined strategic impact of policy-oriented feminists, Washington insiders, and ordinary working women who generated outside pressure by using their newly acquired rights to initiate EEOC complaints and court actions against discriminatory employers and their unions alike. Each story played out against the background roar of the cultural debate on "women's place" in kitchens, bedrooms, and offices. The media described women's political activism with implicitly raised eyebrows, as in this 1973 *Boston Globe* report on a National Women's Political Caucus meeting with state Democratic Party leaders:

> In short, the women are refusing to be taken for granted any longer and are insisting that their voice be heard and that their gender be represented in Democratic decisions and leadership. That's what they'll tell the party brass at a breakfast at the Parker House Wednesday for which the ladies will defy all tradition and pick up the tab.[4]

Critical to women's new political clout were the thousands of women who asserted new rights as soon as they had them. With the passage of the Equal Pay Act in 1963 and Title VII of the Civil Rights Act in 1964, working women had at hand new and powerful legal tools, which they seized vigorously. The Equal Pay Act made it illegal to pay women less than men for the same job. Title VII added "sex" to "race, religion, and national origin" as categories protected by federal law from employment discrimination. The Civil Rights Act also established an Equal Employment Opportunity Commission to hear complaints and enforce compliance with its antidiscrimination rules. In the first year of the Equal Employment Opportunity Commission, nearly 2,500 complaints (27 percent of the total) came from women charging sex discrimination. Individual women often filed their complaints without the support of their unions and in some instances charged the unions with discrimination. Even progressive unions like the United Auto Workers (UAW) and the International Union of Electrical Workers (IUE) that had a history of attention to women's issues and provided leadership to the President's Commission on the Status of Women found their female members restless and willing to use governmental remedies against their unions as well as their employers. The commissioners, however, were for the most part unprepared to consider sex discrimination a significant issue and for their first year made no response to such complaints. Commissioners Aileen Hernandez and Richard Graham and EEOC lawyer Sonia Fuentes, disturbed by their colleagues' inaction, began to articulate the need for an "NAACP for women" to pressure the EEOC to enforce the law. This, of course, was the idea behind the creation of NOW.[5]

Unions and companies often tried to claim that denials of access to overtime and higher paying jobs were necessitated by state protective laws.[6] These laws, many on the books for half a century or more, "protected" women from exploitation by limiting the hours they could work and specifying allowable working conditions, such as limits on the amount of weight a woman could be asked to lift. Such rules, of course, resulted in the exclusion of women from many of the better paying occupations and from opportunities for promotion. Under feminist prodding, courts began to rule that protective laws could in fact discriminate and thereby violate Title VII of the Civil Rights Act.[7]

A landmark case began when Lorena Weeks sued Southern Bell Telephone Company for refusing to promote her to a job she had handled many times as a substitute and instead hired a man with less seniority. When she lost her case in 1967, Marguerite Rawalt of the NOW Legal Committee offered assistance on appeal. Attorney Sylvia Roberts from Baton Rouge prepared the case with Rawalt and argued it before the appeals court. Standing only 5 feet tall, Roberts marched around the courtroom carrying the equipment required for the job in one hand while arguing that the company rules that placed weight lifting restrictions on jobs for women were not a "bona fide occupational qualification." The decision handed down in March 1969 in *Weeks v. Southern Bell* denied the validity of the "bfoq" exemption for Bell's weight-lifting restrictions and set a new standard of proof. No longer would a demonstration that many, or even most, women could not perform a specific job requirement justify such a restriction. Instead, employers (and states) would have to show that all or "substantially all" women could not do so. The choice to accept a particularly difficult job should rest with women as it already did for men.[8]

The greatest political goal of all, the Equal Rights Amendment, had divided supporters of women's rights for nearly half a century. A legacy of the suffrage era, the ERA had first been proposed in 1923 by the National Women's Party, to remove in one fell swoop the remaining obstacles to full legal equality. With a constitutional amendment mandating that "Equality of rights under the law shall not be denied or abridged by the United States or by any state on account of sex," legal restrictions like Southern Bell's would tumble in a hurry. Progressive reformers and their labor union allies, however, who had fought long and hard for laws to protect working women from excessive low wages and harsh working conditions, were horrified. To them, legal equality would only worsen the situation of the most disadvantaged, forgetting that protective laws were passed solely for women in an era when that was the only way to get any kind of protection. Since the 1930s, however, courts had dropped their opposition to legislation protecting all workers, such as minimum wage or occupational safety and health rules. Leaders' realization that protection could be discrimination grew in response to initiatives and protests from below.[9] By 1970, however, the ranks of ERA supporters had come to include most of its former opponents: the League of Women Voters, Business and Professional Women, the YWCA, the American Association of University Women, Common Cause, and the United Auto Workers. Together they formed a coalition capable of mounting a massive 2 year campaign that generated more mail on Capitol Hill than the Vietnam War.[10]

The ERA received "official" support in 1970 in the report of President Nixon's short-lived Task Force on Women's Rights and Responsibilities, appointed to gather information for his State of the Union address. Under the leadership of Virginia Allen, the Task Force produced a sharply worded pro-ERA report, *A Matter of Simple Justice*, which the administration quickly suppressed. Elizabeth Koonz, Director of the Women's Bureau in the Department of Labor, finally succeeded in publishing the report (after it had circulated underground for several months) in time for the Women's Bureau's Fiftieth Anniversary Conference in June 1970.[11]

Among the 800 contentious women at the Women's Bureau Conference was Arvonne Fraser, a longtime activist in the Democratic Party. She had managed her husband's successful campaigns for election to Congress and then staffed his congressional office. She listened raptly to Elizabeth Koonz, an African-American Republican, speaking about unity among women toward the goal of women's full participation in American life. Fraser jotted notes to herself so that she wouldn't forget: "*Koonz*—standing ovation—beautiful voice, resonant, deep with a lilt and humor. . . . At [the] end of her speech a young women's lib type stood up and said she didn't see many lower class women or many young women in the audience . . . immediately to her left an older black woman in [a] pink outfit came up and demanded: 'what do you expect a lower class woman to look like?' [T]he whole audience hooted and clapped and Mrs. K responded: 'we don't judge people by their outward appearance.'" Koonz indicated that some welfare mothers had been invited and when she asked young women to stand, " . . . they included young black women as well."[12]

Even as this feminist intergenerational clash occurred at the Women's Bureau Conference, Representative Martha Griffiths filed a discharge petition to force the ERA out of the House Judiciary Committee and onto the floor of the House. The previous month the ERA had received its first congressional committee hearing since 1956 as a result of a NOW demonstration in February. Twenty women from the Pittsburgh chapter, under the leadership of Wilma Scott Heide, had disrupted a hearing on the vote for 18-year-olds to demand immediate action on the ERA. With a constant flow of letters and telegrams to re-luctant congressmen, the petition reached the necessary 218 signatures on July 20 and thus bypassed a committee vote. On August 10 (after a debate in which Emanuel Celler argued that there was "as much differ-ence between a male and a female as between a horse chestnut and a chestnut horse"), it passed the House 350 to 15.[13]

On March 22, 1972, both houses of Congress finally approved the ERA. By the end of the year, 22 of the needed 35 states had ratified it. No one could know that the rate of ratification would decelerate sharply as opposition forces began to organize themselves. The early victories, how-ever, were a sign of women's political self-organization at the state level that paralleled and reinforced their new national visibility. Political cau-cuses and commissions on women in most states coordinated their efforts to increase women's political participation, to press for the elimination of discriminatory laws, and to generate new initiatives. In Minnesota, women formed feminist caucuses in both major political parties.[14]

In Congress, 1972 turned out to be a banner year for women's rights legislation. In addition to the ERA, Congress passed Title IX of the Higher Education Act, providing "No person in the United States shall, on the basis of sex, be excluded from participation in, be denied the benefits of, or be subjected to discrimination under any education pro-gram or activity receiving federal financial assistance," setting the stage for the growth of women's athletics later in the decade. The Equal Op-portunity Act broadened the jurisdiction of the EEOC and strength-ened its enforcement capacity. Working parents received a tax break for their child care expenses. Representative Bella Abzug recalled 1972 as "a watershed year. We put sex discrimination provisions into every-thing. There was no opposition. Who'd be against equal rights for women? So we just kept passing women's rights legislation."[15]

Arvonne Fraser was one of the Washington insiders whose linkages with feminist outsiders made for such a powerful alliance in these golden years. As she describes her own story, she came into the women's movement much the same way thousands did around the country, by organizing her own support group. Schooled in organizations, she tried first to join NOW in 1968 or 1969, but her letter was returned—probably a casualty of NOW's disorganization after the UAW withdrew financial support or perhaps NOW's early policy of restricting membership to professional women.[16] So, she invited 20 women to her home to talk about the new women's movement. They would not have called themselves a consciousness-raising group. That was a label for younger radicals. But they easily adopted the small group-organizing strategy of women's liberation. At the first meeting, women decided not to introduce themselves in terms of their relationships with men precisely because most of them were in Washington because they were on the staff of, or married to, prominent male politicians. As word of the group spread, reporters tracked Fraser down at her husband's congressional office. "The reporter's first question was: 'Who are their husbands?' I refused to answer, and the group began to call itself 'the Nameless Sisterhood.'"[17]

The Nameless Sisterhood linked an important underground of feminists in key policy-making positions in Washington. It spun off organizations—as when Bernice Sandler urged Arvonne Fraser to organize a Washington chapter of the Women's Equity Action league (WEAL), which rapidly became a major source of activism on both legal and legislative fronts. It also initiated legislation. The story of the Women's Education Equity Act (WEEA) shows how informal networks can work when the timing is right.

The idea for the Women's Education Equity Act originated with Arlene Horowitz, a secretary on Capitol Hill who had worked for 3 years for a House Education Subcommittee. Frustrated that "the males on this committee felt that women were only good for typing and carrying out their wishes," she "ran out of typing one day, so I decided to knock off a bill."[18] The idea was to create a Council on Women's Educational Programs in the Department of Education that could devise programs to address discrimination against women in educational access, in curriculum, and in hiring by funding small, innovative projects that could document problems and develop model solutions. Horowitz approached both Fraser and Sandler, who were initially dubious but responded to her persistence by calling a meeting to work on the draft and to ask Representative Patsy Mink to hold hearings. Fraser recalled,

We met one night in 1972 at George Washington University to draft the bill. Present were Shirley McCune, who was working on sex-equity problems for the National Education Association, and Marguerite Rawalt, who came to ensure that the bill would be consistent with the ERA when it passed. Sandler, Horowitz, I and a few others rounded out the group. When we came to the authorizing of funds, we laughingly entered $30 million, fantasizing about what that amount of money could accomplish.[19]

As the bill progressed through Congress, sponsored by Representative Mink and Senator Walter Mondale, female networks went into action to generate publicity and support. Hearings aired the issues. Fraser's longtime political ally, columnist Geri Joseph wrote a widely reprinted column, "Women's Rebellion Against Dick and Jane," which linked the proposed WEEA to myriad feminist grassroots efforts to document the ways educational systems tracked girls into traditional roles: a WEAL study on vocational education for girls in Waco, Texas, NOW task forces "around the country poring over children's readers," and Princeton NOW's widely read study entitled "Dick and Jane as Victims." Joseph also quoted Fraser's own testimony at hearings on the bill: "We have looked at the education of girls as a kind of life insurance, something they need, 'just in case'—just in case they can't find a husband or in case they need to support themselves while looking for a husband."[20] The Women's Educational Equity Act became law 2 years later.

As women like Arlene Horowitz throughout the country began to rethink aspects of their everyday lives they had never previously questioned, they generated a barrage of new issues for feminist policy activists. Suddenly, concrete evidence of discrimination was easy to find and to present to courts and legislatures. Wave upon wave of new leaders and organizations arose. The surge of energy around each issue could carry it forward with astonishing speed. When the National Commission on Consumer Finance initiated hearings on the problem of women and consumer credit in the spring of 1972, policy makers were stunned by the flood of complaints and demands for action. NOW, WEAL, Parents Without Partners, and the American Civil Liberties Union all conducted investigations on consumer credit, finding that the credit industry consistently marked women as "poor risks." If single, they might marry; if married they might become pregnant. In either case it was presumed that they would stop working, so their income was not considered a valid basis for credit. Divorced and widowed women found that they had no credit record. Married women's income was commonly not considered in mortgage applications, although some companies would reconsider on the basis of a physician's assurance that the woman was sterilized or taking birth control pills.[21]

Two NOW members, economist Jane Roberts Chapman and attorney Margaret Gates, established the Center for Women Policy Studies in March 1972 with a $10,000 seed grant from Ralph Nader's organization. Later that year they garnered a $40,000 grant from the Ford Foundation to investigate the problem of women and consumer credit (an interest created when "a female employee of the Ford Foundation was turned down on a credit application and senior staff there became interested in this economic issue").[22] Their research, in turn, both galvanized other networks and produced a systematic body of "expert" information for presentation to legislative hearings and briefings for interested organizations. The result was the passage in 1974 of the Equal Credit Opportunity Act, followed by 2 years of careful monitoring and pressure to ensure that the Federal Reserve Board's regulations to enforce the EOCA would have the necessary "teeth" to protect women. Problems persisted, but credit was substantially more available to women by the 1980s than it had ever been.[23] Another response to the revelations about women and credit was the creation of feminist credit unions and banks, illustrating again the two-pronged strategic approach that characterized the movement as a whole: change the rules but also build institutions that can function as if the world were feminist.

The most powerful organizational expression of the insider-outsider alliance was the National Women's Political Caucus (NWPC), which formed in 1971. In the tradition of the women's suffrage movement, NWPC set out to use the vote "to influence the priorities of our nation away from war and toward dealing with the diverse critical human problems of our society."[24] "The time has come," its leaders asserted, "to assume our rightful place as decision-makers and to raise our voices for life-enhancing priorities."[25]

The vision of NWPC was somewhat muddy at the outset, which turned out to be a strength, at least for a time. Fundamental was the demand for equality, for full participation on the grounds of simple equity:

> Certain facts of political life still shock and anger us. Women are 53 percent of the population. They turn out at the polls in larger numbers than men. They do most of the drudge work in politics. But of the 435 members in the House, only 12 are women. Out of 100 senators, one is a woman. There are no women Governors, few big city women mayors, only a scattering of women in state and city government.[26]

They also suggested, however, that "women's political power" could "redirect our nation toward peaceful goals," a perspective that would have been very familiar to their suffragist foremothers. One of the founders recalled later the belief

> ... that women shared a common perspective based on their roles outside the power structure as nurturers and consumers or as victims of sex discrimination in education and employment. ... Some [founders] thought consensus would arise out of women's innate humaneness, an alleged quality which made them more responsible in relation to power than men. The assumption that women were by nature more humane made some of the women uneasy, but since the case for political equality did not depend upon it, it was allowed to pass largely unexamined.[27]

When Betty Friedan, Bella Abzug, Gloria Steinem, Representative Shirley Chisholm, and Representative Patsy Mink called an initial meeting to announce their intention to form a national women's political caucus, more than 100 showed up. The initiating committee then invited women from across the country to attend an organizing conference on July 10–11, 1971, in Washington, D.C., the meeting that

Newsweek described as "rowdy." They articulated from the outset a "strategy of inclusiveness" that made NWPC one of the most racially diverse of all the new feminist organizations. For the first year and a half, the national leadership of NWPC consisted of a national policy council that included feminist media "superstars" like Friedan (originator of the caucus idea), Abzug, Chisholm, and Gloria Steinem; women with powerful media and political connections, like Shana Alexander (editor-in-chief of *McCall's*), Liz Carpenter (former press secretary of First Lady Lady Bird Johnson), Virginia Allen (former chair of Nixon's Task Force on Women's Rights and Responsibilities), Elly Peterson (former Vice Chair of the Republican National Committee), and Jill Ruckelshaus (aide to President Nixon); but also key leaders from minority communities, labor unions, and organizations of the poor: LaDonna Harris (Indian rights leader), Myrlie Evers (civil rights activist), Dorothy Height (President of the National Council of Negro Women and a leader in the YWCA), Fannie Lou Hamer (civil rights leader), Olga Madar (United Auto Workers), Beulah Sanders (Vice President of the National Welfare Rights Organization), and Wilma Scott Heide (NOW president).

At the organizing conference three caucuses formed immediately: black women, radical women, and younger women. Although the initiators were experienced with strong, national organizations, their inclusive strategy drew in many who preferred local experimentation and resisted centralized authority. As founder Rona Feit put it, there was no money and no staff and "infighting was common at every level."[28] Yet they launched a local organizing process that inaugurated 30 state caucuses by December 1971.

Enthusiastic state caucus founding meetings focused on gaining access to party presidential nominating conventions in 1972.[29] The result of this effort was astonishing. Both political parties increased the representation of women enormously. Female delegates to the Republican Convention rose from 15 to 30 percent, Democrats from 13 to 40 percent.[30] Each party also included a "women's plank." Shirley Chisholm's presidential candidacy (the first black woman ever to run) and the influence of feminists in the McGovern camp made the Caucus extremely visible at the Democratic convention. Chisholm never really had a chance. McGovern supporters withheld some commitments out of concern about Caucus members' loyalty to Shirley Chisholm, but she and her strongest supporters were distressed at the weakness of her support. It stung that even Bella Abzug was unwilling to cast an initial, symbolic vote for Chisholm on the first ballot.[31]

By 1973 the Caucus was ready to hold a founding convention in Houston, Texas: 1,500 women came to establish " . . . the organizational basis upon which to build a national political movement for women." Shirley Chisholm argued that "the function of the National Women's Political Caucus is not to be the cutting edge of the women's liberation movement, but the big umbrella organization which provides the weight and the muscle for those issues which the majority of women in this country see as concerns."[32] Arvonne Fraser was assigned the impossible task of chairing a workshop to design the structure for NWPC. Those who envisioned a muscular, centralized, and efficient organization quickly realized that power and responsibility would have to reside with the state caucuses. A wave of antielitism, emanating from the grass roots and reflecting the spirit of the women's liberation movement, led current "superstar" leaders, one after another, to offer to step aside in favor of grassroots leadership. Chisholm was the first, urging others to do the same. Friedan and the rest followed.[33]

Perhaps most startling about the NWPC—apart from the fact that it survived its own centrifugal stresses—was its sheer diversity. Mary Ziegenhagen wrote in a report to members in Minnesota,

As we listened to speaker after speaker, each more impressive than the last, we were struck by the astonishing diversity of the crowd. Gloria Steinem said what we've always known, "You see, women come in all sizes, shapes and colors," and to be in the midst of it was a kaleidoscopic delight. A vast room crammed to the corners with every description of female persons: worried blue permanent waves, smart Afros, long black braids; silk print dresses with pearls, blue jeans, pants suits, who-cares-which-dress, and a delegate from California in a sun-colored muu-muu and lavender head scarf. And no less varied and diverse were the political hues of that rainbow, as we were soon to learn when we got down to the business of deciding what shape the Caucus was to take.[34]

In contrast to more radical feminist groups, women of color were part of NWPC from the outset. At stake was access to public power: representation in parties, in elected office, in appointments. Avis Foley, an African-American delegate from Minnesota, reported that "there must have been nearly 100 black women at the conference—enough to be truly visible and that really set the stage for me." After noting the diversity of black women there from across the country and their varied political persuasions, she described their tactical solidarity: "An unexpected opportunity for black solidarity arose when Gwen Cherry, Chair of the Convention and Democratic Florida State Legislator, was threatened with removal." Criticism focused on Cherry's failure to control the unruly crowd, many of whom were unaccustomed to abiding by parliamentary procedure. In response, members of the black caucus " . . . stationed ourselves at each mike to prevent monopoly by one person or group, guarded access to the rostrum until aisles were clear to ensure true count of a standing vote. No more was heard of Gwen's removal."[35]

Similarly, a Chicana caucus made up of members of La Raza Unita Party functioned as "a highly disciplined group with articulate and feisty leaders." One observer reported that "with no small amount of courage and by paying attention—and undoubtedly, suppressing internal disputes—they succeeded in electing three of their members to the national steering committee and in gaining substantial concessions. . . ."[36] NWPC incorporated these diverse groups by agreeing to the formation of permanent minority caucuses for blacks, Chicanas, Puerto Ricans, and Native Americans with representation on the National Steering Committee. It also guaranteed representation of Republicans (who were in a distinct minority). In subsequent years, permanent caucuses emerged also for Asian-Americans, lesbians, and Capitol Hill staff members.

It was a black Congresswoman from Texas, Barbara Jordan, who reminded the assembled women that the Declaration of Independence was not written overnight nor was the Constitution drafted without conflict and strongly worded dissent. Toni Morrison later articulated the vision that made a diverse group of women willing to go the distance despite inevitable conflicts:

> The winds are changing, and when they blow, new things move. The liberation movement has moved from shrieks to shape. It is focusing itself, becoming a hard-headed power base, as the National Women's Political Caucus in Washington attested last month. Representative Shirley Chisholm was radiant: 'Collectively we've come together, not as a Women's Lib group, but as a women's political movement.' Fannie Lou Hamer, the Mississippi civil rights leader was there. Beulah Sanders, chairman of New York's City-wide Coordinating Committee of Welfare Groups, was there. They see, perhaps, something real: women talking about human rights rather than sexual rights—something other than a family quarrel, and the air is shivery with possibilities.[37]

Shortly after that founding meeting, Lael Stegall walked into the Washington NWPC office with her 3-week-old son on her hip. After a stint in the Peace Corps she had returned in the late sixties "to be part of the social revolution at home." Interested in policy, she worked in Bella Abzug's first congressional campaign in 1970 and in 1971. After that she threw herself into George McGovern's campaign. It was a Republican neighbor who said to her late in 1972, "Have your second baby and [come] help us form the NWPC. We need women like you." That first step through the door "began a decade of politics for me." Despite the high-powered group at the helm—a set of accomplished women including Doris Meisner, Myrlie Evers, Fannie Lou Hamer, Sissy Farenthold, Millie Jeffrey, and Ronnie Feit—Stegall remembers a sense of revolutionary new beginning that echoes the experiences of women's liberation groups. "[We were] clueless about how to build an organization. Dues? Planning? What do you do with a steering committee? Next thing I knew someone said 'someone has to learn how to raise money around here; do development; go talk to Roger Craver at Common

Cause. You are entrepreneurial, why don't you do that?' So I said, 'oh, OK.' In those years, you just did it. . . . By 1979 I knew as much about women, money, and power as anyone."[38]

Involvement in NWPC brought women of color together not only with white women but also with each other. Their caucuses further nourished growing networks among minority feminists, who increasingly felt the need for organizations that could articulate their needs and their perspectives directly. The black caucuses of the NWPC and NOW led to the formation of the National Black Feminist Organization (NBFO). In response to a call in the summer of 1973, over 100 African-American women gathered in a New York church "to find out what this women's lib thing is all about." A reporter for *Essence* described the gathering:

As the meeting progressed with women shooting hands into the air to speak, a testifying filled the crowded room like vapor. Applause, laughter and 'right ons' greeted the different chapters of each woman's life as recognition and empathy flashed through the women's minds. The talk was of being on welfare, of not having day care facilities and black men; of color discrimination within the race, salary and job discrimination, of being a lesbian, of being treated as a sex object, of learning to love oneself and black men.

Black men have confidently scoffed at "those crazy white women who just want out of the kitchen." As one brother said to me "Our women got more sense." But black women, regardless of their attitudes toward the women's movement, are largely disregarding male rhetoric about "stepping back" and the benefits of the "prone position."[39]

At a press conference, founders of the NBFO announced that

The distorted male-dominated media image of the Women's Liberation movement has clouded the vital and revolutionary importance of the movement to Third World women, especially black women. The movement has been characterized as the exclusive property of the so-called 'white middle class' women and black women seen involved in this movement have been seen as 'selling out,' 'dividing the race,' and an assortment of nonsensical epithets. Black feminists resent these charges and are therefore establishing THE NATIONAL BLACK FEMINIST ORGANIZATION, in order to address ourselves to the particular and specific needs of the larger, but almost cast aside, half of the Black race in Amerikka, the Black woman.[40]

Their militant rhetoric, including spellings that visually link the United States to its racist past (the KKK or Ku Klux Klan), marked the continuing influence of black separatism and identification with Third World revolutions.

Carolyn Handy, an early member of NOW in Syracuse, New York, described the two reasons for founding NBFO. First, founders recognized that predominantly white feminist organizations may have tried to address the concerns of black women but had failed to do so effectively. As a result, black women felt a need "to get their heads together over issues—independently" as black women. Their second purpose however, was " . . . to make the movement—the women's movement—stronger and to attract and support all those black women with questions—even though the media keeps saying 'minority women aren't involved in the movement because they are already liberated.' . . . It's time that minority women stand up and say, 'Listen, it's our movement, too, and we're supportive of our white sisters, and if you have any questions about our commitment, here we are. Ask us.'"[41]

An East Coast regional meeting of NBFO in November drew 500. Black women who attended spoke afterward of healing, of energy, of no longer being alone. Francella Gleaves wrote, "Never before have I felt such genuine sisterhood with other black women. A longtime feminist, I have often felt I was a pariah, since very few black women I knew ever admitted sharing my views."[42] Suzanne Lipsky approached the meeting cautiously, tentatively, with low expectations. "But I came away with a feeling that something had been fulfilled; that I had been waiting for this weekend; that something very important and personal had been confirmed."[43] Alice Walker wrote lyrically about the power of being in a room of black women who were not afraid and who talked about "things that matter. . . . So the air was clear and rang with earnest voices freed at last to speak to ears that would not automatically begin to close." She pondered the need to retrieve the history of black women, to persevere despite criticism from other black people and especially the fear of lesbians. "I only met other black women, my sisters, and valuable beyond measuring, every one of them. And we talked and we discussed and we sang for Shirley Chisholm and clapped for Eleanor Holmes Norton and tried to follow Margaret Sloan's lyrics and cheered Flo Kennedy's anecdotes. And we laughed a lot and argued some. *And had a very good time.*"⁴⁴ Within 4 months NBFO had a mailing list of 1,000.

With less fanfare, Latinas also created new organizations, but they found that identity politics was a continuing obstacle to unity among themselves (Mexican, Chicana, Puerto Rican, Cuban, etc.) as well as with other groups. Early groups of Puerto Rican women had begun to meet in Washington, D.C. and New York City in 1970–1971. Efforts to meet with Mexican-American women led them to believe they needed to develop separate organizations. As one of the early Puerto Rican activists recalled, she had "been deluded by the North American idea of Hispanic homogenization," which overlooks differences among the groups. "Latinas were not ready to have that kind of unity, for each group needed first to develop by itself." Lourdes Miranda also remembers her group meeting in the Cleveland Park Library in Washington D.C., where she and Carmen Maymi brought their daughters. One time her daughter came running down the hall saying that there was another group of women in the building "just like you" and asking why the two groups didn't meet together. As it turned out, there was a NOW chapter just beginning to form that also met in the library, but "of course" the two could not unite at that time. "We needed space to develop our brand of feminism. Our issues were not strictly gender issues, but racial as well." In 1972 the National Conference of Puerto Rican Women held their founding meeting at the Dupont Plaza Hotel in Washington. Despite mutual suspicions between professional women and community activists, the women who gathered discovered the power of Puerto Rican sisterhood. "What happened was so beautiful" that it inspired participants to build a national organization that quickly grew to more than 20 chapters and endured for 25 years. Facing suspicion from other Puerto Rican organizations, chapters of NCPRW focused on the needs of specific communities, violence against women, employment inequality (linked to racial discrimination as much as sexism), and the broader issues of racism, poverty, and education. The leadership of NCPRW were also positioned to have a voice in such organizations as NWPC and a network of presidents of national women's organizations initiated by Dorothy Height.[45]

By the time Eliza Sanchez moved to Washington, D.C. in the summer of 1975, Chicanas there had been meeting for several years. At the age of 8, Sanchez had walked union picket lines with her Mexican immigrant mother in the 2 year (1950–1952) strike by Chicano mine workers in New Mexico, later immortalized in the movie *Salt of the Earth*. When a court injunction enjoined workers from picketing, women in the community not only took over the picket lines but also insisted that their issues—having to do with sanitation and lack of hot water in company-owned housing—be on the table alongside hours and wages. That was, for Sanchez, "a defining experience. I knew what the power of women could be." During the early years of women's liberation, however, she was cutting her own activist teeth in the black civil rights movement as an organizer for Community Advancement Incorporated, an OEO (Office for Equal Opportunity, the federal "antipoverty" program) organization in Baton Rouge, Louisiana. She had no idea that "her" movie, *Salt of the Earth*, had become a staple of women's liberation events.[46] Soon, however, the growing assertiveness of women within the Chicano movement drew her in. "In Dallas in 1974, several women friends and I got on the nomination committee of the local IMAGE [Mexican-American Government Employees] chapter. [We were] tired of all those men, decided to make our votes count, [and] took over the chapter. The guys were pissed. We were beginning to feel more like 'Hey, wait a minute. We can think, strategize, run meetings, etc. as well as you can.'" The next year when she arrived in Washington and heard that women were organizing she thought "wow, this is where I want to be." What she found was a group calling itself the National Mexican American Women's Association (MANA), whose meetings involved 25–30 at any one time, eager to "do something" and willing to weather the stress and tension over leadership and power that inevitably followed.[47]

Multicultural feminism also found a small niche within the federal bureaucracy. Carol Bonasarro attended the Houston founding conference of NWPC as director of the Women's Rights Project of the Federal Civil Rights Commission. She had served on the Commission staff since the mid-1960s, and when Congress mandated that the Commission must include issues of sex discrimination within its jurisdiction, she received the appointment to head the Women's Project. A white woman, Bonasarro was acutely aware that the leadership of the commission viewed feminism as a "white women's thing" and had resisted previous efforts to place women's rights within its jurisdiction. As a civil rights veteran, she set out to win the Commission over to a vision of a multicultural, multiracial women's rights program. Bonasarro undertook a series of trips around the country to meet women in the movement and get responses to her program. She met with Hispanic, Asian, and black women, as well as noted white feminist leaders. It was an experience of "light bulbs going off, chords being struck." Things she had known all along "were up there in neon." Suddenly she had names and explanations for her "year from hell" as an electrical engineering undergraduate at Cornell whose classmates refused to be her lab partner and whose advisor continually asked, "when are you going to liberal arts where you belong"—and for the frustrations in her career when men received recognition and awards that she knew she deserved. Finally she could link her own anger together with her passionate commitment to racial equality. For Bonasarro, the Houston conference was utterly enthralling.[48]

With the support of the Commission's Staff Director, John A. Buggs, Bonasarro hired a diverse staff and set out to educate the Commission and its staff on the issue of women's rights. Of course she ran into prejudices. When she brought in Gloria Steinem and Margaret Sloan to speak, she was unprepared for the negative response of black women on the staff (Sloan was black but also lesbian). Bonasarro's goal, however, was to link the issue of women's rights to every other issue considered by the Commission.[49]

Carol Bonasarro discovered a multicultural women's movement because she was looking for it. The work of the Civil Rights Commission, which focused on investigation and policy recommendation, further strengthened the participation of minority women by linking them not only through openly feminist organizations but also in their communities. The difference was that organizations like NOW focused strictly on women's rights; the Civil Rights Commission refused to separate issues of sex and race, and they understood the political necessity of giving each group an opportunity to speak in its own voice. With a multicultural staff, the Women's Project published a special women's rights issue of *Civil Rights Digest* in 1974, in which they gave voice to the specific concerns of Chicanas, Native American women, Puerto Rican women, Asian-American women, Chinese immigrants, Issei women, and black women. The issue was titled, "Sexism and Racism: Feminist Perspectives."[50]

Similarly, the National Council of Negro Women (NCNW) began to assert leadership in the women's movement through a contract with the Office of Equal Opportunity of the Department of Housing and Urban Development to generate data on discrimination against women in housing. A leadership policy statement in 1974 claimed the feminist legacy of their founder: "Mary McLeod Bethune's idea for uniting women to secure justice, the idea on which she founded the National Council of Negro Women, never had more relevance than in this day when women throughout the nation are raising their collective voices demanding their rights as persons in all areas of life." Having worked with HUD to develop a home ownership opportunities program, NCNW leaders had learned "from this and our own life's experiences, . . . [that] sex discrimination is pervasive in every area of the housing industry."[51] Shortly thereafter, NCNW President Dorothy Height wrote to the presidents of major national women's organizations "to fulfill this idea of unity of women . . . [by coming] together to develop collective strategies concerning two basics of life—shelter and food."[52]

BY FAR, THE SINGLE greatest impact of the women's movement was in the American workforce. Beyond housing, beyond day care, beyond issues of housework between husbands and wives, it was issues of career and work opportunities that allowed women to remake the nation. Whether they worked in factories, in offices, or as professionals, the politics of work was an abiding concern for feminists.[53] Consciousness-raising groups facilitated the decisions of millions of women to take advantage of crumbling barriers to professional education and occupational advancement, but women also brought concerted pressure to bear on the workplace.

When Helen Dudley conducted Seminars for Women Executives in the Federal Government in 1968, she introduced an analysis of sex discrimination as part of the curriculum. Dorothy Nelms, an African-American woman working in the Social Security Program, attended one of the seminars as part of an executive development program. Recently divorced, raising two children on her own, Nelms was seeking ways to enhance her career. During the 2 day meeting, leaders invited participants to describe their experiences of sex discrimination. Dorothy recalls that they all said, "we know what it is but it doesn't affect us." So the leader went around the circle asking, "Did you ever come up for promotion in your job? Did you get it? Tell me what happened." She "made us all relive things we had experienced but had buried. Within four hours we were raging maniacs, we had become so livid." After a series of such seminars, a few women took the next step. They called themselves Federally Employed Women, with the pointed acronym, FEW. Nelms, who had already joined NOW and the International Toastmistress Clubs, joined FEW as soon as she heard about it in late 1968: 10 years later she was its president, and 30 years later she served a second term.[54]

Highly focused on job discrimination in the federal government, FEW set out to train members in administrative skills and to give them the knowledge and tools they needed to challenge discrimination. It also set out to train the government itself. An executive order in 1967 had set up a Women's Program throughout the government, appointing people to see that antidiscrimination rules were enforced, but it was FEW that saw to it that the women placed in those positions were properly trained, for example, in how to read statistics and how to frame policy recommendations. Soon FEW was also heavily involved in lobbying on Capitol Hill on such issues as the Equal Rights Amendment and affirmative action.[55]

Similarly, professional women began to organize themselves. In academia, professors of sociology, history, political science, psychology, and modern languages organized caucuses to pressure their associations to set up formal committees on the status of women.[56] Soon their example spread to fields in the natural sciences as well as the rest of the humanities and social sciences. Between 1968 and 1971, 50 such women's groups were established. Between 1969 and 1972, such groups sparked 30 studies on women in academic disciplines, documenting the extent of discrimination in detail.[57]

Academic women's caucuses did not simply pressure for professional advancement: some went so far as to challenge the intellectual premises of their professions.[58] In 1970, a panel of young, feminist historians (including Bread and Roses founder Linda Gordon) at the American Historical Association (AHA) accused the profession not only of ignoring women in the historical narratives presented in textbooks but also of treating women, when they did so, with condescending stereotypes. Male historians reacted with incredulity, claiming the mantle of scholarly objectivity and accusing the women of political bias. It was a turbulent, angry meeting at the usually decorous AHA.[59]

Bernice Sandler initiated one of the most far-reaching challenges to discrimination in colleges and universities after she was denied tenure at the University of Maryland. Upon discovering that her experience had been repeated many times over, she approached WEAL about taking action. In January 1970, WEAL filed a complaint with the U.S. Department of Labor demanding a review of all colleges and universities holding federal contracts to determine whether they complied with antidiscrimination regulations; 250 institutions were targeted for more specific charges of sex discrimination. By the end of the year, suits brought by individual women and for women as a class had been brought against more than 360 institutions of higher education.[60]

In response to similar pressures, most professional schools not only began to pay new attention to their own employment patterns but also to drop barriers and quotas designed to limit the enrollment of female students. The revolution was quiet. Two decades of rapidly increasing access to higher education had prepared a large number of women for law school, medical school, and the like. As the floodgates opened, thousands seized the opportunity. The number of female applicants to law school, for example, grew 14-fold between 1969 and 1972.[61] By 1976, women were more than 19 percent of medical school graduates, up from 7.5 percent in 1969.[62] Stories of hostile treatment in this formerly male terrain abound. Doctoral students in chemistry found dog feces in their desk drawers.[63] Less hostile departments simply reminded women from time to time that they didn't quite fit. Kathleen Graham's female classmates at Stanford Law School (1968–1971) developed intense bonds to help them cope. What they faced was not hostility but a generalized inability of those around them—both in and out of school—to entertain the category female lawyer. "It took a lot of energy to think about how to respond to the broad spectrum of response to us that suggested we weren't serious. . . . [We were] being constantly, subtly undercut and relegated to a complementary, soft, feminine role that [undermined] the possibility and opportunities and reality of being intellectually rigorous and articulate and strong."[64]

The dramatic increase in the number of women "in the pipeline," in turn, began to change the workforce, heralded by a growing number of "firsts." Among the earliest were women who had been waiting, fully prepared, for ordination. In 1970, two major Lutheran denominations approved the ordination of women. In 1972, Sally Preisand became the first female rabbi. Most major Protestant denominations experienced turbulence as "women's liberation" presentations appeared on the agendas of major national meetings. Episcopalians in 1970 seated female deputies for the first time but denied ordination on the grounds that women were not in the "image of Christ." Sandra Hughes Boyd had been devastated by the rejection of women's ordination. When she heard that 11 women deacons and several bishops planned an "irregular" ordination in Philadelphia on July 29, 1974, she "knew [she] had to be there."

A group of us borrowed a van to drive to Philadelphia. En route we emerged only shaken up following a triple spin on the wet, slippery Pennsylvania turnpike and left unspoken the extent to which we believed this somehow confirmed the rightness not only of the event itself but also of our own participation in it. . . . Despite the considerable anxiety about the potential for violent reaction against this open challenge to the church's authority, it was a day of unforgettable joy and celebration.[65]

The church quickly declared such ordinations "invalid," but after 2 more years of intense debate and politicking, in 1976 the Episcopal Church reversed itself, recognized the ordinations of these rebellious pioneers, and allowed future women's ordination.[66]

ALTHOUGH MANY OF the most powerful and visible symbols of women's new access to the world of public work were highly educated professionals, greater numbers lay in the tenacious and courageous challenges raised by women in the "pink and blue collar" ghettos of factories and offices. In 1974, clerical workers in Boston and Chicago created a new kind of workplace organization using the techniques of community organizing pioneered by Saul Alinsky rather than traditional trade union methods.

Day Piercy, as an undergraduate at Duke University and then a student in social work at the University of North Carolina in the late sixties, had become intensely involved in community organization and briefly connected to women's liberation groups. After moving to Chicago in 1969, she served as the first staff member of the Chicago Women's Liberation Union (CWLU), working out of a small office in the YWCA. She convinced the YWCA to hire her "to do rap groups with working class women," which led to a strong interest in day care. She and Heather Booth (one of the founders of the West Side Group and later the CWLU) created an action committee for decent child care through the CWLU despite serious debates about "whether it was correct to work on issues like child care."

It was the demise of the day care project—in the aftermath of Nixon's veto of federal child care funding—that provoked Piercy to shift her focus toward organizing working women. Heather Booth had recently founded the Midwest Academy, a training center for community organizers. Together they and several others debated the possibilities of organizing women workers. They modeled themselves on the farmworkers' union led by Caesar Chavez. Piercy recalls thinking that the development of the Farm Workers, which began with civil rights issues and then moved to more traditional forms of collective bargaining, "was totally parallel to feminism in many ways. I began to wonder if you couldn't [use] those same principles: dignity for women workers, equal opportunity for women, equal pay for equal work—by the end of 1972 [these were] widespread."[67]

Women Employed, then, was founded by two women in their middle twenties who had been active in the women's liberation movement, influenced by civil rights, farmworkers, and community organizing, and who had an institutional connection to the YWCA, where Piercy was still employed. Aware that labor unions denigrated the possibility of organizing women, they set their sights on women workers in the Chicago Loop.

One of their first steps was to conduct training sessions for women at the Midwest Academy. Ann Ladky and Ann Scott from Chicago NOW showed up. Piercy quickly discovered among them a capacity for strategic and pragmatic thinking and a strong interest in organizing she had missed in more ideological groups. Ellen Cassedy arrived from Boston, where she worked with an organization of Harvard office workers started by Bread and Roses member Karen Nussbaum. Cassedy recalls that after her years of antiwar and women's movement activism in Chicago and Berkeley, she was stunned by discussions that began with "'OK, what are you going to win?' Just the word 'victory' felt weird." She spent 2 months more working with the fledgling Women Employed and returned to Boston inspired to change their small group into an organization that could win concrete changes for working women.[68] That group became 9 to 5, ultimately a national network of organizations of clerical workers.

Women Employed and 9 to 5 took the insights generated by several years of consciousness-raising and applied them to the problem of organizing women in one of the most female-dominated sectors in the labor force. Instead of focusing on the traditional labor union issues of wages and hours, they talked about the little daily humiliations that reminded office workers of their subordinate status *as women*. Highly trained legal secretaries made coffee for the entire office; secretaries performed personal services outside their job descriptions—shopping for presents for their boss's wife or children and delivering and picking up laundry; office workers regularly trained inexperienced men to take over senior positions for which they could never be considered and endured sexual harassment from men at all levels; and clerical pay remained extremely low on the assumption that women didn't really need the income. Aware that office workers were often isolated from one another and extremely vulnerable, WE and 9 to 5 developed methods of gathering information and feeding it back in a public forum. They passed out questionnaires at subway stops and near office buildings. Then they announced survey results at a press conference and through flyers that invited clerical workers to meetings at the end of the workday. In the flyer, secretaries could read information about salary discrepancies, about limitations on advancement, and about how these practices were not only unfair but illegal.

Like the Farm Workers' Union, Women Employed proposed to begin with an assertion of legal civil rights, win some early victories, and move from there—perhaps—to more traditional forms of union organization. Using information gained from questionnaires, they filed suits against major corporations, including Kraft, Sears, and banks and insurance companies, for violations of Title VII. They also held flamboyant demonstrations that were empowering for women previously considered "unorganizable." Darlene Stille, for example, worked in an insurance company where despite her hard-won college degree (against her parents' wishes) she found herself " . . . in a great bullpen with a lot of other people. It was noisy; it was uncomfortable; it was gloomy; it was depressing. I just couldn't believe that after all those years of effort, this is what it had come to." Then she was rejected for a supervisory post because she was a woman. "I just had this notion that I could pull myself up by my bootstraps. And my bootstraps kept breaking." In April 1973, however, a friend in NOW persuaded her to attend a Women Employed demonstration and for the first time she saw that change was possible. She joined a WE picket line at Kraft Foods 2 days later. "It was wonderful, feeling that all this anger that had been backing up inside me now had a release, that I could bark back somehow . . . that I could find my voice in a larger community of women." Inspired, Stille became an activist and eventually served as Chairperson of Women Employed.[69]

Demonstrations not only recruited members, they were carefully designed to provoke media coverage and spread the word. Iris Rivera was an excellent legal secretary in a major Chicago law firm. When her supervisor ordered her to prepare the office coffee every morning, she refused on the grounds that "I don't drink coffee; it's not listed as one of my job duties, and ordering the secretaries to fix the coffee is carrying the role of homemaker too far." When she was fired, Women Employed saw a wonderful opportunity to dramatize their issues. They held a demonstration at the law office, national media in tow, and presented the lawyers with a bag of used coffee grounds and a flyer on how to make your own coffee. Step 5 was "Turn switch to on. This is the most difficult step, but, with practice, even an attorney can master it." Iris Rivera's face and words flashed across the country on TV screens and in newspapers, sparking debates and small revolutions in thousands of offices. She got her job back.[70]

Both 9 to 5 and Women Employed inspired similar groups in a number of other cities and a movie starring Jane Fonda, Lily Tomlin, and Dolly Parton. Actress Jane Fonda, who knew Nussbaum through antiwar movement networks, arranged a conversation with members of 9 to 5 who were invited not only to tell stories of office work from the point of view of secretaries but also to imagine changes they would like. These became grist for the script writers. The movie used comic exaggeration to portray scenes that any woman who ever worked in an office would recognize: incompetent men whose offices run only because of the behind-the-scenes competence of women, secretaries with skill and ambition who experience routine harassment and discover that promotion is impossible. The sequences in which women take over the office, exact revenge on evil bosses, and run it more effectively than ever were drawn directly from the fantasies of members of 9 to 5.[71]

In 1981, 9 to 5 agreed to become District 925 of the Service Employees International Union (SEIU) and to take on the unionization of clerical employees using their new methods.[72] The labor movement, however, had in the meantime enjoyed its own upsurge within the ranks in which women began to work together to build a Coalition of Labor Union Women (CLUW). The initiative that led to the formation of CLUW came from women who had been active in the formation of NOW and the NWPC.[73] Most important were the Women's Department of the United Auto Workers, which had housed NOW in its first year; the International Union of Electrical, Radio, and Machine Workers (IUE); the Communications Workers of America (CWA); the American Federation of State County and Municipal Workers (AFSME); and the American Federation of Teachers (AFT). UAW and IUE, with their deep roots in the radical unionism of the 1930s, had provided leadership on women's issues from the very beginning of the Second Wave. AFSCME, CWA, and AFT had organized constituencies in the growing female sectors of the labor force. But traditional union divisions not only prevented concerted action, for the most part they kept female activists in different unions from being aware of each other, even when they worked in the same city. By the late sixties and early seventies, however, they were meeting on other grounds.[74]

Several CLUW founders recalled the charged atmosphere in the early seventies. Those who were active in NOW, WEAL, or commissions on the status of women were constantly asked, "When are you people going to do your part [i.e., begin to raise women's issues within the labor movement]?" Female workers now regularly resorted to government intervention against both their employers and their unions. The IUE, for example, in 1966 expanded its Civil Rights Department to a Social Action Department in order to incorporate women's issues; the following year it held a national women's conference that spotlighted the problem of sex discrimination.[75]

It was difficult to organize across union lines. A few leaders got to know each other in the aftermath of the President's Commission on the Status of Women, and then through state commissions, NOW, and WEAL. A few more met at the roundtable discussions of women union leaders hosted by Elizabeth Koonz at the U.S. Women's Bureau. Others, like Olga Madar of the UAW and Addie Wyatt of the Amalgamated Meatcutters Union, met in antiwar activities or in support of the farmworkers' organizing efforts.[76]

More than 3,000 women showed up at the founding meeting for CLUW in 1974, twice the expected attendance. Joan Goodin described the excitement as "electric." "I remember being hugged in a jammed elevator by a stranger who proclaimed: 'Sister, we're about to put trade union women on the map.'"[77] Founders were surprised at how exciting it was simply to establish a network among union women. Addie Wyatt, elected Vice President, proclaimed, "CLUW has been a shot in the arm to the total labor movement. It has brought trade union women to the surface . . . never again will they be content to be absent from the world's agenda."[78] In subsequent years, despite serious internal divisions between 1974 and 1977, CLUW became an important training ground in leadership skills as well as a support group for women. For many, leadership in CLUW has translated into further leadership roles in local unions.[79] Joyce Miller, the first woman on the AFL-CIO Executive Council in 1980, was a president of CLUW.[80]

Yet CLUW also fueled a serious internal struggle with some radicalized graduates of elite colleges, determined to spread revolution. The effort of leftist sectarian groups to infiltrate and take over CLUW provoked a strong reaction by the founders of CLUW and forced a relatively closed hierarchy to seal its borders. CLUW was also shaped by the nature of the labor movement. Careful not to encroach on the organizing territories of individual unions or to appear in any way to be competitive with them, CLUW forswore any effort to reach out to unorganized workers.

At the height of the movement, women were not only challenging employers and political parties, they were rewriting the language itself. The story of Women in Publishing shows how a social movement can find its way into newspapers, textbooks, and schools across the country. Ann Ladky, a founder of Women in Publishing, attended one of Day Piercy and Heather Booth's training sessions at the Midwest Academy in 1972 and went on to become a leader in Women Employed. Her path to activism, however, had been through an eclectic mix of grass roots consciousness-raising that surged through workplaces, kitchens, bedrooms, and even car pools. After graduating from Northwestern University in 1970, Ladky found a job in publishing as a writer in the promotion department of Scott Foresman. The car pool she joined in April 1971 to get to her office in the Chicago suburbs was filled with women "who were all reading and talking about the women's movement." Several were members of NOW, and in the car they would debate the sexism of textbooks, offering examples from their own experiences as well as from discussions in NOW. Soon they began to ponder setting up a women's group at work. They also urged Ladky to join the Chicago NOW chapter. "I didn't see myself as a joiner at all, but I was disturbed the longer we talked." Late in 1971 a dozen or so women working for different publishers decided to create a citywide organization, Women in Publishing. Their first concern, that language itself encodes the subordination of women at every turn, drew on the insights of numerous CR groups and task forces. They drew up guidelines for nonsexist language use and set out to persuade major publishers to adopt them.[81]

In October 1974 the *New York Times Magazine* published excerpts from "Guidelines for Equal Treatment of the Sexes in McGraw-Hill Book Company Publications," an 11-page statement that had been distributed to all editorial employees and to 8,000 nonfiction authors of textbooks, reference works, trade journals, educational materials, and children's books. These guidelines inscribed the key elements of feminist ideas about sex roles and individual choice by the middle 1970s: "Men and women should be treated primarily as people, and not primarily as members of opposite sexes." Thus the guidelines advised avoidance of typecasting either men or women either by the type of work or by level of authority. "Members of both sexes should be represented as whole human beings with *human* strengths and weaknesses, not masculine or feminine ones." Not only were authors advised to avoid stereotypic and simplistic presentations, they were also warned to deal with women and men in the same terms (negative example: "Henry Harris is a shrewd lawyer and his wife, Ann, is a striking brunette"), to avoid patronizing, "girl-watching," and sexual innuendo, and to treat women "as part of the rule, not as the exception" (e.g., woman doctor).[82] The grammar of sexism was spelled out in admonitions to avoid the generic use of "man" or male pronouns (with numerous examples to illustrate possible substitutions: firefighter, not fireman; chair, not chairman; humanity, not man) and the many ways that women can be diminished by being referred to by first names when men are designated with full names and titles or by identification in terms of roles as wife, mother, sister, or daughter regardless of relevance, or by such pairings as "man and wife" and "the men and the ladies," and by never being first in order of mention. The disquiet of the *Times* editors, who themselves had not adopted such guidelines, was reflected in the subtitle: "The Mc-Graw-Hill Book Company's guidelines for equal treatment of the sexes, in which the average American loses *his* pronoun, Betty Co-ed becomes simply *student* and boys shall henceforth grow to *adult*hood."[83]

By the time publishers began to pay serious attention to the grammar of sexism, women's liberation had been a major force in the mass media for several years. Feminists communicated among themselves in a startling array of journals and newsletters. By 1975 there were upward of two dozen feminist presses and nearly 200 periodicals.[84] The most prominent bridge between the internal conversations generated by these publications (often within very specific groups, such as professional caucuses or feminists interested in such topics as abortion or therapy referral) and the broader public was *Ms.* magazine, whose preview edition, enclosed in an issue of *New York* magazine, appeared at the end of 1971.

Ms. set out to compete with mainstream women's magazines on the shelves of grocery stores. Glossy, slick, professional—run by professional journalists Gloria Steinem and Pat Carbine (former editor of *Mc-Call's* and *Look*)—the first "stand-alone" issue of *Ms.* sold out 300,000 copies within 8 days, generating a modest but encouraging 36,000 subscriptions and an astonishing 20,000 letters.[85] On the cover, a figure of the Hindu goddess Kali brandished in her ten arms the tools of women's daily lives: an iron, a telephone, a hand mirror, an automobile steering wheel, a clock, a feather duster, a frying pan, and a typewriter.[86] In that issue women first read about "the click" in Jane O'Reilly's "The House-wife's Moment of Truth." Gloria Steinem explained "Sisterhood" as "deep personal connections of women . . . [which] often ignore barriers of age, economics, worldly experience, race, culture—all the barriers that, in male or mixed society, had seemed so difficult to cross." Judy Syfer humorously addressed working women's exhaustion with "I Want A Wife"; Letty Cottin Pogrebin explained how to raise children without imposing traditional sex roles in "Down with Sexist Upbringing," and Cellestine Ware interviewed Eleanor Holmes Norton on "The Black Family and Feminism." Additional articles on welfare as a women's issue, how to set up child care centers, abortion rights, where to complain about job discrimination, and lesbian love portrayed a significant range of feminist concerns and activities.[87]

This first issue was the brainchild of Gloria Steinem from start to finish. She chose its contents, and the authors were drawn from her own circle of friends.[88] Steinem is an interesting link between the various branches of the Second Wave. Generationally she was a bit older than the founders of women's liberation and a bit younger than the founders of NOW. Already a professional journalist, she was drawn into the professional and political circles around NOW and WEAL, but she was radicalized, fundamentally, by radical feminism. With her media connections, and good looks, Steinem was quickly anointed a feminist leader and spokesperson by journalists. For this she came under considerable fire. Yet because most of her close political connections were through networks of policy activists, she could be a superstar like Bella Abzug or Shirley Chisholm without being driven from the movement. Hers was always a multicultural vision of feminism. Through the 1970s she insisted that she share the platform with a woman of color at all her speaking engagements. A founder of NWPC, activist in the Democratic Convention in 1972, and founder of Women's Action Alliance in New York, she continually functioned as a link between groups and a popularizer of some of their more radical ideas.[89]

Ms. lacked the raw angry passion of women's liberation manifestos, but neither was it a dry, policy-oriented brief. It packaged feminism in an optimistic and personalized frame using the approaches of traditional women's magazines, such as "how-to" articles with an altogether new twist: how to raise children without imposing stereotypic sex roles or how to file an EEOC complaint about discrimination on the job. Through *Ms.*, a new form of address entered the popular culture. Many Americans found it odd, even insultingly strange, but *Ms.* defined its title as a "form of address meaning whole person, female" that did not define women according to their marital status (as Miss and Mrs.)."⁹⁰

Women's liberation found another institutionalized and mainstream outlet in the creation of women's studies programs on campuses across the country. Women's studies started with informal courses at "free universities" and other alternative settings. Indeed the campus setting of much of the New Left made it natural for consciousness-raising groups and women's caucuses of New Left organizations to offer courses as a form of outreach. Leaders of such courses made no pretense of expertise, but they wanted to spread the word that women were oppressed and needed to band together. They used courses to extend their own understanding of women's history and the nature of female oppression, to review classics like Simone de Beauvoir's *The Second Sex*, as well as to read the new feminist literature that was growing with breathtaking speed.⁹¹ To colleges and universities, they began to make the claim that women were a worthy subject of study.

Just as the civil rights movement had stimulated a demand for black history and African-American studies, the women's liberation movement posed questions that challenged the standard content of traditional courses in history, literature, and social sciences. Feminists who were already in positions of academic leadership played critical roles in launching women's studies. Sheila Tobias, Associate Provost at Wesleyan University, teamed up with Betty Friedan as visiting professors at Cornell in January 1969 to teach what may have been the first women's studies course for credit,⁹² Gerda Lerner taught a women's history course at Sarah Lawrence, and courses on "Women in History," "Women in Literature," "The Politics of Male-Female Relationships," and "The Evolution of Female Personality" appeared in college catalogues from Cornell to San Diego State and from the College of St. Catherine to Princeton, in 1969–1970. In 1970, Tobias put together a collection of 17 syllabi and bibliographies. The Commission on the Status of Women of the Modern Language Association 2 years later compiled 66 syllabi from about 40 different schools for the publication of *Female Studies II.* Nearly half the courses concerned women and literature or cultural criticism—understandable because of the networks closest to the compilers—but they also gathered descriptions of 9 history courses (several on women's social roles, 2 specifically on the history of women's rights movements), 15 social science courses (e.g., "Sex and Politics," "Linguistic Behavior of Male and Female," "Psychology of Women," and "Women in the U.S. Economy"), and 11 interdisciplinary courses (e.g., "Philosophical and Psychological Aspects of Women's Roles," "Women as a Minority Group," "Biology and Society," and "Sex Roles in American Society and Politics").[93]

Word about women's studies spread through movement channels as well as academic ones. At many universities, students were the first to demand a women's studies course and they frequently participated in teaching experimental and interdisciplinary offerings. At Old Westbury Community College on Long Island, students and faculty jointly taught a course attended by students, secretaries, and even the wife of the college president.[94] Karen McTighe Musil remembered that those early courses were interdisciplinary and closely connected to students' lives. She had taken her first teaching job in 1971 at LaSalle College just as the college went coed. Eager to offer the women students a course about women, she teamed up with Judy Newton, who arrived the next year, and together they taught the first women's studies course in 1973. Female students flocked to them, acutely aware of the differential treatment of male and female students. "It was heady times. The students fired us up."[95]

The handful of scholars already studying women, people like Alice Rossi, Jesse Bernard, Gerda Lerner, and Anne Firor Scott, suddenly found an audience and an intellectual community. A generation of young professors with activist leanings but trained in traditional disciplines suddenly changed course. They left behind standard dissertations framed in the traditions of their disciplines and moved quickly into the forefront of the new feminist scholarship and the creation of women's studies programs.[96] Kate Millett, galvanized by her participation in New York Radical Women, wrote a dissertation entitled *Sexual Politics* that broke open the field of feminist literary criticism and feminist theory when it was published in 1970.[97] A total of 150 women's studies programs were established between 1970 and 1975, offering everything from a small cluster of courses to full-blown undergraduate majors. By 1980 there were 300.[98]

WITH THE ISSUE of women's equality a matter of continuing public debate, on September 20, 1973, 48 million Americans were glued to their television sets, watching "The Battle of the Sexes," a tennis match between tennis pro Billie Jean King and a former male tennis star, Bobby Riggs. King was at the top of her form in 1973. For several years she had used her prominence to publicize the inequities faced by professional women tennis players and to build a grassroots movement of female athletes. In 1970 she was the first professional woman tennis player to earn more than $100,000 in a single year, yet the top male player earned three times as much for winning only one-third as many tournaments. King organized a boycott in protest of the pro tennis tour because of the income differences between women and men. Subsequently she played a prominent role in the new all-women's pro circuit (the Virginia Slims Tour); forced the U.S. Open to equalize prize money for women and men; and organized the Women's Tennis Association. For many women, and especially budding young female athletes, Billie Jean King symbolized their hopes.[99]

Billie Jean had no need to defend her skill against the taunts of a 55-year-old hustler and former tennis star, Bobby Riggs. Proclaiming himself a "male chauvinist pig," Riggs needled, "You insist that top women players provide a brand of tennis comparable to men's. I challenge you to prove it. I contend that you not only cannot beat a top male player, but that you can't beat me, a tired old man." When he goaded the second-ranked player, Margaret Court, into a match—for which she did not train or prepare—and won, King accepted the challenge, because she understood the power of a symbol. She trained hard and joined in the hype. At the Houston Astrodome, the two contestants met at center court. Riggs entered the arena in a ricksha pulled by "Bobby's bosom buddies," five young women in skimpy attire. King appeared on a brilliant red divan borne by four men in Roman slave costume. Riggs' hustle worked. Las Vegas bookies set the odds at 5 to 2 in his favor, but King won the three sets with ease 6–4, 6–3, 6–3.[100] Shouts of jubilation echoed in homes and bars across the country. For a moment, at least, it seemed that nothing could hold women back. From the protests of a few militants the Second Wave had swept to the forefront of American society, changing everything from language, to etiquette, to who cooks dinner and who can be a sports star.

The national organizations, campaigns, and institutions feminists built in the golden years only hint at the massive upsurge in state and local activism. Yet it is too easy to tell the story as if the movement was invincible and internally consistent. Within the growing surge of the feminist tidal wave the undertow of internal strife always coexisted with innovation and creativity.

CHAPTER 4

Undertow

EVEN AS THE MOVEMENT gathered strength, as Billie Jean King whipped Bobby Riggs (1973) and women's groups pushed the ERA through Congress (1972), there were signs of trouble for anyone who was looking for them. The paucity of memoirs from the first years of the Second Wave until recently indicates that in these years intense pain and ecstasy, utopian expectation and despair, were sides of the same coin. Dana Densmore recalled with some puzzlement that her Boston group (later Cell 16) published a journal in August 1968 with no name and no date. "Looking back as editor and publisher of some of the later six issues, it seems strange that it never occurred to us to date the first issue, but it accurately reflected our state of mind then. We didn't foresee an orderly future that would in turn become history and require documentation. Instead, we saw ourselves on the verge of a great upheaval. Perhaps it was like the anticipation of the end of the world for early Christians."[1] Like the nineteenth century American apocalyptic believers, these activists were destined to suffer great disappointment. The undertow of division and internal conflict, however, was part and parcel of feminism's creative power. Conflict and creativity alike flowed from utopian hopes in a turbulent historical context, and each flourished on the boundary between public and private, political and personal.

Feminist radicals were hardly the only apocalyptic activists in the late sixties and early seventies. Violence was ubiquitous—in Vietnam, in urban riots, on campuses like Kent State and Jackson State where the National Guard killed demonstrating students, in a few acts and a lot of talk of political terrorism (banks bombed and robbed, a campus building blown up), and in widespread talk of "revolution," whatever that meant. It was an era of immense countercultural experimentation with new ways of living—from diet to work to sexuality to family formations. It was also a time of high hopes in which change increased at an exponential rate, leaving people dizzy and breathless, whether with exhilaration, dread, or despair. By the middle seventies, as if in reaction, the country seemed to have retreated into the imagined safety of private life, earning the (mis)nomer "the me decade."

Challenging old rules, activists analyzed the many ways that traditional hierarchical structures enforced the subordination of women. While looking for ways not to replicate the evils they wished to overthrow, they sometimes made new rules as rigid as the old. Wave after wave of division swept around the country, wracking some groups with conflict, touching others only slightly, leaving some individuals too wounded to continue while others found new and more effective ways to carry on. Many of the battles in retrospect seem as difficult to grasp as ancient debates about how many angels can dance on the head of a pin, but they were immensely real to participants, and they set up a dynamic that persisted for decades. It may help to imagine this process of internal disintegration and re-creation to look at one example, in this case the history of the women's liberation movement in Washington, D.C. between 1968 and 1971. It was born, grew large and complex, and then imploded over one of the many "splits" that occurred around the country, in this case the "gay-straight" split. The group that forced this explosion called themselves "the Furies." They did not last long, but their ideas remained influential, appearing and reappearing in other contexts for years to come. Having explored this case study, we can look at the broader pattern it exemplifies and reflect on the historical reasons and the dynamics within the movement that made these creative years simultaneously so divisive, fusing political innovation with personal and ideological discord.

WOMEN'S LIBERATION in the District grew from the New Left in 1968. With leadership from Charlotte Bunch and Marilyn Webb based at the Institute for Policy Studies, D.C. Women's Liberation grew rapidly but was plagued by persistent self-criticism. How could radicals be sure they were revolutionary rather than merely Band-Aid reformists? In the summer of 1969, one subgroup issued a paper complaining that "Washington Women's Liberation is presently without energy or passion, amorphous with respect to priorities, . . . undefined with respect to strategy and organizationally uncoordinated." A second group responded that this approached the problem backward, that it was useless to create a structure before reaching political agreement. Liberation, in the latter view, was "not possible given a system of capitalism; it is only possible to think about after that system is destroyed."[1] Given the high polemical pitch of the remnants of the New Left around them, most of the women involved shrank from the debate itself, choosing instead to continue working in a variety of projects on the assumption that a common political analysis would emerge from this practice.

So the women in the District worked, and their projects proliferated. The "do-everything" ethos of early women's liberation was as exhilarating in D.C. as everywhere else. Playgroups led to the creation of a day care center. Proliferating invitations to speak to high school classes inspired an education project. Discussions of physical vulnerability produced self-defense classes. Participation in environmental activities (the first Earth Day was April 22, 1970) prompted a women and ecology study group and a paper on the link between sexism and environmental destruction, long before anyone had heard of eco-feminism. Activists freely, and playfully, conducted WITCH actions, among them hexing the Justice Department as a bastion of male supremacy.

But their longing for fundamental change could make it difficult to carry through on more short-term activist successes. For example, health care activists worried that abortion counseling was insufficiently radical, and yet as elsewhere the demand for it would not abate. They formed a brief alliance with a welfare rights group to explore the links between racism and women's health issues. Later they disrupted congressional hearings on the pill to demand attention to the risks to women from the new medication that had not been widely tested (indeed, early hormone doses in the pill were very high). Out of this came national attention, a national survey, and a sit-in at the office of HEW

Secretary Finch when he failed to carry out a promise to include warnings in every package of birth control pills. Yet in each case success and self-criticism went hand in hand. In retrospect this intervention had a long-term impact, but its initiators floundered strategically, unclear how to link a specific issue to their broader vision. Thus, health care activists concluded in 1971 that "we were not successful, however, in making this a useful local organizing project; only a few women were continuously and actively involved after the Finch sit-in; we were unsure where to move next with the issue."[3]

D.C. Women's Liberation rented an apartment, set up an office and a coordinating committee called Magic Quilt [designed to discourage takeover efforts by the Socialist Workers' Party], offered courses, sponsored projects, saw the movement grow in Washington suburbs, and began to spin off "collectives" that hoped to avoid the stifling slowness of consensus-based decision making. *Off our backs* was one of the first collectives and it grew rapidly into one of the most important national feminist newspapers. Playfully named groups like Daughters of Lilith and Coral Conspiracy and an experimental women's commune all set out to figure out what to do in the stage beyond initial consciousness-raising. Each in turn was charged with elitism.[4]

According to D.C. Women's Liberation's own analysis at the time, "While this was an active period with many political debates, by the end of May [1970] when over 60 women came together for a weekend retreat, it was clear that there were unresolved political problems. There was still no agreed upon political program; many new women felt left out and confused about our directions; many other women felt held back by the large number of new women and the need for consensus to act."[5] Those who were most involved in trying to maintain a central office and communications network felt overburdened and burned out while activist energy continually emerged at the periphery. By the fall of 1970 there were 24 discussion groups and 14 projects in D.C. Women's Liberation, but little communication among them except for the weekly meetings of Magic Quilt, which were, by turns, bureaucratic and contentious.[6]

This was a volatile mix of utopian expectations, high energy, and a yearning for certitude and consensus in the face of constant argument. Seeking to claim the "radical" or truly "revolutionary" high ground, differences of opinion quickly became polemical absolutes. Fearing rupture, activists continually suppressed differences rather than engage them. With their horizon set on revolution, wanting every act (public or private) to be politically pure, they were unable to grasp the amazing success of their proliferating activities or to create structures capable of sustaining them. Instead, they debated things like how to "smash monogamy" in a desperate search for the "fundamental contradiction" that would hold the key to revolutionary change in their lives and in the world. Beneath the tension and self-scrutiny there was also an erotic current. Thrilling to some, frightening to others, lesbianism provided the political solution for a small group who broke the political stalemate decisively, traumatically, and creatively in the spirit of radical, utopian experimentation.

What was happening in Washington in 1970 and 1971 was of a piece with the rest of the nation. Participants wrote, "The most burning controversial issues of the fall [1970] were racism and relating to the Panthers, Imperialism and what it means to be international, and the smoldering controversy over lesbianism. Generally, we were asking how do each of these relate to building a revolutionary women's movement."[7] As their own experiments gained in intensity, Washington women's liberation's relationship with the left, in particular with the Black Panther Party, deteriorated beyond repair. At two national conferences in the fall of 1970, the Panthers exhibited great disdain for the white women who showed up. In an interesting twist, though, it was at one of those meetings that Washington women came in contact with Radicalesbians from New York and were swept off their feet by their energy, their conviction, and their sheer radicalism.[8]

Inspired by the actions and writings of "Lavender Menace" and the arrival of Rita Mae Brown, a founder of Radicalesbians in New York, several women in Washington developed the conviction that lesbianism and feminism were one and the same and that women's survival depended on the possibility of complete autonomy from men. They had found the "fundamental contradiction": heterosexism. Lesbianism became the key to overcoming male supremacy and—given that many of them had become lesbians through the women's movement—they believed it could be a political choice for any woman, in fact the only way a woman could be free. "Lesbianism is a threat to the ideological, political, personal and economic basis of male supremacy. . . . The Lesbian's independence and refusal to support one man undermines the personal power that men exercise over women. . . . We offer the beginning of the end of collective and individual male supremacy."⁹ Their evolution wracked the D.C. Women's Liberation Movement with conflict. Were lesbians appropriate models in the child care center? Could male children be allowed to come with their mothers to "all-women" events? At a spring 1971 retreat to assess the state of the movement and define directions, one group consciously and deliberately forced the discussion of lesbianism into every session, demanding that all women who were serious about feminism make the choice to become lesbian or at least talk about it.¹⁰ This group, who all lived together, later became known as the Furies.

The 12 women who named themselves the Furies in the manner of many revolutionary groups set out to erase the boundaries between public and private by eliminating the latter. If communist states had set out to create a "new socialist man," the Furies were going to create a "new woman." Founding member Rita Mae Brown articulated the vision this way:

We must move out of our old living patterns and into new ones. Those of us who believe in this concept must begin to build collectives where women are committed to other women on all levels—emotional, physical, economical and political. Monogamy can be cast aside; no one will 'belong' to another. Instead of being shut off from each other in overpriced cubicles we can be together, sharing the shit work as well as the highs. Together we can go through the pain and liberation of curing the diseases we have all contracted in the world of male dominance, imperialism and death. Women-identified collectives are nothing less than the next step towards a women's revolution.¹¹

They set out to cure these diseases with searing criticism and self-criticism sessions, a well-known practice on the left, in which they challenged each other's political imperfections, pointing out instances of racism, classism, heterosexism, and ageism. Charlotte Bunch remembers it as a time when "we were obsessed" with creating an identity. As a consummate coalition builder, she found this detour into "the most extreme thing I ever did" a kind of liberation, an "exhilaration of just being bad" by taking one issue to its logical extreme and not worrying about bringing others along. Having splintered the women's movement in D.C., however, they burned themselves out in about a year and a half. Soon they realized they were talking only to themselves. "It was great for about a year or so. Then, 'so what?' What do we do strategically, politically?"[12] The extreme form of separatism the Furies tried to live out proved a dead end. Politically, at least, there was nowhere else to go because the rest of the world did not follow them. Their experiment, however, especially, the fiercely radical and uncompromising thinking in their newspaper, which began publication in January 1972, pushed lesbian feminism to the forefront of radical feminist thought, where it has remained, though in far different forms.

THOUGH THE FURIES represent an extreme example, the women's movement as a whole was prone to schism from the start. When Charlotte Bunch said that the Furies did not know any other way to do what they set out to do, her criticism was of the "all-or-nothing" dynamic not only within women's liberation but also within the remnants of the New Left that entertained grandiose fantasies of revolution.[13] Such movements (which sociologists have called "totalizing") took over virtually every aspect of one's life: relationships, recreation, and work as well as politics. "Living and breathing" the movement was a source of great exhilaration, but it was also draining and impossible to sustain, and it raised apocalyptic expectations that could not be realized. The rhetoric about "revolution" was not just about making history but about the *end* of history in which the movement becomes the entire society. Change (i.e., history) would become irrelevant because people would finally have gotten it "right" and understand the "truth."

The early struggles about the definition of the emerging movement were themselves framed by a left-wing form of argumentation filled with invective and charges of reformism and selling out. For example, a widely read paper by Beverly Jones and Judith Brown in Gainesville, Florida, "Toward a Female Liberation Movement," criticized a 1967 manifesto from the SDS women's caucus as "soft-minded NAACP logic and an Urban League list of grievances and demands." With such adjectives as "ludicrous" and "pathetic," the authors accused women in SDS of "mimicking dominant groups' rhetoric on power politics" and trying to advance personally in a male power structure. Against this background, they made their case for an autonomous radical women's liberation movement.[14]

Of course, they were responding to similar rhetoric from leftists (both male and female), who freely accused women who chose to organize separately as lacking "revolutionary potential."[15] Marge Piercy reflected on her years in the Left when men insisted that " . . . for a woman to think of herself is bourgeois subjectivity and inherently counterrevolutionary": "I once thought that all that was necessary was to make men understand that they would achieve their own liberation, too, by joining the struggle for women's liberation: but it has come to me to seem a little too much like the chickens trying to educate the farmer."[16]

In Boston, Cell 16, under the leadership of Roxanne Dunbar, advocated a strictly separate radical women's movement. In the first issue of their journal, Maureen Davidica called for "radical women to dissociate themselves from male-oriented, male-dominated radical organizations and join together in Women's Liberation groups." Not only had women played secondary roles in radical movements and achieved their status by association with radical men, but Davidica also maintained the radical movement was "irrelevant" to women. "War is male. The draft is male. Power structures are all male."[17] Radical women in Boston who disagreed with Cell 16 founded Bread and Roses with the hope of building an autonomous women's movement that could remain connected to the issues and concerns of the Left.[18]

In its first, formative year, women's liberation meetings roiled with such debates. The Lake Villa Conference in November 1968 was the first effort to bring together a national gathering of women's liberation, and at least some of the planners had hoped that there might emerge from it an embryonic national organization. Reports from that conference, however, were extremely polarized. At a series of "body feminism" workshops on sexuality and lifestyle, participants were thrilled by the sense that they were pushing the edges of what they knew or thought possible. Together they explored what a feminist lifestyle might be like and how they felt about their bodies. But Charlotte Bunch, who chaired the final plenary, says it took everything in her to keep people from killing each other (metaphorically speaking) in a meeting that reenacted the worst of New Left-style debate. Women from New York arrived with a plan for consciousness-raising that became foundational for practices around the country, but they also believed that they had the TRUTH and that any deviation from their tightly defined way of conducting a consciousness-raising session constituted an unbearable dilution and loss of meaning. When others appropriated and improvised on their theme, they reacted fiercely. Little wonder that no one left that conference inspired to try to build a national movement organization.[19]

Most cities managed to avoid the sectarianism that characterized the New York women's movement, where one group after another broke off to pursue its own utopian vision. New York was not so much different in kind, however, as in intensity. Everywhere, groups formed, grew large and unwieldy, divided, and battled over ownership of the movement. Characterized by an enormous intellectual creativity, the New York Radical Feminists (the initiating group and the one that invented consciousness-raising as a technique for building theory) also drew in a number of leaders with impressive egos and ambition. Some of them, like Shulamith Firestone, Kathie Sarachild, Carol Hanisch, Anne Koedt, and Susan Brownmiller, had roots in the civil rights and antiwar movements, but their connections with New Left organizations were relatively tenuous as the women's movement began. They were primarily intellectuals, not organizers, and they believed deeply in the power of ideas. Several of them wrote classic works—obviously at white heat when you realize it was late 1967 or early 1968 when they first started to meet: Shulamith Firestone's *The Dialectic of Sex* (1970), Kate Millet's

Sexual Politics (1970), Robin Morgan's edited collection *Sisterhood Is Powerful* (1970), and Susan Brownmiller's *Against Our Will* (1975). New Yorkers also had to deal with a part of the left that was notoriously schismatic, flamboyant, doctrinaire, and male-dominated. They led the effort to define "radical feminism" as a movement to eradicate sex roles and to criticize those who continued to have other social movement connections as hopelessly "politico."[20]

The so-called politico-feminist split raged on ideological issues but frequently rested more on differences of emphasis, tone, and style. Often these issues boiled down to a willingness or unwillingness to work with men under any circumstances. Semantic games about who is the enemy (men or "the system") masked these other differences. In part it was an argument about priorities, but in the polarized version of the debate, "feminists" cast everyone with any attachment to other movement issues as traitors to feminism and willing subordinates of men; "politicos" (who for the most part did not accept that label) accused feminists of being reformist and bourgeois. Each charged the other with failing to be truly radical and betraying the "real" revolution. In most cities there were debates but not a split. For 3 years before the Furies, in Washington, D.C., women's liberation "the usual D.C. response to these debates was to discuss the issues, to agree we had to combine some of both sides (i.e. we agreed with feminists that women should organize separately and that men were individually oppressive to women and we agreed with 'movement' women that the real cause of our oppression was the system, not the men who were agents of it, and that while organizing separately we still had to address ourselves to other than women's issues as well), and to breathe a sigh of relief that we in D.C. were not so factionalized."[21]

But those who broke away from the male Left under the banner of "radical feminism" found that division was far from over. Alice Echols has traced in some detail the schisms among radical feminists and their strenuous efforts to get it right: New York Radical Women, Redstockings, the Feminists, and Cell 16.[22] Several of these groups were utopian and sometimes authoritarian experiments organized around a charismatic leader (Roxanne Dunbar dominated the early months of Cell 16;

Kathy Amatniek, Redstockings; Ti-Grace Atkinson, the Feminists). Efforts to realize ideals rapidly evolved into rules. In many cities, popular leaders and public speakers were ordered not to accept invitations lest they become "heavies." Radical feminism as "the advocacy of the total elimination of sex roles" was a powerful vision but a quixotic one that led to excesses. While the pioneering groups splintered, their patterns of experimentation, rigid rule making, and sectarian division echoed across the country, although often with less intensity.

When Robin Morgan set out to promote *Sisterhood Is Powerful* in 1970, she was astonished to discover that the exhausting debates that consumed her in New York were fundamentally irrelevant to most of the groups springing up across the country.[23] Indeed, in most cities the decentralized nature of women's liberation groups meant that schism was avoided for several years. By the early seventies, though, women's liberation organizations across the country were wracked with tension over seemingly irreconcilable perspectives.

After only 6 or 7 years, the women's liberation movement had splintered. Naomi Weisstein lamented the dissolution of the Chicago Women's Liberation Rock Band in 1973, which " . . . broke up in an agony of hatred and hidden agendas. . . . The band was a microcosm of what was happening all over the country: we were losing our women's movement and there was no one to tell us how to stop the dissolution."[24] It was not a simple story of decline, however, but rather one of change and transformation. For some, this meant a turn toward other forms of activism in socialist feminist groups, in labor organizing, in academia; others could only see loss and disintegration. In 1975, Robin Morgan circulated an essay, "Rights of Passage," to other editors of *Ms.*, in which she optimistically described her own emergence into a broader vision of feminist radicalism, including activism on the part of the "reformist wing" she previously reviled. Ellen Willis fired back an angry memo challenging Morgan's optimistic rendition of the state of the movement: "The movement is fragmented, confused, torn by major political splits, dominated by its most conservative elements. . . . I would say the movement is *in crisis*—and what we need is to analyze the real situation, not pour honey all over it."[25]

The crisis splashed across the Family/Style section of the *New York Times* after reporter Lucinda Franks visited Sagaris, a feminist summer institute in rural Vermont in August 1975. A few months before, some of the founders of Redstockings had circulated an attack on Gloria Steinem alleging that "Gloria Steinem has a ten-year association with the CIA stretching from 1959 to 1969 which she has misrepresented and covered up. Further, we have become convinced that *Ms.* magazine, founded and edited by her, is hurting the women's liberation movement."[26] When Steinem did not dignify the charges with an immediate response, many longtime activists gave them credence because of their own experience with government surveillance and sabotage. Indeed, as historian Ruth Rosen has demonstrated conclusively, during this time the FBI infiltrated many women's groups, and it seems likely that agent provocateurs exacerbated some internal divisions.[27] At Sagaris, a battle erupted when participants learned of a new (and much needed) grant from the *Ms.* Foundation. Ti-Grace Atkinson charged, "You can't take that money. The Redstockings have just accused Gloria Steinem of being a CIA agent. The money is tainted, that money is suspect, and you're going to pollute Sagaris with it."[28] Soon after, a third of the faculty and students walked out to set up an alterative institute, and the *New York Times* reporter arrived to find, as her article headlined, "Dissention Among Feminists."[29]

Competition for ownership of the movement had reached a fever pitch across the political spectrum. Betty Friedan, never subtle about her irritation at the attention paid to Gloria Steinem, fed the speculation about Steinem. Through news reporters, she demanded a response and wondered aloud whether the CIA was behind a "paralysis of leadership."[30] For the original founders of the Second Wave across the political spectrum, the fact was that the movement had grown beyond their control, and they found themselves in the position of hearing words and slogans they had coined coming from groups with whom they disagreed. Envy and loss expressed themselves with the traditional arsenal of left-wing paranoia (indeed, a strange parody of McCarthyism).[31]

Inside NOW, the struggle for leadership was less personalized but equally fractious. In its first contested election, the 1974 NOW convention selected New York lawyer Karen DeCrow as president; supporters of her opponent, Mary Jean Collins-Robson from Chicago, dominated the Board as well as the Chicago office staff. Ostensibly the conflict had to do with whether NOW should continue as a mass-based, grass-roots organization or shift to a more streamlined structure emphasizing the catalytic importance of leadership on a more radicalized set of issues. DeCrow's slogan, "Out of the Mainstream and into the Revolution," signaled the influence of women's liberation, as she called for a greater emphasis on lesbian rights, racial minorities, and working-class women. Her opponents' anxieties about the emergence of lesbians as a political force in the movement were expressed in a strategic complaint: "NOW is concentrating unduly on lesbians . . . and that's not where the mainstream is."[32] Collins-Robson and many of her supporters had been trained at the Midwest Academy founded by Heather Booth and Day Piercy. Their Alinsky-style organizing approach, emphasizing local mobilizations around concrete issues like pay equity, affirmative action, and daycare never had an opportunity to flourish.

By the end of 1974, 12 board members had joined DeCrow in calling for structural change, filing a lawsuit (alleging violations of the by-laws), and placing their dues in escrow. Calling themselves the Majority Caucus, they waged a tightly organized campaign at the 1975 convention at which the American Arbitration Association had been contracted to oversee the election (for $100,000). There were in fact no deep ideological differences between the two factions, each of which agreed that the continuing existence of a national organization was paramount. The Majority Caucus's narrow victory paved the way for a streamlined organization that, under the subsequent leadership of Eleanor Smeal, turned in a more focused political direction. Rather than "do everything," they built a disciplined and massive campaign in support of the Equal Rights Amendment.[33]

Conflicts in liberal organizations, however fierce, were less likely to be waged in the press because they had, through the process of elections, a more direct method of contesting for power. Furthermore, as long as all sides agreed that the continuing existence of the organization was important, it was essential to keep the infighting behind the scenes as much as possible. The result was something more like the "machine politics" in NOW, where behind the scenes machinations and coalition building only occasionally erupted into public view. In a number of other organizations, those with a different agenda would quietly withdraw and go off to create new mechanisms to carry out their work. For example, while the NWPC created a lively grassroots organization, it was not an easy vehicle for the kind of disciplined political training some of those most closely involved in party politics thought was needed. So Arvonne Fraser, Frances Farenthold (a political activist in Texas), Millie Jeffrey from the UAW and the Michigan Women's Commission, Rosalie Whelan (partner in a Democratic political consulting firm), and others created the National Women's Education fund, a nonprofit corporation, "to draw women into leadership in public and political life . . . by training them in the techniques of political action—organizing, lobbying, and elective politics."[34]

How do we explain the fragmentation of women's liberation and the continuing internal conflicts in more liberal groups? On one level this can be understood historically by placing it within the tumultuous political and economic context of the time. An economy that had been driven from expansion to inflation by the war in Vietnam, slowed and then shifted in the early 1970s. The dual shocks of an oil embargo in 1973, which doubled the price of gasoline and oil, and military demobilization meant that the previously expanding "pie" had begun to shrink. As rampant inflation diminished wages, the nation finally felt, full force, the decline in basic industries and the shift to a service economy that had been underway since World War II. Unemployment rose from 4.9 percent in December 1973 to 8.2 percent by June of 1975.[35] In such a setting, redistributive social movements seeking a more equitable share of jobs, wages, services, and other social goods found many previous supporters becoming cautious or even hostile. Affirmative action, once generally understood as a policy designed to give minorities and women a fair chance to overcome long histories of injustice became "reverse discrimination" as dominant groups faced a tightening job market.[36] Even the "friendly" Democratic administration of Jimmy Carter, elected in 1976, which appointed Sarah Weddington to a key White House post and Bella Abzug to head the 1977 International Women's Year celebration, could deliver very little in the way of dramatic victories for women.

Economic stagnation interacted with the cynicism resulting from the Watergate scandal that forced President Nixon into a humiliating resignation and with the national disillusionment with the war in Vietnam. In one sense, the antiwar movement triumphed when the United States pulled out of Vietnam in 1975, but the war, and efforts to stop it, had been waged for more than a decade. Only near the end did most Americans realize that for years their government had falsely, and knowingly, assured them that victory was in sight. The denouement represented a kind of national humiliation: the first war that the United States had lost and an utterly unnecessary one at that. Anger and sorrow at the loss of 58,000 American lives cast a long shadow over American politics and foreign policy for decades to come.[37]

Conservatives, upset with the loss in Vietnam, angered by policies like affirmative action designed to give minorities and women greater access to job opportunities, and alarmed by the rise of feminism, sought new constituencies. The New Right that coalesced in the mid-1970s appealed to traditional values on such cultural issues as abortion, the ERA, affirmative action, and school prayer in place of the Old Right's emphasis on laissez-faire economics and anticommunism. Thus, feminist gains and goals became contested everywhere, from national political parties to local school boards. In 1975 voters in both New Jersey and New York defeated equal rights amendments in statewide referenda. Feminists became defensive. Abortion rights activists had thought most of their work was accomplished after *Roe v. Wade*. The National Association for the Repeal of Abortion Laws, founded in 1969, changed its name in 1973 to the National Abortion Rights Action League (NARAL) but it had little left on its agenda. The emergence of a vehement antiabortion movement describing itself as "prolife" reinvigorated NARAL, however, and led its leaders to coin the label "prochoice."[38] *Roe v. Wade*, it turned out, had not resolved the issue at all. Instead that decision became a rallying point for an emerging New Right coalition that would continue to gain momentum through the 1970s and into the

1980s. Similarly, the easy ratification of the Equal Rights Amendment by 30 states in the first year could not be replicated for the remaining nine needed states. In 1972 Phyllis Schlafley formed a new association, STOP ERA, built on anticommunist networks forged in the Cold War. She reached out to vulnerable women and played brilliantly on cultural anxieties.[39]

Faced with a spreading backlash after 1974 that focused on abortion, ERA, and women's athletics (like *Roe*, Title IX didn't solve things either), and with a declining economy that made women and minorities easy scapegoats, policy-oriented feminists shifted gradually from offensive to defensive, from ebullient optimism to tenacious persistence. Feminists could no longer successfully frame the changes they advocated in terms of simple fairness and equal opportunity. They faced opponents who appealed to fears about the dissolution of all traditional and communal institutions, redirecting many women's anxieties (especially the growing sense of vulnerability and marginalization among housewives) into opposition to "equal rights." Opponents suggested, for instance, that an ERA would allow men to abandon all responsibility for their families and further diminish the grounds for female distinctiveness and respect.[40]

Ironically, while the Right gained strength by reacting against the victories of the Left (blaming the loss of Vietnam on the antiwar movement, blaming the rise of divorce rates on feminism, and blaming affirmative action for the loss of jobs), the Left fragmented in frustration over its *lack* of total victory. Talk of revolution drew on the disillusionment and despair about a seemingly endless war and the violent racial polarization of the late sixties. Many New Left activists came to believe that American society was not salvageable and required a total transformation. The most influential organization on the Left in the late sixties and early seventies was the Black Panther Party, which envisioned itself as a paramilitary, revolutionary movement.[41] Their example shaped the offshoots of white student movements, such as the Weatherman faction of SDS, which briefly became a terrorist underground until several members blew themselves up while making bombs. As it became clear that the tiny communist-led country of Vietnam could not be defeated by massive American firepower, many activists were drawn to the revolutionary certitudes of Marxist-Leninism.

In this broader political and economic context, the women's movement was part of the final devolution of the New Left on the one hand into highly authoritarian, sectarian Maoist and Marxist-Leninist groups and on the other into a utopian and radically personalized, antiauthoritarian counterculture. Both sectarianism and the counterculture reached an apex in the mid-1970s. Feminist radicals exhibited much of the rhetorical style of the Left, but at the same time, the decentralization of the women's movement and its hostility to structures left it extremely vulnerable in the face of efforts by leftist sectarians to infiltrate and take over. Marxist-Leninist sects that lacked any substantial base of their own often tried to take over groups they believed to be strategically located or were seen as likely recruiting grounds. Early efforts on the part of the Socialist Workers Party to take over NOW ultimately failed, but in subsequent years most socialist-feminist groups were weakened or destroyed by similar efforts on the part of several sectarian groups. The Coalition of Labor Union Women, never structureless or leaderless, nevertheless faced a strong internal challenge, which had the effect of making it a tighter, more hierarchical and bureaucratic organization.[42]

Women's liberation groups believed themselves to be fundamentally different from one another, signaled by such labels as radical feminist, socialist feminist, or lesbian feminist, but they struggled with the dynamics of personal politics in markedly similar ways. The personal search for authenticity that had flourished in the student movements of the sixties remained a powerful force within women's liberation.[43] Similarly, the hostility to hierarchy (presumed to be male) and ingrained suspicion of leaders, which led to structurelessness in more radical groups, was also a powerful and disruptive force in many mainstream organizations. As a result, from the beginning and in evolving ways over subsequent decades they clashed over a series of identifiable issues all linked to the pursuit of that illusive ideal in which the personal becomes fully politicized. These issues were the intersection of race and sex, the quest for ideological purity, lifestyles and sexual identities, and the ongoing problem of organizational structure and leadership.

RACE AND SEX

PERSONAL POLITICS was a variant on the emerging identity politics of the late sixties, and it was shaped by the racially polarized context of those years. Nationalism, emphasizing racial solidarity, identity, and separatism, was the dominant language among militants in the black community and increasingly within other minority groups as well. This was the era in which the Black Panther Party advocated violent resistance and other black nationalists sought African roots; Chicanos reclaimed their Aztec heritage, and American Indians forged a militant pan-Indian organization, the American Indian Movement (AIM). Within such movements the narratives of racial oppression frequently revolved around the loss of manhood. Women didn't easily fit in and sometimes became targets of attack. By the late sixties strong black women had become the scapegoats for angry nationalists who charged that they had emasculated black men.[44]

Minority women faced sexism inside as well as outside their own communities. Feminism, however, especially in its radical varieties, posed serious problems even for sympathetic minority women. Many of their grievances as women were rooted in race. Black women, for example, were acutely and angrily aware that American popular culture had never deemed them "feminine" and that their job prospects were far more restricted than those of whites even within a sex-segregated labor force. Most minority and working-class women had not been in a position to invest their entire identities in the roles of housewife and mother. Indeed, to be a housewife was a luxury that they simultaneously envied and held in contempt. Their work experiences, on the other hand, provided plentiful evidence of discrimination on the grounds of both race and sex as well as an underlying sense of independence and self-respect. Given their own images of white women—"Miss Ann who can't even clean her own house or care for her own children even though she appears to have little else to do"—they found it difficult to identify with the struggles of white women for identity, autonomy, and self-respect.[45] Hence the ambivalence that characterized black women's responses to the reemergence of feminism.

The leadership of minority women in NOW and NWPC contrasts with the near absence of women of color in early meetings of women's liberation. In Washington, D.C., women's liberation made a conscious effort to reach out, forming a "women and racism" group "which had some good dialogue with local black women, but did not succeed in involving black women or in challenging the racism in the movement." In a collectively written history of the DC Women's Liberation Movement in 1971 they acknowledged, "While trying to reach out to women different than ourselves, we still did not basically change the nature of our group. Instead, we required that they become more like us to participate. Some did, but others found this impossible."[46] The result was that their evolving theories consistently failed to incorporate more than a narrow range of women's realities.

Younger black women who joined the feminist movement found themselves on the margins of both the women's movement and the black movement. Frances M. Beal's experiences as founder of the SNCC Women's Liberation Committee in 1968 were typical of the few who spoke out. Rarely did she receive public support from other black women. Behind the scenes, however, there were words of encouragement that " . . . showed us that in speaking up for women's liberation, we were speaking for many more who were not ready to speak for themselves."[47]

Indeed, polls showed that black women approved of the women's movement in substantially greater numbers than white women, yet those who joined were continually charged with betrayal of their racial community. The publisher of the *Black Scholar* wrote an editorial in 1971 entitled "Will the Real Black Man Please Stand Up":

This is the day of the black male, when we must take up with ever more resolve the role of liberator. . . . [B]ecause it is the era of liberation the black man will be able to bring the woman along in our common struggle so that we will not need a black women's liberation movement. . . . The black woman is, can be, the black man's helper, an undying collaborator, standing up with him, beside her man.

Feminism, in this view, was a white women's issue being foisted divisively upon the black community.⁴⁸

Toni Cade edited a collection published in 1970 entitled, *The Black Woman: An Anthology*, in which author after author described the dilemma:

> ... the black movement is primarily concerned with the liberation of blacks as a class and does not promote women's liberation as a priority. Indeed, the movement is for the most part spearheaded by males. The feminist movement, on the other hand, is concerned with the oppression of women as a class, but is almost totally composed of white females. Thus the black woman finds herself on the outside of both political entities, in spite of the fact that she is the object of both forms of oppression.⁴⁹

Comparable rhetoric can be found among Asian-American, Latina, and American Indian women activists. In every group, some women picked up on the issue of women's rights very quickly and ran headlong into charges that to do so was divisive. At the same time, their experiences with white feminists proved disappointing.⁵⁰ Sometimes white feminists responded angrily when assumptions about women's oppression, based on their own experiences, were challenged. More often they simply did not understand, and insofar as their fervor was rooted in their own personal lives, they could be downright uninterested. Chicanas, for example, resented the antifamily and antireligious rhetoric of many feminists, and those women, consumed with analyzing old wounds linked to family and church, had a very hard time listening to such a different point of view.⁵¹ Among minority women in policy-oriented women's groups who had begun to build caucuses, militants felt themselves to be tokens. Paula Giddings argues that feminism within the black community has historically gathered strength as nationalism ebbs.⁵² Certainly this was the case in the 1970s.

When Barbara Smith graduated from college around 1970, " ... I had thought that I would never be involved in political work after I graduated from college because that was the height of black nationalism and I felt like I just wasn't permitted to be the kind of person I was in that context. . . . [M]y job was to have babies for the nation and to walk seven paces behind a man and basically be a maid/servant. I didn't get involved in the women's movement for a few years after it became very visible because my perception was that it was entirely white."[53] Smith attended the founding meeting of the National Black Feminist Organization (NBFO) and helped to organize a Boston chapter in 1974, but she did not feel politically "at home" even so. After participating in the Yellow Springs Socialist Feminist Conference in 1975, Smith returned to Boston fired with a new vision. Her chapter decided to break away from the NBFO and form the Combahee River Collective, a nonhierarchical, socialist, African-American feminist group. It was a small and relatively short-lived group, but because they articulated a belief that feminism was an essential element of the struggle against both racial and economic injustice, their statement provided many women of color with a way to express their feminist commitment without ambivalence and white women with a useful starting point for theory that explored differences as well as similarities among women. As Smith explained,

> Combahee was really so wonderful because it was the first time that I could be all of who I was in the same place. That I didn't have to leave my feminism outside the door to be accepted as I would in a conservative black political context. I didn't have to leave my lesbianism outside. I didn't have to leave my race outside, as I might in an all white women's context where they didn't want to know all of that. So it was just really wonderful to be able to be our whole selves and to be accepted in that way.[54]

Smith also pointed out that minority women who were also lesbians experienced a painful silencing within their own communities. "In the early 1970s . . . I didn't see any way that I could be black and a feminist and a lesbian. I wasn't thinking so much about being a feminist. I was just thinking about how could I add lesbian to being a black woman. It was just like no place for us."[55] As lesbian feminism emerged in the predominantly white movement, minority lesbians understood deeply that they had a powerful stake in the success of a feminism in which their lesbianism was welcome. As a result, women like Barbara Smith, Margaret Sloan, Audre Lorde, Gloria Anzaldua, Cherrie Moraga, Betty Powell, and Paula Gunn Allen became critical links between movements, articulating the perspectives of one group to the other. Until they could find a "home base" like the Combahee River Collective, however, they also experienced ongoing fragmentation of a highly personal sort.

Nevertheless, the continuing assumption that the women's movement in the 1970s was by and large a middle-class white phenomenon falls short. By the mid-1970s, minority women's literary voices were among the most powerful expressions of Second Wave feminism, and most of them continued to speak through subsequent decades. The novels of writers like Alice Walker, Toni Morrison, and Maxine Hong Kingston were widely read across racial lines, as was the poetry of Audre Lorde, Gloria Anzaldua, Maya Angelou, Paule Marshall, Toni Cade Bambara, and Paula Gunn Allen. By the late seventies they were joined by a series of theoretical and polemical challenges to the underlying "whiteness" of most feminist theorizing. The radical women's liberation movement, however, was no longer available as an arena in which to debate the challenges of feminists like Bell Hooks, Bonnie Thornton Dill, Barbara Smith, June Jordan, and Cherrie Moraga.[56] By the late seventies and early eighties the problem of difference would rapidly become an acknowledged dilemma within feminist theory, but the contexts had changed.

IDEAS AND IDEOLOGIES

IDEAS WERE CENTRALLY important to feminists with roots in the New Left in a way that they were not for the older, more structured branch of the Second Wave. The older generation was focused on results. They did not contemplate overthrowing capitalism or the family. They simply wanted equality between the sexes and concrete changes that make women's lives better. Over the long haul, the radicals achieved a dramatic intellectual ferment in virtually all of the basic academic disciplines of the arts and sciences. Some of their ideas even found their way into public policy proposals. In the beginning, however, the clash of ideas was a source of continual fragmentation.

In the context of a liberal interest group there were numerous models: Women could be an interest/pressure group like the NAACP, the AFL-CIO, or even chambers of commerce. For women's liberation, politics itself had become a kind of identity ("radical") built around a critique of inequalities in American society and a commitment to change. Arguments often took the form of demonstrating that one was "more radical" than others by showing that one had identified the root cause of inequality (and was therefore the group best positioned to challenge it). By the late sixties, for example, as black nationalists claimed primacy for race, and therefore themselves as a vanguard, radical whites who did not accept this view (as most, in fact, did) countered by arguing for the primacy of "youth" (Yippies and Weatherman), students (a "new class"), or the working class (various groups of Marxists and Maoists). The form of this argument echoed a century of Marxist debate over the place of workers, peasants, women, and intellectuals in the "revolutionary process." Every new group had to contend with the traditional Marxist assertion that the class struggle was the "primary contradiction" and that only the victory of the working class would allow secondary forms of oppression (such as sex) to be overcome.

In this vein, "radical women," "radical feminists," and "radicalesbians" all fought to prove they were *radical*. The first clear position to be staked out in this way came to be known as radical feminism. Its many versions held in common the assertion that women constituted a "class," that gender rather than race or class was the "primary contradiction," and that all other forms of subordination could be traced to the original domination of women by men.[57] As position papers proliferated and groups divided and subdivided, a number of more fully argued explanations were offered. Women's liberation groups eagerly read and debated each new mimeographed paper as it circulated throughout the country. In an intense search for the certainty of an ultimate truth, some groups would seize on a particular position and then exclude all but the "true believers." As a consequence, from time to time the development of new ideas stalled as positions froze, cutting off genuine deliberation.

For example, the "politico-feminist debate," which dominated the first 2 years, was often referred to not as a debate but as a split. Those on the feminist side, especially in New York, not only advocated the creation of an autonomous women's movement but also feared contamination if there were any association between this new movement and other forms of radical activism whether civil rights, antiwar, or labor related. Politicos on the other hand, were likely to be active in such organizations and to have intimate ties with male activists as well. The middle ground in this split was occupied by groups that provided the rootstock for what came to be called socialist feminism, an extremely influential branch of the women's movement. Bread and Roses, for example, the Boston group that formed partly in reaction to the separatist radical feminists in Cell 16, tried to remain linked to the Left but discovered with considerable pain that they were not welcome. Their initial response was intense anger at the male friends and comrades from whom they had expected support, not ridicule, and soon they were furious with men in general.

Gradually "male supremacy, the system, replaced male chauvinism, the attitude, as the target in the struggle."[58] Nonetheless, although Bread and Roses came to a conclusion similar to that of radical feminists, they did not accept the radical feminist assertion of the absolute primacy of gender. As socialist feminists they blamed both capitalism and male supremacy, concluding that the structural foundation of male supremacy was the subordination of women within the bourgeois family.[59]

LIFESTYLES AND IDENTITIES

THE DEBATES WERE as much about identities as they were about ideas.[60] If women needed a separate movement, what was it separate from? The Left? Society? All men? Should participants reject not only the "male movement" but also all "male thinkers" (e.g., Marx)? Few writers offered much clarity. Hundreds of groups disbanded after the initial consciousness-raising phase, having facilitated personal decisions regarding career and marriage. The groups that continued either fixed on a specific project (a day care center or a battered women's shelter) or found themselves floundering, wrestling with the problem of what to do next.

What frequently filled that gap were debates over lifestyle. If feminism had become an identity, how was one to live it? If marriage and the family, for example, were sites of female oppression, then perhaps individuals who were married were consorting with the enemy and not to be trusted. Feminists partook of the late sixties radical youth culture, which emphasized resistance to authority and convention, sexual expressiveness, and experimentation. A feminist "style" of dress and demeanor developed rapidly, eschewing makeup, high heels, and other fashions designed to contort (and reveal) the female body. It even became a uniform of sorts. When the founders of 9 to 5 in Boston wanted to broaden their membership, Ellen Cassedy described the response to their first newsletter with revealing irony: "We started attracting people who were *more real* [emphasis added]. I remember one woman came in with make-up."[61]

Lifestyle debates reached their apex in the aftermath of Lavender Menace and the Furies as the "gay-straight split" wracked the women's liberation movement for about 3 years. With lifestyle and sexual experimentation widespread in American culture, the confluence of cultural revolutions where women's liberation converged with gay liberation engendered the vigorous emergence of lesbian feminism. Lesbian feminist leaders argued that "Women who love women are lesbians. . . . It is a life determined by a woman for her own benefit and the benefit of other women. It is a life that draws its strength, support, and direction from women."[62] If lesbians were the only women truly independent of men, and independence (emotional as well as political) were a prerequisite of feminism, then it made sense according to Sidney Abbott and Barbara Love to argue (in their book *Sappho Was a Right-on Woman*) that "Lesbians provide an example of Feminist theory in action . . . for lesbians live what Feminists theorize about; they embody Feminism."[63]

Lesbians in women's liberation heard or read such words with great emotion. The polarized forms of early debates and the anxieties and resistance of heterosexual feminists caused numerous women's liberation groups to rupture. These included Boston's Bread and Roses, Minnesota's Twin Cities Female Liberation, and most spectacularly D.C. Women's Liberation. For a while, just as granola was correct food, lesbianism was correct sex, and a middle ground in which differences could easily and respectfully coexist was hard to find. Yet those ruptures also signaled the emergence of a self-defined community against some of the most powerful taboos in the culture. The intellectual and psychological energy generated by their collective coming out could only have been explosive.

STRUCTURELESSNESS AND LEADERSHIP

A FINAL SOURCE of fragmentation generated by the intense personalism of the early women's liberation movement was its deep opposition to hierarchical structures and to leadership of any kind. Early groups were explicit about their intention to be structureless, leaderless, and radically egalitarian, a deliberate antithesis to what they had experienced as a male-dominant, ego-strutting, macho New Left. Reflecting on that experience and adding to it stories of the ways women's potentials had been crushed in schools, by parents and husbands, and in legal and religious structures and systems, they came to the conclusion that hierarchy itself was a male phenomenon. Formal leaders in positions of structural authority, it seemed, would almost by definition behave oppressively to their "followers." Their alternative models, however, had deep roots in the student movements of the sixties. They drew on memories of endless meetings in SNCC, where the ideal of the "beloved community" made every decision subject to discussion until consensus could be reached and similar meetings in SDS under the banner of "participatory democracy." At the time of their formation, the anti-authoritarian anarchism of the counterculture's "do your own thing" flourished all around them, making the idea of structureless, leaderless collectivity seem eminently reasonable.

Yet structurelessness became its own form of tyranny, no less striking than highly authoritarian organizations like the Weather Underground or the Black Panther Party. Women's liberation groups sought absolute democracy and remnants of the New Left conceptualized themselves as revolutionaries, but both deliberately erased the boundaries between public and private, inventing a personalized political world that consumed every aspect of participants' lives. Within the women's movement the critique of all structures, divisions of labor, and processes of accountability represented a top-to-bottom rejection of life as most people lived it. As a consequence, they often failed to perceive their own public impact and they eschewed the very tools they would have needed to build upon it.

Radical egalitarianism was subverted in the women's liberation movement, as it had been in the New Left, by the undemocratic potentials inherent in "structurelessness." As Jo Freeman explained in a classic article in 1973, leaderlessness generally meant that leaders were unnamed and unaccountable, not that they did not exist. Freeman charged that "the inevitably elitist and exclusive nature of informal communication networks of friends" dominated groups that lacked formal structures of responsibility and accountability.[64] Having defined ambition as "male," a group of extremely ambitious women, many asserting themselves for the first time, self-consciously squelched themselves. Some did it by "trashing" others (no one should have more visibility or power than I have), only to find themselves trashed in turn. In many cities, for example, as founding groups grew large and began to spin off additional groups, the originators came to be seen as elitist insiders. Individuals who were assertive and articulate found themselves accused of egotism, hogging the limelight, and hampering the opportunities for other women to play leading roles.[65] In the beginning of the women's liberation movement in Chicago, Naomi Weisstein discovered her own oratorical powers. As she put it, "I could speak to 3,000 Loyola Catholics, insult their favorite priest, and get a standing ovation nevertheless." She loved speaking, and audiences loved her. When others criticized her, however, she agreed to stop accepting speaking engagements and instead to run training workshops to teach other women. No one at the time knew how much it hurt that the movement that gave her a voice then took it away.[66]

Such attacks were extremely painful. Their effectiveness depended on a value system shared by both attackers and their targets. In Naomi Weisstein's description, "Utopianism morphed into cannibalism, and the movement ate its leaders in city after city, they went down."[67] This may explain why in the radical branch so many women withdrew, causing a major loss of leadership. Vivian Rothstein wrote in 1973 to friends from the West Side Group, "It is so hard—when we once felt we were making history and the lives of hundreds of people were dependent on our actions—to resolve ourselves to less significant and far less ambitious work. I feel that shift tremendously. Now that I don't feel I'm making history, I don't know exactly what to do with my life."[68] In policy-oriented organizations, perhaps because leadership, though contested, was never totally devalued, and perhaps also because support networks were more focused on practical results than ideological purity, leaders who were attacked were far less likely to feel driven out of the movement.

THE POLITICIZATION of private life in a search for political purity characterized the Furies as well as other small groups on the Left, but within the broader women's movement the scrambling of public and private introduced what quickly became a "therapeutic" language into public settings. "I feel" became a "point of order," trumping any other priority. The originators of consciousness-raising were extremely upset by this therapeutic turn away from politics, but in retrospect it seems inevitable. The very capacity to speak from feelings unleashed a river of need that flooded everything else for a time and continually, in one setting after another, welled up and took over. It became a power resource, adeptly used by those who could link "feelings" to "victimization," thereby claiming a moral high ground.

The therapeutic turn emphasized the power of confession. Elinor Langer described a public setting in which Kate Millett responded, with real discomfort, to highly personal questions about her lesbianism. She drew a contrast between the women's movement and other public settings in which leaders (politicians and artists) refuse to answer questions or decline to perform an encore: "The rituals of these occupations permit it: leader and led; star and audience. But the ritual of the women's movement is different. It is disclosure; in fact, confession. Accepting leadership in an anti-elitist movement is asking for trouble. You become both show-off and cop-out."⁶⁹

In the context of consciousness-raising, however, confession could be empowering. The migration from politics to therapy lay in the fact that this empowerment was experienced by many as a new sense of control over their individual lives: to marry or refuse marriage, to claim a lesbian identity despite social taboos, to have children or not to have children, to pursue a career. As one woman described her experience in a CR group, "I realized for the first time in my life that I had choices . . . and that the only person responsible for making those choices was me. Me and me alone. The changes began inside." Having experienced her consciousness-raising as a very effective form of assertiveness training, this person returned to school, got paralegal training and then went to law school.⁷⁰

This therapeutic turn, utterly congruent with an inward-looking national mood in the mid-1970s, was an ironic, if understandable evolution within some parts of the Second Wave. The perceptions of many founders, however, that their movement was disintegrating into individual therapy on the one hand and cannibalistic self-destruction on the other represented a partial view. The radical feminisms of the late 1960s and early 1970s constituted a wave of utopian experiments, none of which achieved the impossible goals that they set for themselves. Even though most groups lasted only a few years, the patterns and ideas they set up were reenacted again and again. Conflicts over ideology, lifestyle, race and class, structure and structurelessness, leadership and egalitarianism showed up in virtually every version of feminist activism in the coming decades, yet the movement surged on.⁷¹

Given the power and persistence of the disintegrative forces both internal and external to the movement, the amazing thing is the movement's persistence, the ongoing effort to try again and to "get it right" with new projects, new issues, new organizations, and new ideas. Part and parcel of these crosscurrents and undertow was the astonishing force of this tidal wave that fostered growth and innovation even as some of its founders succumbed to despair. By the mid-1970s, the dramatic decline of the New Left and the rise of a New Right changed the political context for feminist activism. Many early leaders believed by the mid-1970s that their movement was in decline, but they were wrong.[72] It was changing so much that the transformations made it hard for some to recognize.

CHAPTER 5

Crest

If you think I'm going to slave
In the kitchen for a man who is
Supposed to be brave,
Then I'm sorry to say
But you're wrong all the way,
Because I'm going to be an astronaut.

—ANITA BUZICK II, 9 YEARS OLD, JUNE 1975[1]

TIDAL WAVES OCCUR when strong forces coincide. Storms build huge waves offshore. If they ride into shore on an in-rushing tide their energy is multiplied both by the powerful pull of the moon and by the compression of the rising seafloor. The wave doubles in size, rising to a great wall of water and sucking up sand, earth, anything in its path. As it washes across the land, reaching into spaces untouched by the sea for hundreds or thousands of years, destruction and creation go hand in hand. New land appears; former shorelines drop into the sea.

In the mid-1970s, the women's movement seemed everywhere and ever-changing as the "do-everything" ethos of women's liberation surged across the landscape, rearranging everything in its path. Certainly by 1975, the speed of change meant that no one could "own" this movement nor could anyone ignore it, whether they were thrilled or dismayed. Many early activists mourned the fact that the movement as they had known it in the first 5 years was no longer recognizable, and they did not always understand that it had moved into a new era of institution and theory building. As the crescendo of activism continued to swell, creativity outpaced disintegration. By the end of the 1970s, however, while feminist mobilization around the Equal Rights Amendment further enlarged the movement, there was also an increasingly sober awareness that change would not be easy, that a counterforce was mobilizing, and that the next decade would be filled with challenge.

Institutionalizing Feminism

As feminism moved into the mainstream once marginal and radical experiments took on the trappings of institutions and began to build national, issue-based networks. From another direction, mainstream institutions experienced feminist challenges and organizing from within, as newly trained professional women sought new ways to build feminist careers. Liberal political activists, with the advent of a Democratic administration in 1976, began to imagine the possibilities of real political power when new issues like sexual harassment and comparable worth catapulted onto the political agenda. In the courtroom or on the tennis court, women's activism was everywhere. By 1977 feminists staged a massive, multicultural celebration of the women's movement in Houston, Texas, honoring International Women's Year. A few stories of these building blocks of change can at least trace the trajectory.

By 1975 localized projects had grown into institutions. Byllye Y. Avery was one of three women at the University of Florida who provided abortion counseling in the early 1970s, primarily by providing a contact in New York. "But then a black woman came and we gave her the number, and she looked at us in awe: 'I can't get to New York. . . .' We realized we needed a different plan of action, so in May 1974 we opened up the Gainesville Women's Health Center." Soon they decided they needed to address the needs of women who chose to give birth as well. "So, in 1978, we opened up Birthplace, an alternative birthing center. It was exhilarating; I assisted in probably around two hundred births." Avery went on to found the National Black Women's Health Project in the early 1980s.[2]

Local institutions—shelters for battered women, rape crisis centers, women's health clinics, and feminist media—evolved into national networks.[3] The National Coalition Against Domestic Violence, for example, sprang up overnight. Carol Bonasarro, head of the Women's Rights Project in the Civil Rights Commission, sponsored a consultation on domestic violence in January 1978 to bring this issue to the attention of the commission. She had her staff contact every shelter in the country and invite them. Accustomed to dignified and professional meetings, she was "stunned that so many of the shelter staff came—with sleeping bags." In effect, the Civil Rights Commission provided an arena in which a national movement became visible to itself. Shelter staff shared battle stories, institutional struggles, and strategies and sensed not only their need for a continuing network but also the potential power of a national voice. Before the conference ended they had formed the National Coalition Against Domestic Violence. Bonasarro was "just thrilled."[4]

Women also organized within religious institutions. The National Student Christian Federation, for example, initiated a Women in Campus Ministry Caucus in 1972 to bring together clergy, students, and staff:

We held conferences just prior to each national conference of NCMA [the National Campus Ministry Association] to meet each other and discuss how to change our denominations and our campus ministries. Some of us who attended these meetings were ordained and paid full-time to do campus ministry. Most were not. We were wives of paid campus ministers, office managers, seminary students, YWCA workers . . . and we were thrilled to be together. We shared our stories: the way men in campus ministry were treating us, the way male church leaders were ignoring us, the way the men we lived with were threatened, the sexism we endured at National Campus Ministry conferences, the way our jobs were so part-time or tenuous or even unpaid, the way we risked our livelihood by being feminist activists. These stories helped us make sense out of our isolated experiences as women in the church. And we examined the politics of sexism, racism, imperialism, and heterosexism in order to move from the personal to a systemic analysis of our experience. We laughed and prayed and danced and shared bread and wine. We indeed re-imagined the sexist traditions we had inherited and created liturgies that offered a celebration of our survival.[5]

That energy showed up in many religious contexts large and small. Numerous denominational journals by the mid-1970s published special issues on women and equality in the church or women and ministry.[6] In the Episcopal Church, the struggle for women's ordination between 1974 and 1976 energized a national network, and the debate on women's roles in ministry proceeded heatedly in many denominations. Catholic women, especially those in religious orders, emboldened by the Second Wave and by Vatican II, called a conference in 1975 in Detroit entitled "Women in Future Priesthood Now: A Call to Action": 1,200 attended and another 500 were turned away. A second Women's Ordination Conference in 1978 responded defiantly to the Vatican's 1977 declaration against the ordination of women. Some of the participants urged that Catholic women shift their energies in a more militant and feminist direction to challenge all forms of domination and hierarchy based on gender, race, or wealth.[7]

Theological conservatives also claimed feminism. A small group of evangelical Christian feminists initiated a journal, *Daughters of Sarah*, in November 1974, announcing "We are Christians; we are also feminists. Some say we cannot be both, but Christianity and feminism for us are inseparable. DAUGHTERS OF SARAH is our attempt to share our discoveries, our struggles, and our growth as Christian women." In subsequent issues they earnestly debated sexist bias in liturgical language and hymns, egalitarian marriage, ordination for women, and "the androgyny of Jesus." Within 14 months they wrote, "From a very grass roots beginning among a few friends on the north side of Chicago, Daughters of Sarah has grown to include a subscription list of over 1000 names. Frankly, we never expected this. . . . Obviously there are more of you than we thought." Because of the primacy of their religious identity, Daughters of Sarah aired debates on such issues as homosexuality and abortion without adopting a singular position.[8]

NATIONAL ORGANIZATIONS also proliferated in and around the interlocking networks of NOW, the National Women's Political Caucus, and the Women's Campaign Fund and focused on electoral activity, judicial appointments, and electing women. These liberal experiments, to their participants, seemed revolutionary. Through the middle 1970s, organizations grew in fits and starts, collecting dues and assembling staff and offices, but the process was bumpy. When Lael Stegal walked in to volunteer at NWPC in 1971 the dues were $1. Stegal gradually became a paid staff member and chief fund-raiser for NWPC, but she recalls how traumatic it was to raise the dues to $10 and then $25 and to begin holding fund-raising dinners for $100 a plate. By the time she left in 1979, the founders of this far-flung network of political activists were keenly aware of just how hard was the task they had set themselves.[9] Most of them persevered, some as elected officials, some through government agencies, some with foundations.

Women fired with zeal to change the world began to create new career paths for themselves. Some were in feminist organizations in which women interested in services delivery in particular found outlets for work in health care, education, and psychological counseling. Changes in the law, and the inspiring examples of the Women's Rights Project of the ACLU, WEAL, and the NOW Legal Defense Education Fund, prompted thousands of women graduating from law school to look for ways to use their newfound skills in the interests of women.[10] The stories of Kathleen Graham and Carolyn Chalmers are typical.

Kathleen Graham entered Stanford Law School in 1968, one of the first classes to include a substantial number of women. Fired by the possibilities of legal work against the war in Vietnam and for civil rights, she also began to attend seminars and workshops at conferences on women and the law. Such conferences, unknown in the 1960s, quickly became a regular fixture in the burgeoning world of women's rights lawyers. There she found that across the country, women were using the law to help women as a class. Inspired by the work of Equal Rights Advocates in San Francisco (a public interest law firm founded by three women and funded initially by the Ford Foundation), Graham joined a small public interest private practice in Minneapolis and set out to fight discrimination.

In 1976 Diana Nagy came to Graham with an all too common story. Again and again her bosses refused to promote her, hiring men instead, but the reasons changed. First they wanted someone with greater experience in the company. Then, when she was the insider already doing most of the work, they claimed they wanted a different kind of college training than she could offer. She found herself repeatedly training the less qualified men who were hired over her, and when they performed poorly and departed the process began again. Nagy was furious, ready for a fight. It was a classic case, just what Graham had been looking for. In 1977 Graham filed a class action suit in behalf of the pink-collar, nonunion women at Nagy's company, Jostens, a national retailer for high school yearbooks and class rings.[11] Carolyn Chalmers joined her later that year.

Carolyn Chalmers had entered law school in 1974, where female students were no longer unusual There she found an active women's caucus that included a core group of women in their thirties, like herself, who came to law school inspired by the women's movement. As students they volunteered to initiate a new women's studies course on women and the law, taught collectively by six of them into the 1980s. Carolyn's passion was fair employment for women and minorities. The suit against Jostens was precisely the kind of case she had yearned to work on.[12] With the support of their law partners and financial assistance from the Equal Employment Opportunity Commission and a women's law firm in Cleveland, the two women labored for several years to build a database with which they could prove systematic discrimination. In the process they became nationally visible experts on employment discrimination and models for others who wanted to build a "feminist career." By 1983 they were ready to go to court against Jostens. Their 1985 settlement was a major victory at the leading edge of a series of similar cases that used Title VII to attack sexism in the workplace.

Another group of feminist lawyers linked the antirape movement to the struggle for equality in the workplace by introducing the (then) novel concept of sexual harassment. As Susan Brownmiller recounts the story, it started at Cornell with a speak-out on May 4, 1975 organized by three women (Lin Farley, Susan Meyer, and Karen Sauvigne) who had worked together in New York Radical Feminists, in the gay liberation movement, and in Alinsky-style community organizing. Motivated by the plight of a brave Cornell employee, Carmita Wood, who was willing to tell her story of sexual harassment, they publicized the event to a list of women lawyers and law students, to local factories and workplaces, and to college dorms alike, inviting all to tell their stories. They had also received encouragement from Eleanor Holmes Norton, chair of New York City Commission on Human Rights. The powerful stories told by secretaries, mailroom clerks, shop stewards, and assistant professors who were ogled, pinched, called sexual names, persistently touched and propositioned, pressured for sex, and even raped became grist for *New York Times* reporter Enid Nemy. In August 1975, "Women Begin to Speak Out Against Sexual Harassment at Work" appeared not only in the *Times* but across the country. For the next few years, the concept became an important focus both for journalists and for lawyers like Nadine Taub, Director of the Women's Rights Litigation Clinic at Rutgers and formerly a leader of the ACLU Women's Rights Project. Within 2 years, early cases had begun to establish that a woman could sue on the grounds of sexual harassment under Title VII of the Civil Rights Act, which made the EEOC a critical venue for redress. A large proportion, perhaps a majority of the women who came forward in these early cases were women of color.[13]

Title IX, the 1972 law requiring equal treatment for women and girls by educational institutions, ushered in a revolutionary change in women's athletics. Participation levels in women's athletics at high school and college levels skyrocketed and women's access to Olympic team competition broadened with the approval of women's basketball and women's team handball in 1976 and women's field hockey in 1980.[14] By 1978, *Time* featured women's sports on the cover under the title, "Comes the Revolution." "The revolution in women's athletics is at full, running tide, bringing with it a sea change—not just in activities, but in attitudes as well" intoned the magazine.[15] Of course there was resistance. The National Collegiate Athletics Association (NCAA) lobbied fiercely to exempt athletics from Title IX prohibitions against discrimination, claiming that intercollegiate sports would be "doomed" if forced to share resources with women's programs. Unable to change the law, opponents slowed enforcement efforts so that through the decade of the 1970s, not a single institution was fined for failure to comply.[16]

In the arena of electoral politics, the contagion of feminism touched an enormous range of women's organizations, both new and old. Policy groups buzzed with meetings, plans, and actions. The National Council of Negro Women (NCNW) under the leadership of Dorothy Height initiated a series of meetings of the presidents of national women's organizations " . . . to develop collective strategies concerning two basics of life—Shelter and food. . . . This may be the first time some of us have met together. . . . Let us view this coming together as a launching pad for unleashing the full force of power created by WOMEN UNITED."[17] The Women's Action Alliance in New York called a series of meetings in 1975 to create a national women's agenda. From May to July the meetings drew an astonishing array of 61 women's organizations. The involvement of such a wide-ranging coalition of women was a source of elation for many women of color.[18] A Puerto Rican woman, Paquita Vivo, wrote in the first issue of *Women's Agenda*:

"With the creation of the US National Women's Agenda, the women's movement of the United States has become every woman's movement. For too long we have heard that the movement is not relevant to the *puertorriquena* or the Chicana or the Asian woman or the black woman. By joining forces with scores of other women's groups and participating actively in preparing the Agenda, organizations such as the National Conference of Puerto Rican Women, Mujer Integrate Ahora, the National Black Feminist Organization, the National Institute of Spanish-Speaking Women and the National Council of Negro Women have made it our movement. Our participation has forced other groups to take notice of issues which mean a great deal to minority women but which had not been thought of generally as women's issues."[19]

In the meantime, the Democratic Party Task Force of NWPC, chaired by Millie Jeffrey, was working to build support for a requirement that all party conventions be 50 percent men and 50 percent women. In the months leading up to the 1976 convention, Jimmy Carter, the leading candidate, promised to work closely with them in the future, although he was unwilling to endorse that specific goal in the short term. When Carter's presidency began, the new feminist forces had unprecedented access to the halls of power. Carter appointed National Black Feminist Organization founder Eleanor Holmes Norton to head the EEOC; Sarah Weddington (the young lawyer who had argued *Roe v. Wade*) as Special Assistant to the President; Mary Frances Berry, a young black lawyer who had written the brief on reproductive rights for the Civil Rights Commission's Women's Rights Project, as Assistant Director of the Department of Health Education and Welfare and later as head of the Civil Rights Commission, and former Congresswoman Bella Abzug to chair the International Women's Year Commission. Leslie Wolfe left her work at the Civil Rights Commission to work as Mary Berry's assistant in HEW, where she directed the Women's Equity Education Act program in the Department of Education.[20]

At both state and national levels, feminist elected officials worked closely with grassroots networks to place issues of concern to women on the political agenda. The Congressional Women's Caucus formed in 1976, with the tenacious leadership of N.Y. Representative Elizabeth Holtzman, who joined forces with Republican Margaret Heckler and Democrat Shirley Chisholm.[21] From the beginning the Caucus had strong links to the leaders of national women's groups in Washington. In the early years, their greatest impact was the 1978 mobilization for an extension of the ERA deadline.[22] Similar, though usually less formal, networks in many states drew on strong links with state commissions on the status of women, the NWPC, NOW, and CLUW.

One of the major rallying issues of the 1980s would arise from these networks combined with growing activism among women workers.

"Comparable worth," the idea that women and men should receive equal pay for jobs of equal value to their employers, emerged from the simultaneous efforts of unions in the feminized service sector, active state commissions on the status of women, the new clerical workers organizations like 9 to 5, and feminist organizations. Debates raged in union halls, working women's organizations, professional associations, government agencies, and courtrooms about the causes and possible remedies for the persistent gap between men's and women's wages.

NOW initiated a campaign in the mid-1970s to call attention to the fact that full-time women workers earned less than 60 percent of the average male wage.[23] Pins, bumper stickers, and posters bearing the "59¢" slogan generated widespread recognition of women's low wages.[24] The aggregate data that identified this issue, however, sorted into two different problems with different policy implications: (1) lack of access to traditionally male jobs (addressed by access to education and affirmative action) and (2) the relatively low pay of female-dominated jobs in comparison to the pay for equivalent jobs occupied by men. The latter problem, in a labor market that remained highly segregated by sex, generated the policy called comparable worth, or pay equity, which argues that different jobs that can be evaluated as equivalent in terms of skill level and required training, responsibility, effort (how hard is it to do), and working conditions should be paid along the same scale. EEOC, in fact, was flooded with wage discrimination cases, many of which challenged the lower pay for female jobs compared to "equivalent" male jobs. In one famous case in Colorado, the comparison was between nurses and tree trimmers. Later cases pointed out that school secretaries were paid less than janitors, and that caretakers for retarded adults (mostly female) received less than zookeepers (mostly male).[25]

Several unions took these cases into court and into collective bargaining. The women's caucus of a union local in San Jose, California published its own study in 1977 and in 1978; soon a woman mayor and a female-dominated city council were hearing demands for an "equity standard" for city pay practices. City managers agreed with some reluctance to conduct an official study. When negotiations over wage hikes foundered, the union initiated the first-ever comparable worth strike.[26]

Meanwhile, at the national level the EEOC seemed open to an interpretation of Title VII compatible with comparable worth. EEOC Chair Eleanor Holmes Norton commissioned the National Academy of Sciences to examine the issue in 1977 (a study codirected by Heidi Hartmann and Donald Treiman). By 1980, Norton endorsed comparable worth as "the issue for the 80s," setting the stage for a series of major policy innovations and a national debate.[27]

Another success in the policy arena was the continued funding and expansion of the Women's Educational Equity Act (WEEA). Under pressure from women's organizations (the National Advisory Council on Women's Educational Programs and the Coalition for Women and Girls in Education, which together represented almost 50 education associations and women's organizations), the congressional reauthorization of WEEA in 1978 shifted its purpose toward assisting educational agencies and institutions to meet the requirements of Title IX and required the department to establish priorities for funding. That was when Mary Frances Berry, Assistant Secretary of HEW, appointed Leslie Wolfe to be her assistant and head up WEEA. Wolfe, who worked on the Women's Rights Project at the Civil Rights Commission for several years, brought a new level of feminist energy to WEEA. "By then this was my whole life—building a multi-ethnic feminist movement step by step anywhere you can." She ran the WEEA office "as a feminist collective in the middle of a bureaucracy" with a staff that included two men.[28]

Wolfe and her staff began by soliciting public comments and feedback on proposed priorities and then revised them substantially. All WEEA projects would be "model projects" whose results and project materials could be replicated in other places. Some created new teaching methods. Others generated curricular materials. Their first priority was to assist educational institutions to comply with Title IX prohibitions against discrimination in education on the basis of sex.[29] In addition, separate priorities called for model projects "on educational equity for racial and ethnic minority women and girls . . . [and] for disabled women and girls." Minority women had insisted on the specific focus on the experience of double discrimination based on race and ethnicity, and the emphasis on disability created the first federal program to target the specific needs of disabled women. Additional priorities revealed strategies for change in response to community pressure: "model projects to influence leaders in educational policy and administration" to increase their commitment to Title IX compliance and "model projects to eliminate persistent barriers to educational equity for women." In rural school districts, simply the presence of outside funding could increase the commitment of administrators for equity-based projects and curricula. WEEA projects created a handbook on disability, "No More Stares," with first person stories and guidelines on the needs of disabled girls. An urban school system established a women's studies component in its curriculum with WEEA funding, and WEEA helped to sponsor the First National Hispanic Feminist Conference hosted by the National Conference of Puerto Rican Women, the National Association of Cuban American Women, and the Mexican American National Women's Association (MANA) in March 1980, where over 1,000 women gathered "to discuss topics such as bilingual education, lesbians in the Hispanic community, the socialization process and the Equal Rights Amendment."[30]

HOUSTON 1977: INTERNATIONAL WOMEN'S YEAR

The breadth of the women's movement and the mainstreaming of what had been extremely marginal issues only a decade before became visible in 1977 at the massive International Women's Year Conference in Houston, Texas and the 50 state conferences that preceded it. The idea for the conference emerged from the experience of the U.S. delegation to an international United Nations-sponsored conference honoring the 1975 International Year for Women. Meeting with 6,000 women from around the world and learning that numerous other countries had recognized the year with conferences and commissions, American delegates returned fired up to demand that the United States do the same. The National Women's Agenda discussions call by Dorothy Height provided precisely the broad base needed. Together they developed a plan to present a U.S. National Women's Agenda to the President's Commission on the International Women's Year (IWY), asking for support for a national conference on women. Bella Abzug and 15 other congresswomen agreed to submit a bill to fund such a conference sponsored by the President's Commission on IWY.[31] She embedded into this enabling legislation a vision of a highly participatory, diverse gathering by requiring that delegates to the conference be selected at conferences held in every state and providing funding for low-income women to attend. After the 1976 election, President Carter appointed Abzug to head the commission that planned the conference itself.

Preparation for the conference became a massive organizing opportunity. Because of guidelines that stressed that conferences should be broadly inclusive and provide funding for low-income women, in many states these became the most diverse gatherings yet of the women's movement. In state after state, conferences engaged in a highly visible form of consciousness-raising as they debated equal pay, day care, abortion, sex education, violence against women, and the ERA. Right-wing anti-feminists also organized in response in many states, and they succeeded in dominating conferences in Indiana, Mississippi, and Utah. For some feminists, this was a sobering encounter with the political power and organizing savvy of the anti-ERA, antiabortion, and openly homophobic forces backed by the conservative religious groups (Catholics, Mormons, and fundamentalist Protestants), as well as right-wing organizations (the Moral Majority, Stop-ERA, and others). At the same time, for some conservative women, debating the issues directly with feminists (who turned out to be real people, not ogres) challenged their sterotypes and changed their minds.[32]

The Houston conference, consisting of about 2,000 delegates and 18,000 additional observers, made clear that the women's movement had spread well beyond its original white, middle-class base: 35 percent of the delegates were nonwhite and nearly one in five was low-income. Protestants represented 42 percent of the delegates, Catholics 26 percent, and Jews 8 percent.[33] Those who had organized the conference and developed the proposed plan came together in the conference as a "Pro-Plan Caucus" pledged to work to see that their agenda was endorsed. The gathering was unruly, however, and delegates could not be simply told what to do. There were active caucuses for minority women, lesbians, and numerous others, and the process of passing the plan became yet another exercise in coalition building. When the conference adopted, by significant majorities, the Plan for Action, with the ERA as its centerpiece and major planks on reproductive freedom and minority and lesbian rights, the delegates were elated. Abzug recalled,

> One of the high moments of the conference came when a group of women—Maxine Waters, a young black assemblywoman from California; Billie Nave Masters, a Native American teacher; Mariko Tse, a Japanese-American; Sandy Serrano Sewell, President of the Commission Feminil Mexicana; and Coretta Scott King, the widow of Martin Luther King Jr.—took turns reading sections of a revised plank on minority women that they, with Gloria Steinem of the resolutions committee, had worked on for two days. It was another expression of the remarkable unity . . . that made the conference unique. 'Let the message go forth from Houston,' Coretta King said, 'and spread all over this land. There is a new force, a new understanding, a new sisterhood against all injustice that has been born here. We will not be divided and defeated again.'[34]

Two key behind the scenes figures at the Houston convention were Gloria Steinem, who quietly mediated the relationships among the various minority caucuses and the convention leadership, and Charlotte Bunch, who had long since left separatism behind to work on building broad-based coalitions.[35] The Plan of Action itself made it clear that any sharp division between liberals and radicals no longer made any sense: radicals had brought many of their agendas into mainstream feminist venues, although the planks on abortion and lesbianism in particular provoked intense divisions even as they were adopted. The contacts and conflicts among differing groups of women made for a powerful experience that crossed many of the earlier divisions. One small state delegation of 12, including three Native American women, "developed a deep level of intimacy . . . as the hours went on." One of the whites in the group recalled that "we grew to respect each other's opinions and ended up influencing the delegation on issues, such as reproductive freedom and lesbianism, which the Native Americans had previously been against. When the Minorities resolution passed, we all danced in the aisle and cried tears of joy." Other delegates reported stereotype-shattering conversations on coffee breaks.[36]

One Republican feminist recalled, "Inside the cocoon of those four days of Houston, we women found sisterhood—that universal sense of being together honorably for a great cause. Even now, nearly twenty years later, women who don't know each other will find themselves reminiscing about Houston in the same way war veterans, strangers on sight, quickly become close as they talk about Normandy, Inchon, or Hue."[37]

As the conference had approached, however, opposition grew. The Imperial Wizard of the United Klans of America insisted that a Klan presence was necessary "to protect our women from all those militant lesbians who are going to be there." Phyllis Schlafley's Eagle Forum organized a rally "for the family" of 11,000 men, women, and children on the other side of town during the opening session of the IWY conference. In his keynote address, California Congressman Robert Dornan called the IWY delegates "sick, anti-God, pro-lesbian and unpatriotic."[38] Conference leaders and participants alike went home thrilled by the power of their experience but sobered by the recognition that a counterforce of opposition was also growing.

A New Generation of Feminist Radicalisms

EVEN AS FEMINISM radicalized the mainstream and the early women's liberation groups seemed to disintegrate, a new generation of highly influential utopian visions evolved out of women's liberation. By 1975, both "cultural feminism" and "socialist feminism" were in full sway. Historian Alice Echols has lamented what she sees as cultural feminism's eclipse of the radical feminism epitomized by the early women's liberation groups that sought to create a women's "class consciousness" for the eradication of sex roles. There were two succeeding visions, however, not one, and they were equally rooted in the earliest years of women's liberation. Socialist feminism struggled to build a multicultural feminism that embraced a broad vision of economic equality. Early women's liberation groups self-destructed rather quickly, having fixed an enormous range of issues indelibly on the public consciousness with their rape speak-outs, Miss America demonstrations, and WITCH actions, but socialist feminism grew more slowly, with more focus on organizing than on ideological purity (at least at first), and only later succumbed to very similar internal combustion. Cultural feminism focused on creating a "women's culture" including art, music, and a variety of woman-run institutions. Given its primary emphasis on lifestyle, cultural feminism drew much of its energy from the emergence of a lesbian community, now visible to itself and open to the world for the first time. This evolution of the sexual revolution was only an aspect of cultural feminism, but its influence grew very quickly because the environments called "women's culture," whether living collectives or music festivals, were for lesbians in particular an utterly new kind of public space. At the same time, each of those environments could also be a stage for the many conflicts that haunted feminism in its utopian forms.

To understand how socialist and cultural feminism came to the fore by the mid-1970s, it helps to see their roots in the youth movements that originally gave birth to women's liberation and then trace their evolution from the early women's groups. Cultural feminists drew from the cultural experimentation of the "hippie" counterculture that proposed new, supposedly more "natural" lifestyles with an emphasis on environmental consciousness, on pleasure and self-expression through sex and drugs, on communal lifestyles, and on individual, frequently artistic creativity. Socialist feminists, on the other hand, were the direct heirs of the New Left critiques of capitalism, imperialism, and racism.

The impulses that drove cultural feminism were separatist (women are a people whose liberation will consist in building strong, self-sufficient communities), essentialist (women are different from men by nature—nurturing, earth-loving, cooperative, and peaceful), and esthetic (women's ways of being and expressing themselves in music, art, poetry, literature, and ritual are unique; freeing these capacities will allow the creation of an affirming women's culture, which has been suppressed under eons of patriarchy). In many ways, cultural feminism drew on the common sense of most cultures that assumes a fundamental difference between women and men, except they turned negative stereotypes of women as "weak" and "emotional" on their head to celebrate women as "nurturing" and "relationship-oriented." Cultural feminism's goal was to revalue and reaffirm the female, in contrast to the earliest expressions of women's liberation that rejected the idea that there was anything "essential" about being a woman.

Cultural feminism found expression in an enormous range of alternative service institutions, women's businesses, and cultural events. Its assumptions also found their way into liberal feminist organizations and mainstream institutions far from the feminist counterculture. It did not so much spring up as an alternative to other feminist visions as it evolved out of them. Certainly cultural feminist ideas appeared in women's liberation gatherings as early as 1968. Beverly Jones, at Sandy Springs in the summer of 1968, talked about facing a problem " . . . analogous to black people deciding whether they want a separate state, a separate community."[39] Her colleague Judy Brown asserted that the democratic nature of women's liberation groups " . . . is a much more female type of thing."[40] No one strongly advocated an essential difference between women and men, but many who insisted that men were "the enemy" also maintained that "cultural oppression" was more fundamental than economic oppression. "The idea is to talk about cultural demands politically."[41] As in the black separatist movement, there was a fuzzy line between those who advocated separatism on purely political, strategic grounds to create solidarity and collective power (e.g. the Black Panthers) and those whose separatist vision embraced a cultural sense of "peoplehood" expressed in history, religion and ritual, and artistic expression (music, art, and theater). Those who called themselves radical feminists ultimately were hostile to the latter view, but in the first years, the differences were not so clear.

At the conference in November 1968 at Lake Villa, Illinois, alongside debates over the "correct" method of consciousness-raising[42] and how to go about organizing women across class lines, were workshops on "Sex," "Alternative Life Styles," and "Human Expression—Play."[43]

The alternative lifestyles workshop wrestled with the problem of "what it means to be 'new women'" and tried to imagine communities that "can enable people to live such radical new styles." Participants asked, "Can there exist within a total society, a subculture which would act as a support group to allow individuals to choose from a variety of life styles . . . ?"[44] On the last night of the conference, "almost spontaneously we came together feeling the freedom to move, shout, and respond to each other collectively. . . . Gradually game after game came to us collectively. We went around in circles singing poems about ourselves and expressing them physically. Somehow during this period we began to be more in touch with ourselves, [i]n touch with that greatly stifled creativity which dwells in each of us."[45]

Initially the debate over the "cultural oppression" of women centered on the ways women internalized negative images of themselves. By contrast, the discovery of female strength and creativity was exhilarating. Cultural themes emerged very quickly. In May 1969, the Female Liberation Conference in Boston offered workshops on karate, sex, women and the movement, women and their bodies, working women, high school women, the history and practice of witchcraft, and family, children, and communal living. Planners expected 200 attendees: 500 showed up.[46]

Many artists who began to explore feminist images and possibilities for the self believed they were creating a women's culture. They wanted alternative ways to show as well as to produce their work, and they envisioned their audience primarily as other women. Those, like Judy Chicago, who claimed that female artists expressed uniquely female experiences posed a controversial but thrilling possibility for advocates of the new women's culture. They posited the existence of " . . . a different, women's metaphysics and esthetics. No longer pale echoes of men, women [could be] seen to be generating from the deepest levels of the unconscious, a different universe."[47]

The practice of living in communes led to the formation of all-woman "living collectives" even before the Furies initiated their explosive experiment. A participant in one such group in Iowa City recalled the summer of 1970 as the beginnings of "a female subculture" in a house filled with discussions of women-identified women, "the constant playing of music sung by female singers, and being excited every time we discover[ed] another record by a woman." Other women dropped by frequently, sparking spontaneous dances. Writing in 1971, the author said that while the collective had broken up over issues of "separatism, gayness, and feminism v. humanism. . . . The female sub-culture which has developed and grown here in Iowa City around the living collective during the past year will continue to grow mainly among those of us who are women-identified women."[48]

In 1971 "The Fourth World Manifesto," by a group of Detroit women, argued vigorously that "Although the concept of the 'feminine' was imposed upon women, we have, through the centuries, developed and created within the confines of the feminine, a female culture."[49] Careful not to suggest a biological basis for women's difference, they built their argument on the claim that male dominance over women serves as the archetype for all other forms of domination. "We are proud of the female culture of emotion, intuition, love, personal relationships, etc. as the most essential human characteristics. It is our male colonizers—it is the male culture—who have defined essential humanity out of their identity who are 'culturally deprived.' . . . THE FEMALE CULTURE IS THE FOURTH WORLD."[50]

The Fourth World Manifesto was a harbinger of the shifts toward cultural feminism, full-blown.[51] Soon, writers like Adrienne Rich were even going so far as to say that "feminism must imply an imaginative identification with all women . . ." and that male civilization, patriarchy, threatened life itself. "[W]e have come to an edge of history when men—insofar as they are embodiments of the patriarchal idea— have become dangerous to children and other living things, themselves included."[52] Elizabeth Gould Davis's *The First Sex* provided grist for such imagining by arguing that there had been a matriarchal "Golden Age" destroyed by the rise of patriarchy.[53] Rich celebrated the fact that Davis offered " . . . a historical alternative to a society characterized by dominant, aggressive men and passive, victimized, acquiescent women."[54] Her own poems from 1971 to 1972, published as *Diving into the Wreck*, explored the suppression of the feminine (understood as the

SERVING SANDWICHES This picture from the early 1950s captures the polarized roles American culture prescribed for women and men before the tidal wave began. Women's domestic responsibilities for the home (cleaning, food preparation, and child care) were matched by the male breadwinner role in the world of work outside the home. Though many women found opportunities for pleasure and creativity in their domestic roles, rigid ideas about what women should do frustrated growing numbers while they also justified ongoing discrimination against the millions of women who sought work outside the home, whether by choice or by economic necessity. MINNESOTA HISTORICAL SOCIETY

SHEET CLOSET, 1972 In 1971, the artist Judy Chicago led a collaborative group in the creation of *Womanhouse* in an abandoned house in Hollywood. In a series of fantasy environments they vividly depicted the women's liberation movement's rebellious critique of traditional domestic labor. Calling attention to women's unpaid and invisible work inside the home, they implicitly demanded both recognition and freedom. *SHEET CLOSET FROM WOMANHOUSE* © SANDRA ORGEL 1972, MIXED MEDIA. PHOTO COURTESY OF THROUGH THE FLOWER ARCHIVES.

NOW FOUNDERS, 1966
Founders of the National Organization for Women (NOW) were a strikingly diverse group of middle-class professionals. This picture, taken on October 29, 1966, at the founding meeting in Washington, D.C., includes Dorothy Haener from the Women's Department of the United Auto Workers; Sister Joel Read; Anna Arnold Hedgeman, a Harlem physician and leader of many African-American women's organizations; Betty Friedan, author of the *The Feminine Mystique*; Inez Casiano, Hispanic union leader who later worked for EEOC; Richard Graham, Commissioner on the Equal Employment Opportunities Commission; and Inka O'Hanrahan, a San Francisco biologist. "NOW FOUNDERS" PHOTO BY VINCENT GRASSE, SCHLESINGER LIBRARY, RADCLIFFE INSTITUTE, HARVARD UNIVERSITY

MISS AMERICA PAGEANT DEMONSTRATION, 1968 In August 1968, the younger, more radical branch of the movement known as Women's Liberation organized a protest at the Miss America Pageant to challenge the cultural obsession with women's sexual attractiveness. Their ability to dramatize this issue gained enormous media attention. Thrilled, furious, or merely curious, people across the country were suddenly talking about women's liberation. AP/WIDE WORLD PHOTOS

WOMEN'S EQUALITY DAY, 1970 On August 26, 1970, the 50th anniversary of the ratification of the 19th Amendment granting women the right to vote, NOW called a "women's strike" to direct attention to the upsurge of activism on women's rights. Women staged thousands of demonstrations across the country under the slogan: "Don't Iron While the Strike is Hot."
AP/WIDE WORLD PHOTOS

NATIONAL WOMEN'S POLITICAL CAUCUS, 1971 Keynote speakers at the founding meeting of the National Women's Political Caucus on July 10, 1971, included, left to right: Betty Smith, former vice chair of the Wisconsin Republican Party; Dorothy Haener, International Representative, Women's Department, United Automobile Workers Union; Fannie Lou Hamer, civil rights leader from Mississippi; and Gloria Steinem, member, Democratic National Policy Council and founder of *Ms.* magazine. © BETTMANN/CORBIS

"UP AGAINST THE WALL"—CHICAGO WOMEN'S LIBERATION ROCK BAND
Women's rock bands were part of the women's liberation movement in the early 1970s,
anticipating the Riot Grrrl movement by two decades. They used music to advocate
women's rights, to criticize the misogyny of the male-dominated rock music scene, and
to showcase women's capacity for creativity and assertiveness. Like many early experiments, the Chicago rock band dissolved in the mid-1970s over personal and political
disagreements. New groups quickly appeared, however, and several women's music
festivals founded in the mid-1970s continue into the 21st century. CHICAGO WOMEN'S'
LIBERATION UNION ARCHIVES. LEFT TO RIGHT: PAT MILLER, NAOMI WEISSTEIN, SHERRY
JENKINS, SUZANNE PRESCOTT, FANYA MANTALVO. BELOW: SUSAN ABOD

"MANY WAVES, ONE OCEAN" The Chicago
Women's Liberation Union's Graphics Collective produced dozens of posters in the 1970s.
This one, originally designed by Estelle Carol,
emphasizes the multiplicity of the movement as
well as its international reach by incorporating
the title "Many Waves, One Ocean" in many
languages into the poster itself. CHICAGO
WOMEN'S LIBERATION UNION, WOMEN'S GRAPHICS
COLLECTIVE

JUDY CHICAGO, *THE DINNER PARTY*, PRIMORDIAL GODDESS PLACE SETTING Judy Chicago's massive installation, *The Dinner Party*, completed in 1979, has become emblematic of the feminist art movement in the 1970s. A triangular table, 48' on a side, with 39 place settings for women leaders, both mythical and historic, *The Dinner Party* used imagery that was explicitly female. This place setting, for the Primordial Goddess, highlights the growing interest in spirituality among cultural feminists. PRIMORDIAL GODDESS PLACE SETTING FROM *THE DINNER PARTY*, © JUDY CHICAGO 1979, MIXED MEDIA. COLLECTION OF THE BOOKLYN MUSEUM OF ART, GIFT OF THE ELIZABETH A. SACKLER FOUNDATION PHOTO: © DONALD WOODMAN

HOUSTON, 1977 In November 1977, 2,000 delegates and 18,000 observers gathered in Houston for a national conference honoring the U.N. International Women's Year. Racial minorities constituted fully one-third of the representatives selected by conferences in every state and territory. Here Coretta Scott King presents the resolution on minority women's rights with other spokeswomen from the minority caucus. The passage of that resolution was one of the highlights of the conference. CORBIS, 1977 © BETTMANN/CORBIS

NINE TO FIVE, **1980** On December 14, 1980, Dolly Parton, Jane Fonda, and Lily Tomlin arrive at a benefit showing of *Nine to Five*, their new film about life in the secretarial pool. The benefit was dedicated to 9 to 5, a national organization of office workers that had inspired the film. CORBIS, 1980 © BETTMANN/CORBIS

MORMONS FOR THE ERA, EARLY 1980s When Mormon women began to speak out for the Equal Rights Amendment, church leaders condemned them and even excommunicated their leader, Sonia Johnson, in 1979. These intrepid women, however, refused to be silent. SONIA JOHNSON COLLECTION, J. WILLARD MARRIOT LIBRARY, UNIVERSITY OF UTAH

Do women have to be naked to get into the Met. Museum?

Less than 5% of the artists in the Modern Art sections are women, but 85% of the nudes are female.

GUERRILLA GIRLS CONSCIENCE OF THE ART WORLD
www.guerrillagirls.com

GUERILLA GIRLS, "DO WOMEN HAVE TO GET NAKED," 1989 Guerilla Girls, a group of artists in New York, announced their existence in 1985 with a series of demonstrations and posters protesting the failure of major galleries—particularly the Metropolitan Museum—to include the work of women. To preserve their anonymity, they always appear in public wearing gorilla masks. This poster was originally designed as a billboard for the Public Art Fund in New York in 1989. When the PAF rejected their design, Guerilla Girls rented advertising space on New York's public buses where the poster circulated for several years. COPYRIGHT © THE GUERRILLA GIRLS, 1989, 2002

WOMEN'S ACTION COALITION, 1992 Women's Action Coalition emerged in the early 1990s as a response to the furor over Anita Hill's testimony alleging sexual harassment by Supreme Court nominee (now Justice) Clarence Thomas. Here they participate in a 1992 demonstration in New York City's Times Square sponsored by United for AIDS Action. CORBIS, 1992 © JOSEPH SOHM; CHROMOSOHM INC./CORBIS

U.S. WOMEN'S SOCCER WORLD CUP FINALS, 1999 The Women's World Cup Soccer Finals in July 1999 caught the media by surprise as millions of Americans stopped whatever they were doing to watch the U.S. team win. Suddenly female athletes were national heroes. Billboards shouted "Girls Rule." In the key play of the final game, goalie Briana Scurry blocked a penalty shot by China's Liu Ying during the shootout after regulation time. Few newspapers ran this photograph on their front pages, however, as most opted to show Brandi Chastain's muscled body and sports bra when she ripped off her shirt in jubilation after kicking the winning shot. CORBIS, 1999 © AFP/CORBIS

the fight for social justice ignores no one

THIRD WAVE, 2002 Young feminists in the 1990s declared themselves to be a "third wave" of women's rights activism. Their approach is notably multicultural and inclusive. This picture is from the homepage of the Third Wave Foundation Web site in 2002. THIRD WAVE FOUNDATION principle of nurturance and empathy embodied in mothering) as well as more overt forms of discrimination. Women, still linked to that suppressed culture (" . . . an underground river/ forcing its way between deformed cliffs/ an acute angle of understanding/ moving itself like a locus of the sun/ into this condemned scenery") hold the key to the vision of a redemptive future.[55]

Cultural feminism received an ideological boost with the emergence of lesbian feminism. The experience of separatism, in the words of Furies founder Charlotte Bunch, allowed a process of self-discovery of lesbians "as a people." As Rita Mae Brown, one of the founders of the Furies, put it,

> A woman can best find out who she is with other women, not with just one other woman but with other women who are also struggling to free themselves from an alien and destructive culture. It is this new concept, that of women-identified women, that sounds the death knell for the male culture and calls for a new culture where cooperation, life and love are the guiding forces of organization rather than competition, power and bloodshed.[56]

Such language obscured the conflict that dogged the movement from its inception, especially the painful gay-straight split Brown herself helped to engineer. Its appeal lay in the dream of escape from "male" competition into "female" cooperation. The Furies were only one of dozens, perhaps hundreds, of lesbian communes, many of which persisted through the seventies and into the eighties. In such environments, talk of women's culture seemed natural, linked to a separatist vision of economic as well as cultural independence.

When the Furies broke up in 1972, its members took the quest for female self-sufficiency in new directions. Having given up the view that they could withdraw into an entirely female world, they nonetheless set out to establish women's businesses and outlets for women's artistic expressions. One such company was Olivia Records, founded in 1973 by five women. Former Furies member Ginny Berson described their decision-making process: "We asked ourselves, what are we going to do next in the women's movement? what needs to be done? how can we gain power for women?" They decided that " . . . the way for women to get power was through economics, by controlling our own economic situation. . . . [W]e wanted to set up some sort of alternative economic institution which would both produce a product that women want to buy and also employ women in a nonoppressive situation—get them out of regular jobs. Second, we wanted to be in a position to be able to affect large numbers of women, and that had to be through media. . . . So we put the two together and got a women's recording company."[57] Their first disk, issued in 1974, was a 45 rpm single with Meg Christian and Cris Williamson. Other former Furies were involved in founding Women in Distribution, Diana Press, Moonforce Media, *Quest: A Feminist Quarterly*, and Sagaris Institute.[58]

After 1972, in cities across the country women's institutions flourished. The Women's Action Collective (WAC), an umbrella organization in Columbus, Ohio, was founded in 1972 and grew within 2 years to include a Women's Co-op Garage, a Legal Action Group, a Women's Community Development Fund, Women Against Rape, a Women's Publishing Group including *Womansong* newspaper and Fan the Flames Feminist Bookstore, a concert production company named Women's Music Union, and a lesbian support group. Its leaders were active in the initiation of women's studies at Ohio State. The 1974 WAC "Statement of Philosophy" offered a vision that was widely shared by similar groups across the nation:

> We are committed to change in our lives NOW. We believe the personal is the political and we must live what we believe. We must withdraw our support from existing sexist institutions and create new ones expressive of our philosophy. While we recognize the value of other forms of struggle, we are committed to building an alternative feminist culture NOW, even on a small scale, rather than expending our energy on large scale reformism.[59]

The rush of institutionalization in the mid-1970s ensured the continued existence of thousands of spontaneous, largely volunteer-run feminist experiments. In 1976 Adrienne Rich described the idealistic vision shared by many:

> More and more, however, women are creating community, sharing work, and discovering that in the sharing of work our relationships with each other become larger and more serious. In organizing a women's self-help clinic or law collective or a writing workshop, in editing a magazine or creating a center for women's work like the Women's Building in Los Angeles, in running a press that publishes "lost" books by women or contemporary work that may be threatening or incomprehensible to male editors, in participating in a women's prison project or a crisis center, we come to understand at first hand not only our unmet needs but the resources we can draw on for meeting them even in the face of female poverty, the hostility of institutions, the lack of documentation of our shared past.[60]

Cultural feminism had from the outset a strongly lesbian identity. It allowed lesbians to construct, for the first time, public spaces in which their sexual preference was acknowledged and celebrated rather than hidden and suppressed.[61] As one participant in a very early women's living collective put it in 1971,

> Female culture to me means lesbian culture, and until recently it has been invisible to most and silent. . . . Since Gay Liberation and Women's Liberation, since the women's living collective, since new women, who haven't been hiding all their lives have joined the gay community, Lesbian Culture has come above ground some and broadened. Now I talk about it as women's culture.[62]

The "women's culture" that developed in the 1970s and continued in subsequent decades was a direct continuation neither of the isolated lesbian subculture (most visible in gay bars) of the 1950s and 1960s nor of the traditional "woman's culture" based on women's responsibilities for childbearing, child care, and household labor. Theorists like Adrienne

Rich or the authors of the Fourth World Manifesto made frequent references to the latter tradition and sparked an important reevaluation of mothering and motherhood.[63] In practice, however, the new women's culture expressed a separatist, New Age, lesbian communalism whose lineage could be traced only very circuitously to the many expressions of female collectivity that predated it, including women's missionary societies, women's clubs, sewing circles, mother's clubs, and, most recently, the dense networks of suburban voluntarism. These were of course undergoing their own feminist revolution, but they were worlds apart.

The evolving ideas and practices of women's culture can best be traced in the many conferences and festivals. Conferences reminiscent of the women's rights conventions in the 1850s took place across the country on virtually every conceivable topic. Gradually, however, the emphasis shifted from conferences to festivals, from events whose purpose was to discuss and debate feminism to those in which enacting it took precedence. Conference reports described the intractable divisions in the movement between socialist, cultural, and radical feminisms, separatists and nonseparatists, spiritualists and politicals, and lesbians and heterosexuals, as well as the ongoing self-criticisms of the movement for its failure adequately to address issues of class and race.[64] Understandably, many women were attracted to explicitly cultural events, such as poetry readings, art shows, and music festivals, which were congruent with the therapeutic turn in both feminism and the broader society. There, the focus could be on the art, on feeling good about being together, and when divisions arose, audiences generally suppressed conflict with the view that "we're here to share music, not discuss politics."[65]

Music festivals, in particular, became the most important venue for cultural feminism. Local groups held festivals from the earliest years. The first national women's music festival in 1974 at Champaign-Urbana gave 250 participants a sudden sense " . . . that women's music and culture is growing and flourishing." Ginny Berson, founder of Olivia Records, avowed that at the Illinois festival " . . . for the first time there was a forum to understand and expand the dimensions of the explosion."[66] Participants who were new to the women's music scene struggled for words to convey their excitement. "It was almost like going back to my first consciousness-raising experience years ago. The floodgates opened and just being together strengthened us," wrote one attendee.[67]

The festival in Champaign became an annual event. Because it retained some elements of a conference, however, by its second and third years (1975 and 1976) it showed signs of the strains in the movement. Reviewers for *off our backs* in 1975 said that they had a wonderful time "socially, physically, and musically" but commented that "It was surprising but understandable that a musical event would crystallize the most distressing and still growing splits within the women's movement at this time—between lesbians and straight women, socialists and separatists, blacks (there were no more than 10 at the whole festival) and whites—actually you name it and the need for more outreach was in evidence there."[68] Similarly, the *Ms.* reviewer found that in the "haphazard conglomeration of workshops . . . [e]very one I attended was bogged down in discussions about feminism."[69]

Soon the most popular venues for music festivals were rural settings where hundreds, even thousands, could camp and enjoy the personal freedom of an all-female environment. Such surroundings allowed a playful, sensual, and erotic sensibility full sway. The new sexual revolution in which women claimed the right to enjoy their bodies was powerful for straight and lesbian women alike, and clearly both were present. For lesbians the sudden release of the erotic from the isolation of the forbidden closet into the bright daylight of a women's community was an almost indescribable thrill. Two different reporters at the Southwest Feminist Festival/Retreat in March 1973 described "a weekend of singing, dancing, sunning, discussing poetry reading, film viewing and meeting with other women" with similar images:

I felt so high, playing, touching, dancing, living, and exchanging all sorts of things among women.[70]

The experience . . . of being with 200 women, loving, dancing, sharing, and singing is the closest I have come to my ideal lifestyle. . . . The fact that the majority of the women there were Lesbian probably contributed greatly to the closeness and sisterhood I felt.[71]

Sponsors of the Amazon Music Project in Santa Cruz, California were clear about their expectation that their festival in the summer of 1974 would be a lesbian-defined event. In a report for *off our backs* entitled "Redwoods, Lovely Women, New Culture," Natalie Reuss described the atmosphere after several days: "On Sunday there was a general sense that women had become completely comfortable in this forest space they were occupying. There was a free sharing of wine, beer and herbs, lavender silk-screened t-shirts of an Amazon woman, more dance and music."[72]

This sensibility received its fullest expression in the Michigan Music Festival held on 160 acres of rural land. The Michigan Festival began in 1976 and continues into the 21st century, drawing thousands of women every year. From the beginning it represented an "alternate reality," an embodiment of women's culture, in which "woman" and "lesbian" were treated as interchangeable. The first festival drew 2,000 women; the second probably doubled that number as word of mouth and published reports flew around the country describing a nearly utopian experience. Judith Niemi wrote: "Last August I lived in Lesbian nation for a few days. Our city-state was the Women's Music Festival in Mt. Pleasant Michigan, a lesbian Woodstock. A promise, a piece of the future being lived right now."[73] Another writer echoed similar sentiments the following year: "How often in a lifetime does a woman have a chance to experience an environment created by and for wimmin* only? How often can wimmin walk outside naked without fear or hassle? How often can three to five thousand wimmin gather together for 4 days of wimmin's music on 160 acres of gorgeous land? Answer: once a year in Michigan. . . ."[74]

From the beginning, there were women of color at the Michigan festival. The second festival in 1977 offered a workshop on Third World

---

*Alternative spellings of words like woman (wommon), women (wimmin, womyn), and history (herstory) became common among cultural feminists trying to avoid linguistic subordination. In some instances they misinterpreted the etymology of the word. "History," for example comes from the Latin *historia* and does not refer to the English masculine possessive pronoun "his."

women and social change led by Bernice Reagon, founder of the African-American *a capella* group Sweet Honey in the Rock. Reagon urged a more expansive, diverse ideal of women's culture: "I see a lot of people who think that because we are women that in fact all of our issues are the same. And that is erroneous. We are separated by class, race and all of those things put a strong stamp on us. . . . Women have dual, triple and quadruple identities. . . . Everytime you see a woman you are looking at a human being who is like you in only one respect, but may be totally different from you in three or four others. So when you come together, you come together for your commonness, but give the child some space to be the other people that she is."[75]

Michigan was not a utopia. The physical discomforts of inclement weather, long lines for food (simple, vegetarian fare), insufficient toilet facilities, and inadequate sound systems or other facilities in early years were generally borne with massive patience and good will. Conflict over the definition of separatism, there from the beginning, was more difficult. Women did all of the work; the location was remote, and everyone volunteered several hours of their time for tasks like food preparation and standing guard. Tensions remained on two initially unresolved issues, however: the presence of male performers in a few bands and the attendance of male children. Audience hostility to male performers was so high that after the first year or two they no longer appeared. The problem of boys—the discomfort of some women with their presence versus the anger of mothers about exclusion and discrimination—provides one of the most extreme examples of where a serious effort to separate completely from men and maleness could lead. Those who sought the pure experience of a female-only space insisted that the presence of any male was a violation (in effect a source of pollution, making the space itself impure). Mothers, of course, were enraged and accused those proposing such rules of discrimination. Michigan Festival organizers dealt with it by allowing infants of either gender and setting up a separate camp for boys, 14 miles away, while girls had their own camp nearby and from time to time would join adults at festival events. An even more intractable issue turned out to be the attendance of male-to-female transgendered people whose presence in effect challenged the very idea of an essential, biologically based difference between women and men.[76]

The Michigan Festival dealt with most other conflicts more expansively. Virtually any point of view or activity was allowed, and the personalized, therapeutic trend within feminism bloomed. A medical tent, called the Womb, offered both regular and alternative medicine, for example, and there were separate campgrounds for those who preferred quiet or chemical-free environments and for the physically challenged.[77]

Organizers placed no limits on topics for workshops, which could be scheduled in advance or created spontaneously. Merchants had their own tent, although soon enough they protested that they were forced to "hawk" their wares while musicians were paid for their appearances. "Women's culture," one of them objected, "is tilling the land and planting the seeds of a new way of perceiving the world. Cultural workers . . . are silver smiths, quilters, writers, musicians, silk screeners, woodworkers, potters, photographers, etc., etc. They are all of equal importance in the creation of a true reflection of women's reality, of celebration and expression of a new vision."[78] Workshops on spirituality grew each year, and a tent was set aside for the discussion and practice of religion. New Age spiritualism was more than just a women's practice through the seventies, of course, but feminist New Age spirituality had its own tenets. They sought new forms of ritual based on witchcraft and ancient matriarchal religions. In 1980 Z Budapest, the high priestess of the Susan B. Anthony Coven in Los Angeles, offered three workshops entitled "Goddess Religion for the '80's."[79]

Attending festivals gave participants an opportunity to "visit" their "people," to feel visible and at home at least once a year, but they had few illusions that it would ever be possible to extend that community in its purest form much beyond the episodic boundaries of these events. Thousands of women came to enjoy periodic "visits" to women's culture, but there were others who wanted to live it every day. These were women who embraced the utopian fantasy of a lifestyle that they believed would ultimately redeem the earth. The human complexities of trying to live purely in the "real world," however, intruded at every turn.

The idea that an "all-woman" context would be naturally cooperative, nurturing, and egalitarian shattered as women's institutions—whether service oriented, like health clinics, or businesses—began to grow and to become more diverse. It was no simple matter to diversify the relatively homogeneous environments of these early feminist experiments. Staff turnover meant that new hires were not necessarily feminists (or white and middle class) and had a hard time understanding the constant effort to live up to "feminist values."

Funding sources also placed demands not necessarily congruent with feminist suspicion of hierarchy and organizational structure. For example, the Los Angeles Commission on Assaults Against Women had been founded in 1973 by a group of feminist activists who had been working informally on the issue of rape for 2 years. Like many other such groups with roots in the women's liberation movement, they were deeply committed to collective processes and extremely suspicious of government agencies. From 1976 to 1978, however, the LACAAW received a major grant from the National Institute for Mental Health. "So we really got structured, because it was a research and demonstration center. . . . We had an obligation in terms of products that we had to develop—training manual, educational manual—[we had to] develop the programs, and then evaluate them." In addition, they suddenly had five new staff and their accustomed, informal ways of doing business, including midnight phone calls, no longer worked. "Well, we set ourselves up as a collective. Everybody made the same salary; everybody made decisions together. . . . There was a whole process of trying to develop a decision-making process that included hotline volunteers as well as staff. It meant that every discussion was agonizing."[80]

Health clinics, shelters for battered women, rape crisis centers, bookstores, and collectives of all sorts began with the idea that there should be a total sharing of the work and no differences in salary. Because these were labors of love, intended to be of service to the women's community, there was also an expectation that staff would accept extremely low pay. Several things conspired to disrupt this pattern, however. As founders aged, voluntary poverty was less and less attractive. Collective management, which forbade specialization, too often scorned the development of particular skills and made institutional management extremely inefficient. New hires paid for by foundation grants or government sources, such as CETA (Comprehensive Educational and Training Act funding was relatively easy during the Carter administration), did not necessarily share the missionary impulse of the founders or their grounding in feminist community and values. For them, decent pay, allowances for child care, and the opportunity to develop specialized skills were self-evident necessities.

Frequently these conflicts played themselves out on the terrain of race, which was already a highly sensitive issue throughout the movement. Racial diversity grew dramatically both because a high proportion of clients in service organizations were poor women of color and because the ability to hire staff allowed organizations to act on their egalitarian ideals. Minority women expressed resentment about attitudes and behaviors they experienced as racist, however well intentioned. In a typical response, Women's Advocates in St. Paul, Minnesota (one of the earliest shelters) held a Racism Workshop in May 1978. "Our purpose was to confront and deal with racism, staff to staff, staff to resident, and resident to resident. It was a very hard thing for all of us to deal with, . . ." They decided to establish a policy of ongoing workshops and a statement of principle that "Racist behavior will be confronted and anyone who persists in this behavior will have to leave."[81]

Racism was not a simple matter of attitudes or good intentions, however. It overlapped with class, with unspoken stereotypes on all sides, and with previous history in the movement. Sharon Vaughan, founder of Women's Advocates and later codirector of the Harriet Tubman shelter in Minneapolis, discovered only gradually the deep distrust of her black codirector toward middle-class white women. Sharon had chosen to be downwardly mobile, living on very little to realize her passionate commitment to ending violence against women. Her codirector, however, "never had any choices" and bitterly resented what she probably perceived to be an attitude of moral superiority. They clashed over the issue of merit raises for staff, which seemed logical to one and unbearably hierarchical to the other. "I won that battle," Sharon remembers. "Wouldn't even consider it." A year later, the staff asked for her resignation on the grounds that she was racist. Only after that, going through what she looks back on as her "Barbie Doll Breakdown," did Sharon begin to express her own anger and to believe that "white women's racism is in not being able to be angry. It is disrespectful."[82]

Feminist businesses and cooperatives that were primarily lesbian frequently sought to realize a perfect merging of public and private, work and personal life, but they also found that effort to be fraught with danger. Virago, a Colorado feminist collective that produced cultural events, began as a volunteer effort. "But when they started getting paid through CETA, they didn't do much and had all kinds of internal conflicts. Some women thought it should be fun as a business, others wanted to see it in terms of political culture. At least one person who was paid a salary did not work."[83] Many a business dissolved when primary relationships among key members broke up. Others sought the assistance of family therapists to sort through the tangle of emotional and professional issues that such relationships could engender. Sisterhood at work could, it turns out, lead to a dysfunctional family business.[84] A group in Colorado sat down to record a discussion of what they referred to as "dissolution in the women's movement" and raised many of the most fundamental dilemmas posed by separatism. "Why is it so hard to work side by side with someone you disagree with—why the terrible concern that everyone should agree on everything. . . . I started listening to people outside my circle of friends and workers. It really made my own life much simpler; I found my world was much larger than I thought."[85] Another reflected that in the separatist phase, "Everyone was either in a bookstore collective, newspaper collective, cultural or political collective. Everyone was doing process. For a while the energy was high. Meetings were numerous. We were everywhere. . . . [But] separatism was the isolationism of the purists. We divorced ourselves from money and capitalism. Money was evil; materialism was to be shunned. For many, it was only from the depths of poverty, when we started suffering from having no money for dentists or doctors or clothes or shelter or upkeep, that we came back to the 'system.' . . . In avoiding capitalism, we shunned learning how to deal and survive in a capitalist society. We had trouble running businesses, competing, paying bills, learning to pay women for their work. . . . Other isms are not equal to feminism, but feminism must be available in the market place of ideas. We are learning we can be feminists and new ageists and socialists and environmentalists all at once."[86]

JUST AS CULTURAL feminism grew from the earliest impulses of women's liberation groups, so did socialist feminism, and the boundaries between the two were clearly permeable, as the previous quote demonstrates. Shorter lived, in an organizational sense, socialist feminism flourished between 1972 and 1976. After that its founders moved in two directions. Some turned in the mid-1970s toward work in liberal organizations with a strong bent toward equity and justice for those at the bottom of society, for example, 9 to 5 or policy-oriented groups. Others turned to the realm of ideas, looking for useful theory but not for ideology, questions to pursue more than answers. They emerged in the 1980s as some of the most important and original intellectuals in the academic field of women's studies.

The failure of twentieth century socialist revolutions makes a concept like socialist feminism difficult to grasp in the twenty-first century, yet most left activists in the late 1960s were deeply disillusioned with the inequities of American capitalism and identified in some sense with the political vision of democratic socialism. Schooled in "participatory democracy," few would advocate a massive state bureaucracy (as had developed in the communist world); rather they looked to experimental democratic alternatives to capitalism, such as workers cooperatives. Feminism was not welcomed by rigid Marxists, who insisted that women's oppression was secondary to the oppression of workers, but most of the founders of women's liberation included in their vision of feminism an ideal of economic equality that fit easily within much of the rhetoric about socialism. In such a context, the word *socialism* represented a humane alternative to capitalism, evoking images of a cooperative, egalitarian, and caring society.

The first socialist feminist groups (Bread and Roses in Boston and the Chicago Women's Liberation Union or CWLU) were founded in 1969 by activists who resisted the bifurcation of the movement into "feminist" and "politico" factions. Distinguishing themselves most sharply from "liberal" feminists like NOW, they challenged the idea that equality for all women could be achieved within a social system built on inequality. At the same time they were highly critical of efforts to define sex as the primary source of all oppression and men as "the enemy," and they also dissented from the more extreme visions of lesbian separatism. Their greatest concern was to build a movement that reached beyond the middle class to include issues and concerns affecting poor and working-class women. Thus, in the late sixties and early seventies, as radical feminist groups splintered, fractured, and succumbed to the gay-straight split, socialist feminist groups offered an alternative that seemed less ideologically purist and more oriented toward practical organizing. Because of their focus on outreach and organizing to achieve practical gains for poor and working-class women, their work was in many ways parallel to project-centered NOW chapters, but they were always, in addition, searching for an effective theory that could link an understanding of women's oppression with other systems of economic and racial inequity.

Socialist feminists wrestled with the linked problems of theory (explanatory ideas) and practice (practical actions). Their theorizing not only sought to explain reality and offer a vision of the future, it was also intended to provide a practical method of achieving that vision. Rejecting the Left's traditional emphasis on the primacy of class, as well as the radical feminist effort to supplant class with sex as the primary contradiction, they endeavored to find an effective way to bring these modes of analysis together.

Pragmatism and ideological precision did not always coexist easily, of course, yet the largest, most vibrant, and longest lasting socialist feminist groups were the least ideological, espousing a nondogmatic, highly pragmatic vision of socialism not unlike that of the American Socialist Party early in the twentieth century. Adapting the women's liberation decentralized approach, these groups did not demand ideological purity. Instead they stimulated an array of organizing experiments.

Bread and Roses in Boston arose in part to counter the narrowness of the radical feminist group Cell 16 and to create an autonomous space on the left for a woman's movement to grow. Founders believed that they

were exploring a new stage of activism that would follow the initial experience of consciousness-raising:

> We and many women friends feel like we've been through a phase,
> a stage, of working out our own consciousness, understanding of
> our past. [This] has taken the form of being angry at men a lot, men
> in general, and men of the left for women who've been in the move-
> ment before. That's been really crucial for us, a way of beginning to
> shed self-blame, self-hate for who we are, really feeling instead of
> just intellectualizing—that it's not our fault, as we find other
> women sharing our experience. And now, as we're beginning to dis-
> cover who we are, who we want to be, we're ready to reach out.[87]

At this point, Bread and Roses was little different from women's liberation groups then forming across the country except that they wanted
to articulate their commitment to other struggles for justice and to
move feminist organizing into the Left's tradition of insurgent organizing and mobilization. In the beginning, of course, they had no real
sense of what kind of organizing could achieve these goals, so they set
out to "do everything."

Bread and Roses and CWLU, in their initial years, evolved broad
umbrella structures under which women's liberation activism of all sorts
could coexist. The impressive lists of activities in which they engaged
mirrored those of highly active NOW chapters, which spun off projects
on rape, health, education, or domestic violence and also organized
consciousness-raising groups. Bread and Roses projects included organizing secretaries, organizing high school students, guerrilla theater, ag-
itation-propaganda, study groups, an orientation committee to
introduce new women to Bread and Roses, and a "strategy and tactics
for the women's movement" group.[88] The Chicago Women's Liberation
Union, which lasted until 1977, was even more diverse, encompassing at
one time or another projects focused on day care, women in prison,
workplace organizing, political education, a liberation school, outreach,
a journal (*Secret Storm*), a legal clinic, a lesbian rap group, a rock group,
a poster and art collective, and several health care projects, including an

abortion task force, pregnancy testing, and HERS (health evaluation and referral service).[89]

CWLU also produced some of the first efforts to articulate socialist feminism as a perspective within the women's movement. Given a leadership with strong roots in community organizing, they also consciously set out to provide a political rationale for methods of organizing that might otherwise be criticized as reformist or bourgeois.[90] In a crucial paper published in 1971 they defined a middle path between, on the one hand, an emphasis on "new lifestyles within a women's culture, emphasizing personal liberation and growth, and the relationship of women to women" and on the other hand, "a structural analysis of our society and its economic base. . . . As socialist feminists, we share both the personal and the structural analysis." CWLU drew on the ideas of Italian theorist Andre Gorz, who argued that it was possible to achieve "anticapitalist structural reforms" that, reformist in their specific nature, would nonetheless achieve genuine shifts in power away from the ruling classes.[91] This, then, gave a rationale for socialists, who had agonized over how to link their involvement in issues like day care and health to their long-term goal of an egalitarian, socialist society.

In response to the success of the CWLU model and its theoretical initiatives, over the next few years 18 women's unions formed, primarily on the East and West Coasts and in the industrial Midwest. Another catalyst was a socialist feminist conference over Thanksgiving weekend in 1972 called by a small group in Durham, North Carolina. In standard student movement fashion, 165 women heard about it through the movement grapevine, drove hundreds of miles to get there (oblivious to the holiday weekend they were missing), slept on floors, ate peanut butter, and debated earnestly with one another for several days. Most of them were unaffiliated with any formal group but they returned home to organize.[92] Soon, in addition to the women's unions and Bread and Roses there were a large number of Marxist-feminist discussion groups and several all women's chapters of the New American Movement (a democratic socialist organization founded by former student activists), all of whom shared a sense with the women's unions that they were a vibrant branch of women's liberation.

Tensions in these groups shifted over time. Bread and Roses experienced the stresses of the early women's movement, including the gay-straight split. Most of the socialist feminist groups that formed after 1972, however, included substantial numbers of lesbian members (in some instances a majority) who consciously chose a political environment that was not separatist. Instead, these later groups were torn by ideological struggle over the definition of socialist feminism. The ease with which CWLU had framed a rationale for socialist feminist organizing in 1971 proved elusive for subsequent groups at a time when the rest of the Left was being drawn into sectarian Marxist-Leninism. Indeed, the central task many groups set for themselves was ideological: they wanted to create a global analysis that would explain not only the relationship between patriarchy and imperialism but also all forms of oppression. Such an analysis, once discovered, would point the way to an effective strategy for overcoming these structures of oppression. As Barbara Ehrenreich put it in her keynote speech to the National Socialist Feminist Conference in 1975: "Whatever the issue, we do not seek individual solutions for individual women. We seek collective solutions and forms of struggle that heighten *collective* confidence."[93] What had been a statement of a few paragraphs for CWLU on the meaning of socialist feminism appeared as a 16-page statement of principles in the founding document of the San Francisco Women's Union in 1974.[94]

As in the first years of women's liberation, the search for ideological perfection, coupled with the politicization of personal life, meant that those who could claim greater oppression had a moral upper hand in debate. Because socialist feminist groups believed that working-class and minority women should be their primary constituency, they also continually berated themselves for their failure to attract such women. At the San Diego Women's Union founding conference, for example (in an account published by the Berkeley/Oakland *Union*), the planning committee was " . . . attacked as straight, white and bourgeois. . . . [E]asily guilt-tripped into silence, they totally abnegated their power and women from the audience took the chair . . . the 'confrontation politics' of some of the most vocal women did not allow for dialogue."[95] Thus, in the name of diversity, debate was sometimes suppressed.

In Chicago, sectarian leftist organizations, such as the Socialist Workers Party, the Revolutionary Union, the Communist Worker's Party, and the October League, tried on several occasions to take over the CWLU, seeing it as a quick and easy way to gain influence and a forum for their own "correct line." When a sectarian group organized a chapter of CWLU in 1975, the steering committee decided to expel them (after extensive debate and much angst). These battles, took their toll, however, and the CWLU disbanded less than 2 years later.[96]

Socialist feminism inherited many of the same disintegrative forces that seemed to accompany feminist growth and creativity from the beginning. For a few years, however, it seemed possible to build a national network and perhaps a national organization. Feminists in the New American Movement (NAM) who were also active in the autonomous women's movement called a national conference at Antioch College in Yellow Springs, Ohio in the summer of 1975. It seems odd at first glance that in a movement so focused on separation from the Left, women active in a mixed organization should be the ones to call for a national organization, but women in NAM were the only ones with an effective national network through which they had opportunities to meet and discuss at a national level. Several chapters of NAM were all women (including the Durham group that called the 1972 conference), and their allegiance to the women's movement was as strong as if not stronger than their allegiance to NAM. They had already sponsored one national conference and produced a number of influential theoretical discussion papers.[97] When the call went out, more than 2,000 women responded and hundreds more were turned away for lack of space and facilities.[98] The yearning for a more effective structure and for a sense of national connection and movement was palpable.

Yet the dominant political style of the Left, and the lack of a coherent sense of what socialist feminism was or could be, made this conference one more occasion for the politics of division, blame, and guilt. Ideological conflict overrode any wish for organization building or strategic planning. The middle-class whiteness of those gathered revealed the movement to itself as overwhelmingly white, in contradiction to the values that brought them together in the first place. According to one of the organizers, "Soon into the conference we had to scrap a lot of the agendas and gather on the commons to hear mostly white women denounce the planners as a bunch of racists and then have open mike about that for hours."[99]

While the women's liberation unions and feminists in NAM sought to create a socialist feminist practice, the ground swell of interest in socialist feminism found a different expression in a serious-process of theoretical study and debate. *Quest: A Feminist Quarterly,* founded in 1974, set out to pursue practical feminist theorizing that could bridge socialist, cultural, and liberal feminism. Theory seekers also began to reexamine traditional socialist ideas from a feminist vantage point, engaging in a kind of Marxist-feminist consciousness-raising. Driven by frustrations with the limitations of personalized consciousness-raising, the excesses of the sectarian left, and a hunger for satisfying explanations of the coexistence of economic, sexual, and racial oppressions, a series of Marxist-feminist study groups emerged primarily on the East and West Coasts starting in the early 1970s, peaking sometime in the mid-1970s (probably around the same time as the Yellow Springs Conference), and continuing in some instances well into the 1980s. One of the first such groups, initiated by women in the Union of Radical Political Economists (URPE), brought together people from New York, Boston, New Haven, and other parts of the East Coast for a twice yearly meeting at a camp in Connecticut owned by the Fellowship of Reconciliation (a long-standing pacifist organization). Linda Gordon remembers that it was organized rather like a scholarly conference, with panels and presentations. Key leaders were Amy Bridges and Heidi Hartmann. This large group, which came to be known as MF1 (for Marxist-feminist group number 1), spun off sister groups in several locations. MF3, for example, was in New York City. Another group formed in Boston.[100]

Many more Marxist-feminist groups, quite outside the linked groups of MF1, 2, and 3, sprang up across the country. Alice Kessler-Harris, frustrated with consciousness-raising, started a small Marxist-feminist group with several friends. Joan Kelly, Carol Turbin, Blanche Cook, Marilyn Arthur (now Katz), Renata Bridenthal, Amy Swerdlow, Pamela Farley, and others gathered regularly, first to read the three volumes of

Capital. This was followed by reading and discussion of the works of contemporary European Marxists like Louis Althusser and Raymond Williams, as well as Engels and Mao. "[We were] reading the men stuff to see what we could understand about women. That was the operative question. It was wonderful." Around 1975 or 1976 they joined MF3 as a group because they felt too isolated, but they found the MF3 group was far less rigorous and far more personal in its approach.[101] Debbie Rosenfeldt joined an MF group in the Bay Area after moving to San Francisco State in 1979 to head the women's studies program there. Her group included Judy Stacey, Donna Haraway, Barbara Epstein, and Kay Trimburger. For several years the group was "wonderful for my own thinking," but it eventually followed the pattern of radical feminist groups, succumbing to an ugly, personal split.[102]

According to Alice Kessler-Harris, "The MF groups were a product, not a source, of the ground swell of commitment in the middle 1970s. The socialism and Marxism they espoused was not fully interrogated. [Rather] people came to explore. Many were academics, about two-thirds."[103] Gordon agreed and noted that in Boston the MF group had far more academics than Bread and Roses. Indeed, the membership lists of Marxist-feminist discussion groups reads like a who's who of feminist scholarship in the 1980s.[104] Perhaps because of their academic bent, these groups were on the whole more interested in questions (starting points for research) than in ideological prescription. Historians Linda Gordon, Alice Kessler-Harris, Joan Kelly, and Renata Bridenthal pioneered research on the history of working women, reproductive rights, domestic violence, and the role of the state.[105] Blanche Cook, having written several books on Dwight Eisenhower, went on to a landmark, multivolume biography of Eleanor Roosevelt. Donna Haraway opened the way for a feminist philosophy of science.[106] Economist Heidi Hartmann's work on comparable worth at the National Academy of Science provided a crucial intellectual foundation for this innovative policy. She subsequently received a MacArthur ("genius") awards.[107] Kessler-Harris, Hartmann, Rosenfeldt, and Amy Swerdlow all either founded or later directed major programs in women's studies. Several served on the editorial collective of *Feminist Studies*, one of the longest lived journals in the field. Clearly the MF groups provided a stimulating and richly productive milieu that contributed substantially to the intellectual legacy of socialist feminism.

That socialist feminism dealt so explicitly with race, together with the decline of black nationalist ideology, created some new space for feminists of color. The intense conflicts over issues of race at Yellow Springs and later in the National Women's Studies Association signaled an explosion of interest among women of color. The Combahee River Collective flourished in the late 1970s. At a series of retreats held across the Northeast between 1977 and 1979, they shared information about the dramatic growth of black feminist groups at the community level, in academic institutions, and among artists.[108] One of the founders of the Collective, Barbara Smith, wrote an open letter in 1979 about the fact that " . . . the black community is having to deal internally with the implications of sexual politics, feminism and most crucially *Black* feminism." The April 1978 issue of the *Black Scholar,* for example, "was an astounding mixture of profeminist even pro-Lesbian articles by, for example, Assata Shakur and Audre Lorde [alongside] the most reactionary anti-black women articles by black male writers." Two issues of the same journal in 1979 took up the issue again. "[S]exual politics is finally up for discussion by black people," she proclaimed, but black feminists face "a massive amount of resistance to the idea of black women being autonomous. . . ." Smith expressed frustration that "white women do not grasp that the black feminist movement is in a very different period historically from the white feminist movement." Relatively few black women were willing to identify publicly as feminists, and their emerging movement had not yet spawned the growth of institutions that could sustain it.[109]

The expansion of feminism among women of color, however, contended simultaneously with a backdrop of racial nationalism and the normative whiteness of the feminist movement. White groups founded on the assumption that women of color were "doing their thing" elsewhere suddenly confronted angry claims for inclusion. Anger and guilt played out a familiar duet in organizations, conferences, and the feminist media with increasing intensity throughout the late seventies and into the eighties.

White women's recognition of the importance of multiracial perspectives sometimes led to concrete action. Reproductive rights, for example, could not be confined to the issues of birth control and abortion within poor and minority communities, in which an appalling number of women were sterilized without their consent.[110] A group in New York that included founders both of Bread and Roses and of Redstockings organized the Committee for Abortion Rights and Against Sterilization Abuse (CARASA). They successfully pressured the City of New York and then the U.S. Department of Health Education and Welfare to issue stronger guidelines to ensure that women who were sterilized had genuinely consented to the procedure. Socialist feminist Rosalind Petchesky's theoretical writings framed a broader agenda that linked their work to women throughout the Third World who both lacked access to safe methods of birth control and also were frequent subjects of murderous medical and eugenic experiments.[111] Other times white women's guilt expressed itself as patronizing dishonesty. In a letter to *off our backs* in 1979, Hope Landrine described her experiences of racism in the movement as a mix of "ingratiation and patronage . . . statements of the we're-so-happy-that-ONE-OF-YOU-could-make-it type." She tested the perception that white feminists avoid serious discussion of feminist theory and strategy with women of color at a women's coffeehouse in New York. She would engage white women in discussion, challenging them with more and more outrageously absurd statements. The white women never disagreed with her, just smiled and asked a few questions.[112]

Although the most visible legacy of socialist feminism has been intellectual, it is important not to overlook the role of practice-oriented, practical organizing groups like CWLU and Bread and Roses, which provided the initial spark for the most innovative working women's organizations in the 1970s: Women Employed and 9 to 5 (now District 925 of the Service Employees International Union). They were also critical to the creation of such organizations as CARASA that worked to bring issues of race and poverty into the feminist agenda and feminist perspectives into other struggles for social justice. Numerous socialist feminist activists moved into mainstream organizations as they sought ways of achieving concrete changes. Heather Booth founded the Midwest Academy, which became the core of a national network of community organizations, and she subsequently worked as a political consultant to a wide range of electoral campaigns.[113] In 1987 Heidi Hartmann founded the Institute for Women's Policy Research, which continues to produce studies that serve as ammunition for policy advocates on issues of equal employment, affirmative action, women and poverty.[114] Caryn Nussbaum, founder of 9 to 5, later served as director of the Women's Bureau in the Department of Labor during the Clinton Administration.

THE NATIONAL WOMEN'S Studies Association was perhaps the most ambitious attempt to bring the various strands of feminist radicalism into a national organization linked to mainstream institutions. Women's studies programs had been building on hundreds of campuses since 1970, some responding to student demand, many as a form of outreach on the part of faculty who were activists in numerous other feminist groups and institutions. Frequently they involved many of the same people working in other feminist institutions. Deborah Rosenfeldt had been a faculty member in English at California State University at Long Beach since 1969, where she lived in a political collective of women and men all engaged in political and feminist activism. She was drawn into feminist activism through a women's studies conference in Sacramento, where Florence Howe invited her to come to New York to work with the Feminist Press for a semester. She returned to help found the women's studies program at Long Beach and then went on to San Francisco State where she became involved in a women's studies program that was extremely multicultural from the outset. Despite a hostile administration, San Francisco State harbored a very activist, grassroots program with "lots of adjunct faculty, some students, a few permanent faculty [all of whom] worked as a collective, in meetings all the time."[115]

Regional networks and conferences among women's studies programs led to a growing wish for national connection. The National Women's Studies Association (NWSA) was founded in January 1977 at a gathering of 500 women at the University of San Francisco. Rosenfeldt wrote at the time, "We came with a sense of history—the remarkable growth of women's studies in the seventies, the struggles with skeptical and often hostile institutions, the ideological disputes within the women's studies movement (largely inseparable from those within the women's liberation movement as a whole)."¹¹⁶ Participants were determined to create an organization that was not just another professional association. They wanted it to be an expression of the women's liberation movement itself and to be broadly inclusive. For 4 days debates raged over membership, dues and sliding scales, and ways to include both formal women's studies programs and community education. Five interest groups formed caucuses immediately: Third World women, lesbians, support staff, pre-K–12 educators, and students. On the first day the conference approved resolutions establishing a permanent Third World caucus and agreed that each of the major Third World groups (the term was not used in its traditional geopolitical sense but rather referred to Native Americans, Asian-Americans, Hispanic Americans, and black Americans) would be represented on the yet to be created coordinating council. Other caucuses demanded similar representation.

The resulting council included representatives of geographical regions, educational levels, different educational settings (campuses, schools, and communities), and groups usually excluded from power in other professional associations (Third World women, lesbians, support staff, and students). The unwieldy result totaled 42.¹¹⁷ The preamble to the NWSA constitution stated,

> Women's Studies owes its existence to the movement for the liberation of women; the women's liberation movement exists because women are oppressed. Women's studies, diverse as its components are, has at its best shared a vision of a world free not only from sexism but also from racism, class bias, ageism, heterosexual bias— from all the ideologies and institutions that have consciously or unconsciously oppressed and exploited some for the advantage of others.¹¹⁸

The rapid proliferation of caucuses, however, soon made a cumbersome structure almost impossible. At the first NWSA annual conference, May 30 to June 3, 1979 in Lawrence Kansas, the Annual Delegate Assembly was flooded with resolutions from caucuses. As one observer described it,

> A major issue of this assembly was the racism manifested at the Kansas conference, and the neglect of the needs of poor and minority women. Locating the conference in a "college town" in the Midwest with all the incumbent registration, membership, and travelling costs negated the option for many Third World and poor women to attend. . . . The Third World Caucus . . . offered three pages of resolutions challenging NWSA to confront the rhetoric of its constitution and its commitment to all women, including women of color and to actively work to eliminate racism, classism, ageism and heterosexism from its organization.[119]

NWSA conferences were an amalgam of academic feminism and women's culture, and they rapidly grew to involve well over 1,000 participants. Academic panels sat alongside workshops on feminist spirituality, arts and crafts displays, cultural events (the founding meeting featured a concert by Meg Christian; the first annual conference had a reading by Alice Walker), and highly politicized caucuses. As a rule, half of those in attendance were not even members of the association but came to experience women's culture. Like music festivals, but more intellectual, NWSA provided a public space for an emerging lesbian community. As one participant described the second annual conference in Bloomington, Indiana in May 1980, "When I arrived there, I was immediately caught up in that energizing, celebrating atmosphere which often accompanies large gatherings of women. . . . Although only eleven workshops had titles mentioning the word 'lesbian', I soon felt immersed in a lesbian world of stimulating ideas, networking, art, politics, and high energy."[120] For others, the politics of race took precedence. A reporter for *off our backs* argued that " . . . the most significant aspect of the conference for me was the substantial amount of work done around issues of feminism and women of color." Out of a large number of workshops and the Third World caucus came a call to focus the next year's conference on the theme of racism.[121] Caryn McTighe Musil attended that conference in Storrs, Connecticut and left awed that 1,500 women "sat there and talked about racism. No other group did that."[122]

NWSA's founding meeting and the Houston International Women's Year Conference both took place in 1977, and both revealed feminism moving into the mainstream. Far more Americans, however, were aware of Houston, which revealed that the Equal Rights Amendment had become a critical mobilizing symbol for feminists as well as for their opponents. The Equal Rights Amendment had been the centerpiece of the Houston Plan of Action, and for the next 5 years it provided a focal point for mobilization both of feminists and of their growing opposition. The symbolic power of the ERA in the late 1970s was partly because, beginning in 1972, it had been seized by right-wing leaders like Phyllis Schlafley who used it and abortion to forge a series of new relationships with an emerging religious right. For these conservatives and traditionalists the Equal Rights Amendment symbolized the changes they feared most. The fervor of male leaders who became hysterical over the possibility of "unisex" bathrooms (as if every home in America didn't have at least one) and the possibility of women in the armed forces facing combat alongside men underlined anxieties that feminism challenged the very definitions of "men" and "women." Men were not the only strenuous opponents of the ERA, however.

Historians Jane DeHart and Donald Mathews have analyzed the ironies of a cultural conflict in which women were prominent on both sides. Women opposed to the ERA were often as suspicious of male intentions toward women as were supporters. Their fears, however, did not center on inequality in the public worlds of work, politics, and education. Rather they feared that without the coercion of the state, men would abandon their traditional responsibilities for the family, forcing women into an "unnatural" and unequal competition with men in the labor force. One North Carolina woman summarized conservative hostility to the use of governmental intervention to secure equity on the grounds of either race or gender: "*Forced* busing, *forced* mixing, *forced* hiring. Now *forced* women. No thank you."[123] Similarly, as the antiabortion movement grew, it drew on the (accurate) perceptions of many women that American society devalued motherhood.[124] In both cases, feminist efforts to guarantee equal rights and opportunities for women in public settings created an easy focal point for anxieties about female vulnerability caused by the profound structural changes in American society.

The ERA was a prominent theme in the 1978 elections, on both sides. Feminists struggled to win seats likely to make a few more states willing to ratify. Republicans began to incorporate "social issues" (ERA, abortion, and "women's lib") into the more traditional conservative agenda and to woo southern Democrats, for whom similar forms of negative campaigning on the race issue had long been common. That year Phil Gramm won a House seat in Texas as a Democrat (5 years later he switched parties and became a Republican) by, as one of his campaign officials acknowledged, " . . . [going] after every rural southern prejudice we could think of. . . . [W]e were appealing to the prejudice against working women, against their not being home."[125] The Republican Party 2 years later dropped its endorsement of the ERA in its platform for the first time since 1940.

In this atmosphere, it was clear by early 1978 that the ERA would not be ratified by the 1979 deadline. All of the major feminist organizations devoted to electoral work mounted a major campaign to have the deadline extended until June 1982. The Congressional Women's Caucus, Democrat and Republican alike, pulled out all the stops to achieve this extension. For many feminist radicals who had not paid much attention to the issue of the ERA, thinking it far too moderate a reform, the real possibility of defeat got their attention. For the next 4 years, a very broad spectrum mobilized state campaigns and massive national marches to publicize the fact that in the foundational document of the United States, women were not equal under the law.

A whole new generation of activists was drawn into the final years of the ERA campaign. Under the leadership of Eleanor Smeal, NOW focused on the ERA struggle first to extend the deadline and then to ratify, growing from 55,000 members in 1977 to 210,000 members in 1982.[126] Millie Jeffrey became the president of NWPC on a platform of strong support for the ERA. She established a budget of $1 million, hired a political director, and embarked on an aggressive campaign. "We worked with other women's organizations, particularly in strategies, what states to focus on, where we should put our greatest strengths and energies, reaching out to labor and many other groups, church groups and so on."[127] For many women, the simple, egalitarian words of the Amendment itself could lead to an epiphany akin to the experiences of consciousness-raising groups 10 years before. Sonia Johnson, a Mormon housewife who had recently moved to Virginia, began reading feminist literature in late 1976 at the behest of an old friend. In the spring of 1977 she heard about a meeting at which a Mormon elder would explain the church's opposition to the ERA. Hoping to find a way out of the contradictions she had begun to feel, Johnson and her husband attended the meeting. She was surprised when " . . . he read the short and beautiful text of the Equal Rights Amendment: *Equality under the law shall not be denied or abridged by the United States or by any state on account of sex.*" Those words changed her life. "[W]hen he read those words in that hostile room that night, they took hold of my heart like a great warm fist and have not let go for one single second, waking or sleeping, since. . . . Perhaps it was like being born again."[128] In July 1978, she testified in behalf of Mormons for the ERA before the Senate Subcommittee on Constitutional Rights. There she sparred with Utah Senator Orrin Hatch, who pounded the table and shouted that her claim that an intelligent Mormon woman would support the ERA was an insult to his wife. Headlines around the country blared, "Woman vs. Senator: 2 Mormons Clash Over ERA."[129]

By January 1979, Mormons for the ERA had grown to 500 members and they became a regular fixture at both Mormon gatherings—where airplanes drew "Mormons for the ERA Are Everywhere" and "Mother in Heaven Loves Mormons for the ERA" banners across the sky—and at pro-ERA events. They devoted themselves especially to exposing how the Mormon church leaders organized opposition to the ERA by passing out literature and instructions in churches and busing groups of women to anti-ERA meetings and to lobby legislatures. The model for this new kind of political activism was Houston and its preparatory conferences at which, in Johnson's description, "Mormon men with megaphones, whistles, walkie-talkies and signs shepherded Mormon women about, body and soul, telling them when to sit and when to stand, when to come and when to go, what to say and when to say it and, especially, how to vote on every single issue."[130] Johnson's activist opposition and open defiance of church authorities resulted in her excommunication in December 1979.

Writing in 1981, the final year of the ERA battle, Sonia Johnson spoke (with some hyperbole) for thousands of women who had joined the struggle for the first time:

> I am sure I am not the only feminist who is occasionally clear-sighted enough to be grateful to Phyllis Schlafley for making us have to fight so hard for the Equal Rights Amendment. Whether in the end this amendment is the way women will achieve legal equality or not, it is still true that the struggle over its ratification has provided the greatest political training ground for women in the history of the world.[131]

The momentum had shifted, however, as feminists of all persuasions began to face the necessity to dig in for the long haul.

IN 1978, GLORIA Steinem reflected, "This seems to be where we are, 10 years or so into the second wave of feminism. Raised hopes, a hunger for change, and years of hard work are running head-on into a frustrating realization that each battle must be fought over and over again at different depths, and that one inevitable result of winning the majority to some changed consciousness is a backlash from those forces whose power depended on the old one." On the other hand, she noted, "Serious opposition is a measure of success."[132]

As the undertow of reaction sparked new energy into the campaign for the ERA, it also forced organizations like NOW, NWPC, and numerous issue-based coalitions to struggle with the long-term necessity of hiring paid, professional lobbyists to sustain a more continuous and professional presence in Washington.[133] For many feminist radicals, immersed for years in a counterculture, the late seventies were a time of crisis. In their case, self-reflection and internal criticism could be harsh indeed: they had set themselves on the road to perfection, and against that measure, the distance between the present and the ultimate goal sometimes seemed greater than ever. Institutions were harder and harder to sustain. Issues were no longer simple or obvious. The emergence of active feminist groups among women of color made race one of the most powerful and disturbing issues for feminists by the late 1970s, laying the groundwork for theoretical debates in the 1980s. Whereas in the early seventies white feminists talked about "women" as a relatively uncomplicated category, by the late seventies feminist journals were filled with criticism and self-recrimination about the "whiteness" of the movement in response to the increasingly visible presence of feminist groups among women of color.[134]

For a time the movement had become a world to itself for thousands of women. Collectives proliferated to create and manage bookstores, journals, coffeehouses, health clinics, and numerous small businesses. Attention to process was all consuming and meetings could be endless, but utopian hopes generated wave after wave of new energy. By the late 1970s, however, there were many for whom the lessons of the 1970s spoke loud and clear about the dangers of purism and isolation. Speaking to a Berkeley audience in 1979, Charlotte Bunch outlined a history of the movement from the early consciousness-raising phase through the building of a feminist subculture. "Within that subculture we've gained a lot of skills and strength and the ability to control a few areas of our lives," but she also argued from her own experience of coalition building since 1976 that "We need growth and enrichment, which comes from interaction with people who aren't like us. Sometimes the subculture stymies that growth because we don't put any value on interacting with anybody who's not one of us. . . . You get a tunnel vision of reality. You start to lose a sense of what else is out there."[135] As backlash gained momentum with the election of Ronald Reagan in 1980, the feminist tidal wave faced the necessity of re-creating itself yet again.

CHAPTER 6

Deep Currents

The Reagan administration did it so quietly. . . . [P]icture the Department [of Education] as a big egg. They didn't crack it and break it and make an omelet. They poked a hole in the bottom and all the essence just fell right out. And you still have a beautiful egg, but there's just nothing inside. . . . Today it is a pale, pitiful shadow of what it was supposed to be.

—LESLIE WOLFE, FORMER DIRECTOR OF WEEA
IN THE DEPARTMENT OF EDUCATION[1]

THE FORCE OF THE BACKLASH made feminists more invisible in the media and even to themselves in the 1980s, yet feminism not only persisted but flowed into new channels. It had to adjust, however, to a dramatically altered political context. The conservative ethos of the Reagan administration abruptly reversed the political influence of the feminist movement. As the New Right gathered political force in the late 1970s, it framed its concerns around "family values" (the mother-centered traditional patriarchal family). Making effective use of cultural themes initially politicized by feminists—family, sexuality, and reproduction—the new conservatism reshaped the 1980 Republican Party platform, eliminating its long-standing endorsement of the ERA. Both overtly and indirectly, the Republican campaign tarred feminists with blame for skyrocketing divorce, for rising rates of single motherhood (falsely portrayed as a rising rate of teen pregnancy), for growing welfare rolls, and for the displacement of large numbers of high-paying traditionally male jobs in a deindustrializing economy.[2] When Ronald Reagan won the presidential election in 1980, the force of the recoil was felt by feminists of every stripe.

Hostility to feminism was a key component of the new administration's outlook. Once elected, the new administration removed many feminists from positions on commissions and in federal departments, replacing them with appointees hostile to affirmative action and other governmental activism on behalf of women's rights and civil rights. Overnight the political atmosphere in Washington became overwhelmingly antagonistic to feminists. The elimination of CETA (Comprehensive Employment and Training Act) and LEAA (Law Enforcement Assistance Administration Grants) removed two national programs through which grassroots groups had received funds for staff. Reagan proposed to cut spending on social welfare programs by 17 percent. He accomplished just over half of that, mostly in the first year, and combined with the onset of a devastating recession in 1981 social services and nonprofits found themselves facing higher demand with sharply reduced resources.[3] In addition, that legislative initiatives to restrict reproductive choice and oppose lesbian and gay rights remained at the rhetorical forefront (though for the most part they did not succeed) kept feminists in a defensive posture throughout the 1980s.

The ERA had already lost its momentum by 1980, and in this new atmosphere, even with an extended deadline, it proved impossible to gain the required number of states for ERA ratification. By the time the clock ran out in 1982, several states had even repealed their ratification. Most of the large feminist organizations had focused their energies on this struggle for several years and remained committed to it to the end. With only three states needed before June 30, 1982, they mounted major campaigns in states where victory seemed possible. Illinois, which already had a state ERA and had failed to pass the ERA previously by the narrowest of margins, drew the most attention. NOW held mass marches and a weekly silent vigil, and smaller groups of women initiated civil disobedience campaigns: fasting, chaining themselves inside the capitol, burning ERA into the lawn with a massive dose of fertilizer. Sonia Johnson (founder of Mormons for the ERA) led the group of eight women who fasted for 37 days, drawing headlines as they grew visibly weaker.[4] Nothing worked.

Subsequent analyses highlighted a variety of reasons for the failure to ratify the ERA. Jane Mansbridge pointed to the unintended consequence of allowing the issue of women in the military to become a pivot of the debate. Mary Berry argued that the very process of amending the Constitution is so arduous and requires such a large majority that failure is the likely outcome in most instances. Jane DeHart and Donald Mathews explored the underlying cultural conflicts in a close analysis of the campaign in North Carolina.[5] In addition, many forms of legal discrimination that existed in 1972 had already been changed by legislation or ruled unconstitutional 10 years later. Taken together in the context of a right-wing ascendancy, the outcome seems foreordained. It had sharp consequences, however, for the prolonged losing battle gave a defensive cast to movement organizations, caused a sharp drop in membership, and drove a wedge between activists focused on the policy arena and those who withdrew even further into the utopian hopes of a self-sustaining women's culture or the abstract theorizing of academia.[6]

The personalism and utopianism of the movement proved to be tenacious characteristics, changing form, appearing and reappearing though frequently in ways detached from direct protest. In some arenas, for example, the Catholic Church, feminist radicalism continued to grow. At the same time, many radicals had migrated into liberal forms of activism to work for specific policy changes, sobered by the power of the state both for change and for containment. Greater engagement with the state challenged politically pure ideals but also signified feminism as an ongoing force in the political landscape. What fell between the cracks, given these two directions, was the recruitment of younger women who found their way to feminism, when they did so, pretty much on their own.

SHORTLY BEFORE Ronald Reagan's inauguration in January 1981, the Heritage Foundation released its blueprint for the future, *Mandate for Leadership: Policy Management in a Conservative Administration.*[7] The study had been requested by Edwin Meese, one of Reagan's key advisors, and its editor, Charles L. Heatherly, was subsequently appointed head of the Office of Management in the Department of Education. In a wide-ranging analysis of administrative units and policies (including recommendations to eliminate legal services for the poor and to limit enforcement of Title IX), this right-wing think tank singled out the Women's Education Action Project within the Department of Education for special scrutiny:

> Women's Education Equity is the unit within the office that is, to judge by the content of programs receiving grants, more in keeping with extreme feminist ideology than concern for the quality of education. . . . [Authorization] figures suggest the increasing political leverage of feminist interests. . . . WEEAP is a top priority item for the feminist network and is an important resource for the practice of feminist policies and politics. Its programs require immediate scrutiny and its budget should be drastically cut.[8]

Aware of the administration's hostility (although not of this particular blueprint for the destruction of WEEA edited by one of her superiors), Leslie Wolfe defiantly refused to remove a poster of Cuban revolutionary Che Guevara from her office wall and continued to nurture strong relationships with WEEA supporters in Congress. When the Reagan Administration proposed to consolidate a number of programs in the Department of Education into block grants to the states, congressional advocates championed WEEA with such vigor that it survived, although its funding was cut. Similarly in 1982, when the Administration tried to zero out WEEA as a separate program, Congress voted to continue it with $6 million in funding. As the Heritage Foundation described in a later "case study,"

> Since it became apparent that Congress was not going to unfund WEEA, administration officials began to channel their attention toward gaining control of the mandatory program. The Program Director Wolfe resisted each step in this process.[9]

The attack was launched with an anonymously authored article in *Conservative Digest*, April 1982, charging that Wolfe was a "radical feminist" who handpicked funding recipients who followed her "personal political agenda." "Anonymous" demanded the "swift dethronement . . . [of this] monarch in the feudal Washington bureaucracy, imperiously guarding her fiefdom." Wolfe's boss, Acting Assistant Secretary of Education Jean Benish, called her in, threw the *Conservative Digest* article on the desk, and asked if she had seen it.[10] Several weeks later Wolfe received a memo stipulating that "the formulation and articulation of all policies concerning the WEEA program will be assumed by the Office of the Assistant Secretary," and then she was summarily "detailed" for 90 days to a task force on waste, fraud, and abuse.[11] Wolfe remembers naively taking this reassignment seriously and arguing that she was really not the most qualified and anyway she had a program to run at a critical point in the grant-making process. Her boss "screamed at me, 'no, you're going; leave your office today, leave your key on the desk, and report there on Monday.'"[12]

Once rid of Wolfe, Acting Assistant Secretary Benish set out to override the program's selection of field readers, the people who read and evaluated grants submitted to WEEA for funding. The new readers were people like Grace Bulton, a Republican National Committeewoman from Oklahoma, who told a home newspaper that she was " . . . brought to Washington for a week to help check a controversial feminist agency which the Reagan Administration wants to abolish." Other appointees were affiliates of Phyllis Schlafley's Eagle Forum, a professor from fundamentalist Christian Bob Jones University (notorious for its racial discrimination), and Republican Party activists. Many brought no experience at all in education on women's issues.[13]

But the insider-outsider links, which had been forged in more than a decade of feminist activism, were not so easy to defeat. Wolfe; who had left the interview with her boss deeply shaken, met several staffers in the hallway, worried about how long she had been in the boss's office. "My troops were waiting for me," she recalled. That Friday afternoon "we filled out slips for the staff, sick leave slips," which Wolfe signed so they could take Monday off. Then they hid Wolfe's most important files in the bottoms of drawers so that they could not be found. "On Monday morning, we met at the Hyatt Regency . . . and we plotted what we would do." They knew that the field readers would soon arrive to re-view proposals, so they spent the afternoon mobilizing support among allies in the Women's Political Caucus, the Women's Legal Defense Fund, and members of the Congressional Women's Caucus. Republican Congresswoman Peggy Heckler recruited the "Wednesday Group" of Republican moderates in Congress to write a letter of protest.[14]

The outcry created by their campaign resulted in Wolfe being re-turned to her job after the 90 day exile and a later series of investiga-tions in which the General Accounting Office confirmed her contention that the newly appointed field readers were utterly incom-petent for the job at hand. The Reagan juggernaut was not to be held back for long, however. "Another battle won, another war lost. A year later my job was abolished. I was fired."[15] Within a year, WEEA had been "downgraded from a separate Program Office located in the im-mediate office of the Assistant Secretary for Elementary and Secondary Education to a small section (under a branch, under a division) in the office that administers state and local education programs (including the 'block grant' and impact aid programs)."[16] Wolfe went on to work for the Project for Equal Education Rights (PEER) at the NOW Legal Defense Fund, where Susan Faludi found her in 1984. Faludi was begin-ning to work on a book about the backlash against feminism and had met a number of people who told her she was imagining things. Wolfe filled her ears.[17]

As in the case of WEEA, the Reagan Administration was overtly an-tagonistic to most of the women's rights initiatives that had made some headway in the 1970s. For example, grassroots activism and EEOC sup-port of comparable worth had laid the basis for policy initiatives on this issue at the state level, but the Reagan Administration was notably cool to the idea and, after the 1984 election, openly hostile. Such policies, they said, interfered with the free market and would cause severe dis-ruption and unemployment. Michael Horowitz, counsel to the director of the Office of Management and Budget, pitted middle-class white women and working-class African-American men against each other: "There is nothing the Reagan Administration has done that holds as much long-term threat to the black community as comparable worth.

The maintenance man will be paid less so the librarian can be paid more."[18] Civil Rights Commission Chairman Clarence Pendleton declared comparable worth the "looniest idea since Looney Tunes came on the screen."[19] His assistant, Linda Chavez, campaigned against comparable worth, writing and speaking across the country.

In other social areas, in which the Republicans used rhetoric but achieved only modest policy changes, a grassroots conservative movement accomplished far more than the politicians could. The political power of antiabortion forces had made abortion the most severely polarizing issue in American politics and one of the defining issues for the New Right. At national, state, and local levels, right-wing politicians found a growing number of ways to impose restrictions on access to abortion. Following the successful passage of the Hyde Amendment in 1977, which forbade the use of federal funds (i.e., Medicaid) for abortion, antiabortion forces successfully lobbied for increasingly restrictive state laws, requiring waiting periods and parental notification for minors, for example, and barring poor women from obtaining abortions using state-funded health care programs, and a series of court decisions upholding such laws suggested that the *Roe v. Wade* decision was in jeopardy.

The passage of legal constraints, however, was mild in comparison to the rise of a violent antiabortion movement that focused its attacks on abortion clinics, many of which had grown out of feminist networks. A campaign of both legal protest and terrorist violence began in the late 1970s and persisted through the 1980s. It was the most virulent expression of hostility to changes in gender roles and sexuality. On the grounds that abortion was murder, abortion opponents escalated from civil disobedience and picketing to verbal harassment of clinic staff and clients and, finally, outright violence. Law enforcement officials estimated that by 1990 abortion clinics had experienced 8 bombings, 28 acts of arson, 28 attempted bombings or arson, and 170 acts of vandalism.[20] Women's rights activists offer much larger estimates.[21] At one clinic, which became the weekly target of picketing and vandalism, the director remembered that time as " . . . terrible, just awful. . . . Sometimes there were as many as 150 picketers, and they would be, you

know, just right up against our front door . . . in people's faces, scream-
ing and yelling. . . ."[22]

The political atmosphere of the eighties authorized more open expressions of hostility to women and minorities. Battles to eliminate language demeaning or belittling to women, for example, which seemed to
have been won in the 1970s, turned out to be only partially achieved.
Growing violence against abortion clinics accompanied a growth in
hate crimes (violence or threats of violence against minorities and homosexuals) and a greater tolerance for overt expressions of prejudice.
Perhaps because the boom did not affect everyone—and in fact
squeezed many in the middle as major industries "downsized"—women
and minorities were basically offered up as scapegoats.

Some of the most vivid evidence of growing intolerance could be
found on college campuses. Throughout the decade, campuses became
more diverse than ever as a result of the growing numbers of minorities
and a massive new wave of immigration from Asia, Africa, and Latin
America. By 1987, women constituted 55 percent of all undergraduate
students. At the same time, funding for higher education contracted
sharply, forcing steep increases in tuition, larger classes, and cutbacks in
scholarship funding. The perception that some groups (especially minorities) had "special privileges" in terms of admission and scholarships
certainly added to the tendency to scapegoat those groups.[23] Incidents
of racial name-calling and verbal harassment of homosexuals that would
have been unthinkable in the years immediately following the civil
rights movement abounded on campuses. Half of each of those groups
were women, of course, and attacks were sometimes directed specifically to them, as in the case of a black woman student at Central Michigan University who found trash bags and a sign reading "bitch" taped to
her dormitory door.[24] When it came to women's studies, and homophobic fears, such attitudes sometimes received official sanction from
politicians and administrators. In Southern California, for example, a
group of conservative Christians allied with several state legislators attacked the Women's Studies Program at California State University at
Long Beach for "prolesbianism and marxist revolutionary bias." Certainly it was a program that housed political radicals, but what marks

this incident is that politicians who disliked certain *ideas* could demand, and get, an administrative review that resulted in firing the women's studies director, canceling a course, and closing the campus women's center.[25] So much for academic freedom.

THE POPULAR MEDIA reinforced a sense that the new complexity of women's lives, rather than the inflexibility of the world in which they lived, was the problem. Newspapers and magazines deplored the toll on women trying to meet standards for success as *both* professionals *and* housewives, two full-time jobs. Numerous articles profiled women who dropped out of high-powered, high-paying jobs to have time with their children.[26] In 1986, *Fortune* magazine published a cover article on "Why Women are Bailing Out" of successful careers.[27] Such coverage laid the groundwork for Felice M. Schwartz's idea, promulgated in the *Harvard Business Review* in 1989, that businesses should offer a separate career track for women (later dubbed the "mommy track"), on the grounds that most women are "career-and-family" oriented rather than "career primary."[28] The next year, however, a study of 50 women who left Fortune 500 companies after more than 5 years found that their primary reason for leaving was the limited opportunity for advancement. It was the "glass ceiling," not a lack of family-friendly benefits that drove them away.[29] Both reasons were probably valid: many young professional women felt trapped by the conflicting demands of their professions and of motherhood at the same time that they *also* encountered increased resistance to advancement as they moved through the ranks. What alarmed feminists about the mommy track idea was that it cast aspersions on the ambitions of women in a way that could reinforce the glass ceiling. Furthermore, it failed to entertain the feminist demands for a reevaluation of work and family to make it possible for *both* parents to be significantly involved in the lives of small children without jeopardizing their careers.

Choices that had been cheered as liberating in the 1970s evoked criticism and dire warnings in the 1980s. In 1973, *Newsweek* had praised the emergence of singleness: "Within just eight years, singlehood has emerged as an intensely ritualized—and newly respectable—style of

American life. It is finally becoming possible to be both single and whole."[30] By the mid-1980s, another cover story in the same magazine warned single women that their opportunities for marriage may have passed by. "For many economically independent women, the consequences of their actions have begun to set in. For years bright young women single-mindedly pursued their careers, assuming that when it was time for a husband they could pencil one in. They were wrong."[31] This warning was based on a poorly researched, unpublished study that rapidly had become the basis for numerous cover stories and TV special reports in which single women (but not men) emoted about their loneliness and lost opportunities.

Certainly a higher percentage of women remained single, and many of them hoped eventually to marry. The media played expertly on the anxieties of women living out new life patterns without familiar models to show the way. Despite overwhelming evidence of life satisfaction and mental health among working women, whether married or not, many women began to believe that they *should* be lonely and panic-stricken. Similarly, the changing work patterns of married women provided fodder for divisive coverage. In a 1982 story entitled "Women vs. Women," *Ladies Home Journal* declared that there was a "New Cold War Between Housewives and Working Mothers." Anyone who read to the end of the story would find a plea for communication and understanding, but the large type lead framed a very different message: "During the 1970s there was a lot of talk about 'sisterhood.' . . . In practice, however, the events of the last decade may have done more to divide us than to bring us together."[32]

Film images of women and men had seemed to be moving in the 1970s toward androgyny, but the 1980s saw a return to stories in which raw male violence and aggression dominated and women were either absent or depicted as sexualized accessories. The shift was not immediate, however, as the early eighties saw a number of movies that challenged gender boundaries with men passing as women (like Dustin Hoffman in *Tootsie*) and women passing as men (like Julie Andrews in *Victor/Victoria* and Barbara Streisand in *Yentl*). The waning social movement idealism of the seventies also produced several early 1980s films about activism—*Reds (1981)*, *Gandhi (1982)*, and *Silkwood* (1983)—and a cluster of movies centered on strong female characters (*Country, Places in the Heart*, and *The River*). Such themes rapidly disappeared, however. In the blockbuster *Rambo* series, movie star Sylvester Stallone's untamed, macho screen image displaced the "sensitive man" as portrayed by Alan Alda in the TV series "Mash." Furthermore, the motivations of the Rambo character shifted sharply to the right between 1982 and 1985 as he became a one-man militia.[33] Similarly, fashion sharpened the contrast between aggressive masculinity and sexualized femininity with a return to cinched waists, high heels, miniskirts, and childlike poufs. In the mid-1980s, feminist author Susan Brownmiller attributed the reemphasis on femininity to "a sociological fact of the 1980s . . . that female competition for two scarce resources—men and jobs—is especially fierce."[34] By the end of the decade, fashion photographers were selling clothes with photographs of pale, pinched, and sometimes beaten women, a style that came to be known as "heroin chic."

In the wake of the ERA's defeat, most national women's rights organizations experienced a sharp contraction of membership and cuts in government funding combined with membership losses destroyed many smaller feminist groups.[35] The popular media in the early 1980s discussed the "death of feminism" or, more kindly, "postfeminism." Young women began to perceive feminism as a source of stigma.[36] *Elle* wrote, in 1986, that the new generation of women "no longer needs to examine the whys and hows of sexism. . . . All those ideals that were once held as absolute truths—sexual liberation, the women's movement, true equality—have been debunked or debased."[37]

Like other feminist institutions, *Ms.* had a bumpy ride in the 1980s, struggling for survival against the rising tide of conservatism and the growing invisibility of feminism. New commercial journals, such as *Savvy, Working Woman*, and *Working Mother*, had emerged to reach a market of young professionals. The covers of *Ms.* became less controversial, emphasizing self-help more than consciousness-raising (advertisers, for example, did not want women on the cover who were not beautiful or who did not wear makeup). The number of ads increased and the journal was sold several times in a search for a niche in which it could continue to exist. Simply by surviving, *Ms.* provided a continuing voice on mainstream newsstands that analyzed such issues as the feminization of poverty, provided research about the conservative right, and offered an outlet for feminist writers.[38]

Empowered by the Republican administration, right wingers kept up a relentless criticism of women's labor force participation, successfully blocking most legislation designed to ameliorate the strains of work and family life while turning the blame for those very stresses back on feminism itself. Opposing state subsidies for female-headed households, for example, George Gilder charged that proponents of such measures " . . . want to ratify the female-headed family as the norm in America. They do not want to subsidize families; they want to subsidize feminism. . . . The female-headed families of today create an unending chain of burdens for tomorrow as their children disrupt classrooms, fill the jails, throng the welfare rolls, and gather as bitter petitioners and leftist agitators seeking to capture for themselves the bounty produced by stable families."[39]

Political commentator E. J. Dionne, Jr. pointed out that "feminism had the misfortune of gaining ground in the period when the American economy suffered from its most severe shocks since the Great Depression." As a result, women entered the labor force in two "parallel streams," one highly educated and eager to seize new opportunities, the other forced into work by a declining economy and falling male wages. The latter, of course, ended up in service jobs that were not particularly fulfilling.[40] In light of the ongoing struggles for equal pay and affirmative action it is deeply ironic that conservatives were so successful in casting feminists as antimale and antifamily "dress for success" professionals who cared little for the trials of ordinary women.

Such stereotypes, however, governed the perceptions of the vast majority of young people of the eighties, both male and female. Paula Kamen, writing for the student newspaper at the University of Illinois in the fall of 1988, "quickly learned that taking a stand on anything even remotely construed as a women's issue aroused strange and strong suspicions." When she subsequently interviewed more than 100 women of her own generation, she found that their associations with the word "feminist" were infused with rigid and extreme stereotypes of "bra-burning, hairy-legged, amazon, castrating, militant-almost-anti-feminine, communist, Marxist, separatist, female skinheads, female supremacists, he-woman types, bunch-a-lesbians. . . ." She attributed the power of these stereotypes in part to the sense that young feminists were virtually invisible in the 1980s. "During our 'coming of age' years from 1980 to 1990, young feminists didn't seem to exist."[41]

Indeed, with amazing speed the women's movement receded to the margins of public consciousness. Younger women were left to believe that the problems were solved. After all, they had experienced athletic opportunities unheard of only a decade before as a result of Title IX, unparalleled access to education and jobs, and curricula in both schools and organizations like the Girl Scouts that were explicitly designed to give them a broad perspective on their own potentials and choices. At the same time the utopian optimism of the sixties and seventies no longer found fertile ground after Vietnam and Watergate. Writing in 1989, Amy E. Schwartz described the experience of those who, like herself, left home for college at the beginning of the eighties:

> We are the generation that grew up liberated already; we had no need to rebel. When we hit puberty, sex was OK; when we got old enough to imagine college, girls were already established inside the old Ivy League barricades, with coed dorms and freedom of behavior taken for granted. Girls were as likely as boys to talk about bright futures; more important, primed on the Judy Blume books they were just as entitled to feel lustful. Abortion was legal, contraception was available, drugs were undeniably around.[42]

Another woman in that same generation, Arrington Chambliss, grew up around strong women in the 1970s but heard little or nothing about feminism beyond the popular stereotypes Kamen described. In the early 1980s, at the University of Richmond, she became a rape crisis counselor at the YWCA. "Women in the rape crisis center asked whether I considered myself a feminist." Arrington asked what that meant; they said equal rights, equal pay, etc. "I said 'of course I do.' They were jubilant." Her subsequent experience as an activist in organizations of young people devoted to social service work and active citizenship replicated those of female student activists in the sixties. Men in leadership positions frequently came on to her, leaving her unsure whether her value to the organization was simply sexual attractiveness "or if I was really talented." Young people expected themselves to give everything to the cause, work day and night, sleep on floors. There were no boundaries. "Women had a role in that, but women involved did not identify themselves strongly as women." As a result, women had few defenses against what was already being named in other circles as sexual harassment. For example, when Arrington went to the Democratic Convention in 1984, "It was OK that I was staying in the same room with my boss who was a man I didn't know. 'OK [because] this is the 80s, it's OK to do this. The discomfort I feel right now is wrong.' There was no one to talk to, no support, no one to help identify what was going on or name it." When Arrington began to speak up about sexism, "people said what is the deal about getting on this women's bandwagon?" Social justice issues, in their view, revolved around economic disparities and racial discrimination. To speak up for oneself in the same context was to be self-indulgent, uptight. Her response, however, was "how can you not get on it? It's part of the whole social justice thing!"[43]

Chambliss's story highlights the isolation of young feminists in the 1980s, but it also captures the reality that many did find their way to feminist activism. Even in the 1970s, feminists were a distinct minority of women on most campuses. When political scientist Jesse Donahue interviewed a group of women like herself who had been activists in college during the 1980s, she found patterns not strikingly different from those a few college generations ahead of them. Inspired by strong role models and infuriating experiences of sexism, they joined an array of student groups working on abortion rights, lesbian activism, and women's health, all of which were available on campuses. Missing in their experience, however, were both the early generation of women's liberation consciousness-raising groups and any of the more institutionalized feminist organizations that continued into the 1980s. NOW, in fact, had made a strategic and devastatingly shortsighted decision not to devote resources to organizing the transient population of college-age feminists.⁴⁴

Campuses in the 1980s were not uniform, however. Most young women in the mid-1980s had to stumble their way to feminism (if they got there) through a thicket of stereotypes, but on many campuses, especially among young lesbians, there were enclaves in which the women's communities of the 1970s seemed to continue uninterrupted. Jeannine Delombard recalls coming out as a lesbian during her freshman year at Vassar in 1985, when "political correctness was sweeping American campuses." They were "blissfully unaware" of arguments among feminists about lifestyles and sexuality as well as of the distance most of their generation felt from feminism. Instead they adopted a "standard dyke or lesbian feminist uniform—baggy, rumpled clothes, Birkenstocks, no makeup, unstyled hair" and engaged in "politically correct unions" that were more political than passionate.⁴⁵

THE VIRULENT, even vicious opposition to feminism in the 1980s was less a death knell than an indicator of the fact that feminism had become a powerful force in American society and culture, reworking the shape and mission of numerous mainstream organizations as well as the nature of public life. Backlash was not the dominant reality of the 1980s. Indeed, the new hostility to change reflected the fact that, whether as working professionals or homeless "bag ladies," women had become omnipresent in public life. Although too often still tokens in terms of total numbers, they were there nonetheless—in corporate boardrooms, on highway crews, at truck stops (driving trucks!), in courtrooms (as judges and lawyers and also as the accused), in the pulpit, and in combat fatigues. The simple appearance of a woman in a position of authority no longer provoked disbelief. Furthermore, the joint impact of the feminist and civil rights movements meant that many of these newly visible women were women of color.

The list of "firsts" multiplied continuously. In 1981, President Reagan named Sandra Day O'Connor to the United States Supreme Court. In 1984, the Democratic Party nominated Congresswoman Geraldine Ferraro for Vice President. Wilma Mankiller was elected Principal

Chief of the Cherokee Nation of Oklahoma in 1985, the first woman to lead a major Native American tribe. On May 1, 1986, Ann Bancroft reached the North Pole by dogsled. During the 1988 Olympics in Seoul, South Korea, Americans stayed riveted to their televisions as African-American track stars Jackie Joyner-Kersee and Florence Griffith Joyner set world and Olympic records. West Point graduated its thousandth woman. Charlayne Hunter-Gault (the first African-American woman to attend the University of Alabama in 1963) and Connie Chung anchored network news shows. The Episcopal Church elected an African-American, the Reverend Barbara C. Harris, as its first woman bishop in 1989.

Women's leadership also continued to grow among community-level activists, who further broadened women's participation in public life. Poor and working-class women brought new issues and definitions of public life into the political arena that cut against the grain of the conservative ethos of the 1980s. In San Antonio, Texas, for example, Communities Organized for Public Service (COPS) created a powerful political base for the Mexican community. Building on the foundation of Catholic churches in the community, it tackled problems ranging from poor schools and housing to unpaved streets and open drainage ditches. The effectiveness of COPS depended to a great extent on the talents of women. As former president Beatrice Cortez put it, "Women have community ties. We knew that to make things happen in the community, you have to talk to people. It was a matter of tapping our networks." The program's success provided a model for dozens of new, frequently female-led, community organizations in Hispanic, black, Asian-American, and white ethnic communities across the country. Community-level activism increased the number of female officeholders as well. In 1969, only 3.5 percent of state elected officials were women; by 1983, women held 13 percent of elected state offices. In municipal governments, the proportion of women grew from about 10 percent in 1975 to 23 percent in 1988.[46]

The work of the National Black Women's Health Project offers a more issue-focused example of community-level activism. Founder Byllye Avery describes how she had only recently begun thinking of herself as a black woman, not just as a woman, by the time she left the Gainesville, Florida birthing center in 1981. Working in a community college setting, she came face to face with the stories of other black women and what she came to call the "conspiracy of silence" that surrounds their experience. By 1983 she had organized a group to launch the National Black Women's Health Project at a conference attended by 2,000 women. At the center of the NBWHP was a kind of consciousness-raising to break the conspiracy of silence. Talking with each other they discovered that they were " . . . dying inside. That unless we are able to go inside of ourselves and touch and breathe fire, breathe life into ourselves, that, of course, we couldn't be healthy." Conference planners started to develop a workshop called "Black and Female: What Is the Reality?" "This is a workshop that terrifies us all. And we are also terrified not to have it, because the conspiracy of silence is killing us." Two issues emerged as priorities: "The number one issue for most of our sisters is violence—battering, sexual abuse. . . . If violence is the number one thing women talk about, the next is being mothers too early and too long." Throughout the 1980s, the NBWHP initiated community self-help programs, held conferences and weekend retreats, and produced educational films and publications on black women's health in the context of black culture. By 1988 the NBWHP had created 96 self-help groups in 22 states, with international groups in Kenya, Barbados, and Belize.[47]

Women's athletics, propelled by the requirements of Title IX, continued to trace a profound, if measurably incomplete revolution. Through the 1980s the growth in women's participation continued to the point that young women could no longer even imagine the restraints their mothers had faced. In 1971, 300,000 girls participated in intercollegiate sport; by 1992 that number topped 2 million. From high school teams to offers of college scholarships to international stardom in Olympic competition, female athletes had begun to seem "normal." The apparent sea change in behavior modified the backlash. Few openly dared to argue that women should not compete or that an athletic body was, by definition, mannish. When the NCAA realized that it could not reverse Title IX, however, it made a successful bid to bring women's athletics under its control, destroying in the process the Association for Intercollegiate Athletics for Women (AIAW), which governed and promoted women's intercollegiate sports in the 1970s. The result was a dramatic loss in female leadership for women's athletics as most schools merged men's and women's athletics under male leadership. When coaching positions for women's teams began to receive better salaries, higher status male coaches displaced almost half of the women coaches. Men's programs routinely received twice the scholarship money and three times the operating funds compared to women's. Under a system of shared, male-dominated governance, women's athletics remained second-class.[48]

For women in the military, gains took place despite the ERA defeat in 1982 partly on the grounds that it would expose women to the unacceptable physical stress and the dangers of the battlefield. The first woman astronaut, Sally K. Ride, traveled into space in 1983 aboard the shuttle Challenger. By the time of the Gulf War in 1990–1991, 11 percent of the armed forces were female, and many women, although supposedly not "in combat," served in positions that were within range of enemy fire. Women flew helicopters, reconnaissance planes, inflight fueling tankers, strategic transport, and medical airlifts. They also served on naval logistics ships in the Gulf and the Red Sea. Two women were taken as war prisoners, and 15 women died.[49]

The "do everything" participatory impulse of women's liberation was also working its way through vast numbers of mainstream organizations. New alliances at state and local levels linked the organizational power of working women with that of elected officials, producing policy initiatives that belied the conservative image of the 1980s. Comparable worth, for example, made dramatic headway in a number of states after a 1983 U.S. District Court decision in *AFSCME v. State of Washington* held that the state of Washington had discriminated against women by systematically paying female-dominated job classes lower wages than comparably rated male-dominated classes and awarded 10 years of back pay in compensation.[50] The case was later reversed by the Ninth Circuit Court of Appeals, but for a time there was a surge of hope on the part of proponents. In the meantime, many states were considering legal changes in response to pressure from unions, from feminists active in the policy arena, and from state commissions on the status of women. These factors were prominent in Minnesota, which had a highly unionized state labor force (organized primarily by AFSCME) and an influential feminist community with strong feminist caucuses in *both* political parties.

In the late 1970s the Minnesota Council on the Economic Status of Women, chaired by Representative Linda Berglin and staffed by Nina Rothchild, a suburban school board member and political activist, issued a stream of publications on women in the Minnesota economy. Berglin and Rothchild stood at the center of a network that reached out into grassroots women's organizations, AFSCME, and CLUW, feminist caucuses in both major political parties, and members of the Minnesota Legislature sympathetic to women's issues. Their political skill paid off when, in 1982, the Minnesota Legislature with very little fanfare passed a State Employees Pay Equity Act "to establish equitable compensation relationships between female-dominated, male-dominated, and balanced classes of employees in the executive branch."[51] The thoroughness of its implementation was assured when, with the election of a Democratic governor later that year, Nina Rothchild was appointed Commissioner of Employee Relations.

By the mid-1980s, however, in Minnesota and across the country, what had looked like a fairly uncomplicated drive for legislative and judicial change had run into a buzz saw of opposition to government intervention into "free markets." In 1984, the Reagan Administration shifted from quiet to active opposition. Agencies that had pressed for comparable worth, notably the Equal Employment Opportunity Commission and the Civil Rights Commission, now headed by Reagan appointees, became bastions of hostility. Despite active opposition by the Reagan Administration, however, by 1987 more than 40 states and 1,700 local governments had taken major steps toward implementing comparable worth policies to raise the wages of female-dominated job classes. Such success produced strong backlashes in 1983 and 1984, however, following several key court cases and legislative victories. From that point on, instituting comparable worth policies was increasingly difficult.[52]

The controversy over comparable worth demonstrated the growing credibility and clout of a network of women's policy research institutes that could generate sophisticated data analyses and provide expert testimony for elected and appointed officials. With support from the Ford Foundation, the National Council for Research on Women brought together the proliferating number of research centers (most on campuses but also freestanding think tanks like Heidi Hartmann's Institute for Women's Policy Research and the Center for Women Policy Studies in Washington, D.C.

The receptivity of some corporations to policy-oriented research reflected their conscious need to find ways to attract and sustain an effective labor force with substantial numbers of women at all levels, as well as their desire to avoid litigation around discrimination claims. The authors of *Megatrends* found only 300 corporations in 1980 that offered on-site child care. By 1990 they counted 3,500. A staff member of the Conference Board gave an even larger figure for employer-assisted child care in 1990: 7,000.[53] Sexual harassment training became commonplace as companies sought to avoid litigation by changing work cultures. Gender-polarized images, common in popular culture, also appeared in a new guise when management consultants discovered that the characteristics of what they called the "new leader," as opposed to the outmoded "traditional leader," were culturally coded as female. Thousands of workshops on leadership styles encouraged the adoption of "women's leadership," which emphasized change over control, facilitation over giving orders, empowerment over commands, creativity over discipline, and networking over hierarchy.[54]

The rumbling of feminist ideas through mainstream institutions can be traced in religious institutions as well. Whereas many denominations ordained their first female clergy and rabbis in the 1970s, by the 1980s, seminaries were filled with women and major denominations embarked on inclusive language revisions of liturgies and hymnbooks. "Mankind" and "brotherhood" gave way to "humankind" or "people of faith." Congregations experimented with feminine images of God.[55] Synagogues in the 1980s became as accustomed to *bat mitzvahs* for 13-year-old girls as they were to *bar mitzvahs* for boys.

Catholic women who organized in the 1970s to press for women's ordination turned in the 1980s to building Women Church, a grassroots
network of women who shared liturgy and rituals, celebrated life cycle
events (puberty, menopause, and divorce), and wrestled with theological inquiry. Moderates continued to work within the church structures,
but a national conference in 1983, "From Generation to Generation:
Women-Church Speaks" launched a movement, in the words of Rosemary Radford Reuther, "not in exile but in exodus." Theologian Mary
Hunt proclaimed "a new baptism—a baptism into a Church which acknowledges that it is guilty of sexism, heterosexism, racism and classism."[56] When the Women-Church Convergence held a second
conference in 1987 in Cincinnati, speakers included both feminist theologians and secular feminists such as Gloria Steinem, Eleanor Smeal,
and Charlotte Bunch. Workshops at the conference embraced a broad
vision of social justice: sanctuary movement, antiracism, abortion, the
problem of sexual assault, lesbians keeping faith, community organizing, women and AIDS, and economic literacy.[57]

This radical challenge, however, was at once exhilarating and painful.
As Barbara Moral and Karch Schwarz wrote, "The Roman Catholic
Church is our history and our heritage. It is our spiritual and religious
'home,' an integral and essential aspect of our identity. It is also the
source of our greatest pain and alienation for, as women, we are both invisible and insignificant to this church we call 'ours.'"[58] The church hierarchy responded to the visible threat of feminist activism with
targeted assertions of authority. Several nuns who had become public,
elected officials, for example, were forced to give up politics or resign.
Mary Ann Sorrentino, former executive director of Planned Parenthood in Rhode Island, was excommunicated. Swift discipline was meted
out to the 97 Catholic scholars, social activists, priests, and nuns who
signed an October 1984 ad in the *New York Times* asserting a "diversity
of opinions regarding abortion" among committed Catholics and calling for "candid and respectful discussion on this diversity of opinion
within the church."[59]

Daughters of Sarah, an evangelical feminist group, continued their vigorous discussions via their newsletter and at conferences through the

eighties and beyond. They wrestled with "goddess" language (aware of new directions in feminist spirituality, interested in using female metaphors for God, but concerned to find a Biblical basis), sexuality (chastity, homosexuality, singleness, and celibacy), racism, women in the developing world, health care, reproduction, and abortion (about which they still had no consensus in 1987). A perusal of the newsletter makes it very clear that readers of Daughters of Sarah were aware of, and in conversation with, Catholic feminists, Jewish feminists ("the other Daughters of Sarah"), ecofeminists, and feminist activists in many denominations.[60] Given the cultural authority accorded conservative evangelicals with a political inside track, it is startling to discover such a vibrant, open, and radical ongoing conversation among evangelical Christian feminists. Tidal waves in the open sea, of course, are barely visible.

Lael Stegall, who spent much of the 1970s in the NWPC office learning to raise funds for feminist political causes, argues vigorously that the 1980s were a time for feminist capacity building, not eclipse. Feminist institutions shifted into the mainstream, taking on the formal trappings of social service institutions with boards, directors, accountants, funding from the United Way, or even direct government control. In other instances, feminists developed new ways to mobilize in an era of blacklash. Stegall says that the open hostility of the Reagan and Bush administrations meant that feminists understood the necessity of aggressive political interest groups, and they set about building them. Those that survived did so because they were strong. She reels off a list: the National Committee on Pay Equity, domestic violence networks, the National Committee on Women's Health, Black Women's Health Network, five or six different women's legal defense funds, and a large number of women's funds and foundations.[61] This "deepening of capacity" is probably best exemplified by the story of Emily's List.

In 1982, Ellen Malcolm, former organizer for Common Cause and press secretary for the National Women's Political Çaucus, gained a new perspective on one of the root problems for women candidates. An experience with Harriet Woods' race for Senate in Missouri taught her about the importance of money, early money, to get campaigns off the ground.

When Woods, a veteran city and state politician in Missouri, announced her candidacy for the Democratic nomination to run against Republican Senator John Danforth, her party turned a cold shoulder. "We have to have a man for the job," leaders said to her. She ran anyway, but discovered to her shock that even with party endorsement financial support remained negligible. The Democratic National Committee finally offered $18,000 late in the campaign, not nearly enough to allow her to respond to the onslaught of attacks from her opponent. Woods called Malcolm, who in the brief time left was able to raise only $50,000. Woods lost by less than 1 percent of the vote, and Malcolm believed that she could have won if the resources available to her had not been too little, too late.

Malcolm decided to found a new kind of feminist political action group based on the theory that "early money is like yeast" from which she took the acronym EMILY. Women's increased labor force participation, she reasoned, meant that they had—perhaps for the first time—resources to invest in the political process. At the same time, few women could make the large contributions toward which most political fundraising was geared. Emily's list would be designed to increase women's contributions in ways that were targeted and effective. Malcolm, herself a major philanthropist and heir of one of the founders of IBM, had the resources to get it started.

Emily's List uses a loophole in the campaign finance laws. Political action committees, as a rule, are not allowed to contribute more than $5,000 to any one candidate. To get around this, Emily's List uses a technique called "bundling." Supporters write checks directly to candidates and send them to Emily's List, which sends them to the candidates.[62]

A new member pays $100 to Emily's List in each 2 year election cycle to cover overhead expenses for running the organization and then pledges to contribute at least $100 to each of two candidates recommended by Emily's List. Once enrolled, the member receives regular mailings about candidates endorsed by Emily's List, with profiles of their careers, their stands on issues, and the likelihood that they could succeed. The member is free to contribute to any or all of the endorsed candidates, but the names are rotated from one mailing to the next so that if everyone funded the first two on their list, equal amounts would be raised for all.

Endorsement by Emily's List is a highly centralized process. It is a partisan PAC. From the beginning, only prochoice women in the Democratic Party have been eligible for consideration. A steering committee made up of the founding mothers of Emily's List makes decisions based on staff recommendations. From the outset Emily's List made a point of supporting only candidates who had a realistic chance of winning. According to founder Ellen Malcolm,

> The old boys network in politics didn't believe the women could win. What we did was publicly talk a lot about how tough we were in deciding whom to recommend. And in fact we were. So it started to become a kind of 'Good Housekeeping Seal of Approval' which helped decrease the credibility problem.[63]

Staff recommendations are based on indicators that show a candidate is "viable":

- Demographics and history of the district
- Analysis of opponents or potential opponents
- Analysis of candidate's education, political experience, and so on
- Demonstrated success at fund-raising
- Poll data to demonstrate name recognition and grassroots support

Such indicators have been criticized primarily by supporters of candidates who did not receive an endorsement. The last item has been most controversial. Polling is expensive, costing upward of $14,000. For some candidates this requirement is a catch-22. They cannot receive money without a poll. They can't afford a poll without some money. Malcolm remains adamant, however, that Emily's List is about winning races. Its recommendations are intended to place women's contributions where they can do the most good. This in turn requires a policy that she thinks of as a kind of "tough love": "No poll, no dough" is the rule. She also defends Emily's List's selectivity as a commitment not to waste resources either on races in which the woman is sure to win or on those that are demonstrably unwinnable. By contrast, NWPC and the Women's Campaign Fund, both nonpartisan, tend to support any woman who met their criteria in terms of support for key women's issues. Although they were important sources of support for women candidates in the 1970s and 1980s, neither ever approached the level of fund-raising success or the impact of Emily's List.

Emily's List had some success in the 1980s, including a few striking victories. When Barbara Mikulski ran for Senate in 1986, Emily's List contributed $250,000 to her campaign ($1 of every $5 she raised) and claimed her victory as evidence of a winning strategy. Between 1986 and 1990 Emily's List helped elect seven Democratic women to the U.S. House: Nita Lowey (New York), Jolene Unsoeld (Washington), Jill Long (Indiana), Patsy Mink (Hawaii), Rosa DeLauro (Connecticut), Maxine Waters (California), and delegate Eleanor Holmes Norton (Washington, D.C.). In 1990 it supported Ann Richards (Texas) and Barbara Roberts (Oregon) in their successful gubernatorial campaigns.[64] By 1990, Emily's List donated $1.5 million to 14 candidates and its membership list expanded to 3,500.

Very different evidence of the continuing and growing strength of the women's movement in the 1980s was the growth of women's studies as a field of academic inquiry. By 1980 even conservative bastions like Princeton, which only began admitting women 10 years before, were embroiled in debates over the institutionalization of feminist scholarship. A *Princeton Alumni Weekly* report on "The Controversy over Women's Studies" noted that opponents challenged the academic legitimacy of a field they believe was trendy, faddish, and—worse—political. "For many men and some women, 'women's studies' has a militant sound." The report also made it clear, however, that there was a growing commitment to establishing a formal program with a director and further that Princeton was under substantial pressure to hire, and tenure, more women.[65]

Over the course of the 1980s, women's studies became institutionalized at thousands of colleges and universities, complete with majors, minors, and tenure-track faculty. By the early 1990s over two-thirds of all universities, nearly half of all 4 year colleges, and about one in four 2 year institutions had women's studies courses. In addition, by the late 1980s there were specialized journals for scholarship on women in the fields of literary criticism, sociology, political science, history, and philosophy, alongside the many interdisciplinary feminist publications. Armed with new knowledge, feminist scholars inaugurated a massive effort to transform the entire curriculum in the humanities and social sciences. With initial funds from the Ford Foundation, faculty development seminars at many universities facilitated the revision of courses with the goal of making them more inclusive, not only of women but also of racial and ethnic minorities. Institutes or centers for research on women sprouted on dozens of campuses, winning research grants, developing curricula at the graduate level, and forming a national network through the National Council for Research on Women.[66] It is important to understand these developments as a context for the emergence in the mid-1980s of an orchestrated right-wing attack on liberal education with specific targets feminist and multicultural scholarship and teaching. This was a powerful backlash, but it came from people who perceived, probably accurately, the intellectual influence of such new perspectives. Some disciplines, notably history and English, had been transformed in fundamental ways. History, for example, shifted away from a paradigm of history as public activity focused on the actions of powerful men to include an enormous range of people (powerful and subordinate) and topics (from housework to popular culture to social movements to legislative activity). Scholarly conference programs once focused primarily on political and military history were, by the eighties, replete with sessions on women, race, and class and usually some combination. Older style political historians whose work had defined the discipline since its inception no longer ridiculed women's history. Some welcomed the new developments; others joined the conservative National Association of Scholars, allying themselves with the political forces trying to stem the tide of feminism and multiculturalism.

As with social service organizations, the institutionalization of women's studies led to specialization, professionalization, and fragmentation. Wrestling with the problem of "difference," academic feminists turned to postmodern cultural theories whose language was accessible only to highly trained insiders; to outsiders it was impenetrable jargon. The proliferation of journals drew academic feminists into specialized, disciplinary conversations, and increasingly theoretical approaches signaled a distressing disconnection between academics and activists.[67] Academics debated the "social construction" of gender—questioning the meaning of the very category of "woman" in light of differences of class and race—and activists continued to speak for women as a group. Although sprung from the same roots, academics and activists no longer spoke the same language.

Yet, the institutionalization of women's studies also gave younger generations a new kind of access to feminism. Throughout the 1980s, despite marginalization and stereotypes, on most campuses intense student groups debated the meanings of feminism and its implications for life choices. Indeed, women's studies classrooms became a crucial incubator for a new generation of women whose voices gradually became audible in the late 1980s and early 1990s, challenging the fragmentation of the movement.[68]

THE NATIONAL WOMEN'S Studies Association followed a path familiar to many other institutional experiments in the 1970s. Noted for large, lively conferences that melded academic discourses with free-spirited expressions of "women's culture," NWSA could barely subsist from one year to the next. By 1982 it was in financial crisis, surviving only because its executive committee stepped in to run the organization on a volunteer basis.[69] By 1984 the new half-time director, Caryn McTighe Musil, found to her amazement that the total budget was $85,000. Musil, her staff, and the executive committee plunged into the task of institution building. They learned how to recruit and retain members (little things like business reply envelopes were a surprise), started an in-house newsletter, and began to plan annual conferences systematically to minimize financial risk and and create a dependable source of income. From 1985 on, the association earned $20,000–60,000 at each annual conference. Step by step, NWSA began to take on the accoutrements of a professional association: an academic, peer-reviewed journal, scholarships and book awards, grants from foundations, a tiny endowment, and a responsibly managed budget of more than half a million dollars. In 1989 for the first time NWSA held a separate conference for directors of women's studies programs in which they could discuss the nitty-gritty administrative details of finances, curricula, pedagogy, and institutional politics.[70] At the same time, however, NWSA struggled to remain true to the personalist, cultural feminist politics that had given it birth. Increasingly it was two organizations, one professional and institution building, the other a movement engaged in a continuing search for political purity, given voice by whomever showed up at conferences.

IN THE EARLY 1980s feminists across the board were increasingly divided over what their agenda should include. Reforms like comparable worth involved feminists in a messy real world of compromise and partial victory. When they won through legal changes or collective bargaining, implementation forced them to contend with highly technocratic forms of implementation that relied on methods of job evaluation designed to serve employers and to reinforce market-based hierarchies. They could fight to close the gap between nurses and tree trimmers but not that between nurses and doctors.[71]

The underlying issue of difference between women and men proved sticky as activists discovered that they had no clear answer to the timeless question: are women fundamentally different from men? In the battle to tear down barriers to female participation in all-male clubs and schools, feminists debated whether they should embrace coeducation as better for all or preserve all-female schools for their ability to develop women's educational and leadership potentials. Should all laws be written in a gender-neutral way, they asked, or were there occasions when women needed to be treated separately to make genuine equity possible? Feminists split, for example, over the issue of maternity leave (linked to the biological fact of bearing a child) versus parental leave, over the problem of sex-neutral divorce laws that overlooked economic disparities and differences in earning potential, and over the question of whether restrictions on the growing pornography industry amounted to dangerous (and antisex) repression or an essential prerequisite to female liberty.

This last debate, argued most heatedly at a conference at Barnard College in 1982, became known among feminists as the "sex wars" because each side claimed to have the only truly feminist position.[72] Through the late 1970s, feminist discussions of sexuality focused increasingly on pornography. An important strand of feminist theory by Kathleen Barry, Mary Daly, Andrea Dworkin, and Catharine MacKinnon argued that male sexual domination of women (as expressed in violent pornography) was the fundamental source of women's oppression and that female sexuality was (or should be) diffuse and gentle. By 1980 some feminists yearned to reclaim the lusty and liberating tone of early consciousness-raising sessions that sought a joyous, assertive, invigorating sexuality. They began to challenge the notion that all pornography degraded women and especially the idea that banning or suppressing pornography was an effective strategy. The conversation, however, proved almost impossible as positions on either side hardened rapidly, claiming the mantle of true feminism. When law professor Catharine MacKinnon and writer Andrea Dworkin joined forces with right-wing evangelicals to propose city ordinances in Minneapolis and Indianapolis defining pornography as sex discrimination, other feminists opposed their idea as a violation of free speech and a dangerous step toward sexual repression.[73] On campuses, however, the MacKinnon-Dworkin position usually held sway.

At the same time that some feminists debated whether women were essentially different from men or essentially the same, others were busy deconstructing the category of "woman." The flowering of multicultural feminisms placed differences *among* women at the center of feminist theory. At the 1979 Barnard Conference on "The Second Sex Thirty Years Later," African-American poet Audre Lorde offered a fierce challenge to the 1,000 overwhelmingly white participants:

It is a particular academic arrogance to assume any discussion of feminist theory in this place and in this time without examining our differences, and without significant input from poor women,

black and third-world women, and lesbians. . . . [Differences must
not be simply tolerated] but seen as necessary polarities between
which our creativity can spark like a dialectic. . . . Difference is that
raw and powerful connection from which our personal power is
forged.

She concluded, "I stand here as a black lesbian feminist, having been
invited to comment upon the only panel at this conference where the
input of black feminists is represented. What this says about the vision
of this conference is sad, in a country where racism, sexism and homophobia are inseparable. Yet to read this program is to assume that lesbian and black women had no input into existentialism, the erotic,
Women's culture and silence, developing feminist theory, or heterosex-
uality and power."[74]

In response, the 1980 Barnard Conference took up the topic "Class,
Race and Sex—Exploring Contradictions, Affirming Connections."
Sarah Lawrence College professor and longtime activist Amy Swerdlow
opened the conference with an announcement that the time for the
women's movement to deal with differences had arrived. Black sociologist Bonnie Thornton Dill challenged the concept of sisterhood. She
argued for a more political (less familial) understanding of feminism to
accommodate the reality that women of color identify simultaneously
with multiple movements.[75]

Recognition of the profound differences among women had a powerful impact on feminist theorists, most of whom, by the 1980s, were in
academia. Lawyers and policy-oriented activists struggled with whether
difference between women and men should be inscribed into law, but
academics pursued the radical search for an overarching theory. The
models that had seemed so compelling in the 1970s led in disparate directions. If feminist theories focused on analyzing patriarchy failed to
account for differences of race and class (not to mention religion, ethnicity, and numerous other sources of identity), theories about race or
class similarly rendered women and the dynamics of gender invisible.
An analytical language, with which to think simultaneously about multiple sources of identity and structures of power, was simply not avail-

able. For a time (from about the mid-1970s to the mid-1980s), socialist feminist scholarship made the most serious efforts in this direction, but in the waning years of the Cold War when movements against communist regimes exposed their authoritarian core, socialism was no longer a visionary language. Another alternative was the popularity of postmodern literary theories that challenged the stability of human identities, exploring instead the ways that the categories of language construct gender, race, and class and other sources of human identity and differentiation. Among literary critics, by the late 1980s feminist literary theory had become arguably the most prominent approach in the discipline, prompting many who had fought so hard to be taken seriously to reflect ambivalently on this new insider status.[76] Theorizing shifted away from "the early feminist stress on the sociological and material" to focus "on processes of symbolization and representation."[77] In the hands of postmodernists, the very category "woman" seemed to crumble as their discussions became ever more esoteric and opaque to outsiders.[78]

Race, however, remained at the center of feminist theorizing because emerging voices of feminists of color tended to be literary or academic or both. Such authors as Gloria Anzaldua, bell hooks, and Barbara Smith forged new, multicultural directions within feminist scholarship.[79] The shift in discussions of race, away from a dichotomous focus on black and white, was encapsuled in an anthology, *This Bridge Called My Back: Writings by Radical Women of Color (1981)*, which was widely used in women's studies courses throughout the 1980s.[80]

The emergence of multicultural feminisms and the difficulty of finding a feminist language that incorporated difference also had an impact on the feminist cultural institutions that continued to flourish in the 1980s. In 1981, Bernice Johnson Reagon, speaking at West Coast Women's Music Festival, put it this way: "We've pretty much come to the end of a time when you can have a space that is 'yours only'—just for the people you want to be there. Even when we have our 'women-only' festivals, there is no such thing. . . . we have just finished with that kind of isolating. There is no hiding place. There is nowhere you can go and only be with people who are like you. It's over. Give it up."[81] In 1982,

Cherrie Moraga, Latina lesbian feminist writer, argued that race and class had returned to the forefront of feminist concerns because of the emergence of Third World feminism: "The white women's movement tried to create a new form of women's culture that on some level has denied where people come from. . . . Whether the women were Irish or German or came from working class or Jewish backgrounds, the desire to have a women's culture suddenly became devoid of race, class roots, what you ate at home, the smells in the air. Third-world feminism is talking about the vital, life-giving necessity of understanding your roots and how they influence your entire life."[82]

The annual National Women's Music Festival, founded in 1974, rebounded from financial and organizational disarray in 1982 and within a few years took on formal organizational trappings with a producer and a clear division of responsibilities.[83] "Women's music," with its own stars (Margie Adam, Holly Near, and Sweet Honey in the Rock), labels (Olivia Records), and production companies, flourished through the 1980s.

Many of these activities also represented a new level of public activity and visibility for the evolving lesbian community. Cultural events and annual demonstrations, such as "Take Back the Night" marches in cities around the country, functioned as public rituals in which lesbian feminists remained visible to themselves and to society. For lesbians, as for feminists as a whole, the eighties, despite backlash, were a time of growth and maturation, in which complexity and differentiation coexisted with growing capacity. The separatist lesbian feminism born in the 1970s continued to flourish in a variety of women's culture events, in rural lesbian communes, and in an array of cooperative businesses related to arts, music, and spirituality. At the same time, younger "lipstick lesbians" begin to deride their "granola lesbian" elders' understanding of a "lesbian lifestyle" rooted in 1970s, women's liberation-style feminism. They insisted on their right to play 'with the erotics of self-presentation and gender ambiguity (for example, wearing lipstick with tuxedos). They also refused the assumption that same-sex relationships required them to forego the joys and pains of motherhood. With artificial insemination (either with the help of sympathetic physicians or us-

ing the "turkey baster" method at home) and adoptions by the thousands, lesbians—and a few gay men—began yet another redefinition of
the family.[84] Finally, the sudden appearance of the AIDS epidemic in the
1980s and the homophobic reactions to the initial definition of AIDS as
a "homosexual disease" made separatism of lesbians from gay men seem
less salient for many younger lesbians. They expressed their solidarity
by joining new forms of activism, from professional lobbying operations
to community networks of care for the ill to the theatrical exploits of
ACT UP and Queer Nation.

Feminism also took a new turn in a diffuse women's spirituality
movement linked to a new strand of cultural feminist theory and action
under the banner of ecofeminism. The term "ecofeminism" was coined
in 1974 by French feminist Françoise d'Eaubonne, but it did not
emerge as a theoretical stream within feminism in the United States until March 1980 at a conference on "Women and Life on Earth" in
Amherst, Massachusetts. Carolyn Merchant, one of the key theorists of
ecofeminism, described how

> Over a three day period 500 women explored the meaning of eco-
> feminism as a force for the future. They concluded that, as moth-
> ers, nurturers, and caretakers, women should direct their creative
> energies to heal the planet, bringing to the public sphere the care
> and concern of women for all of life, and that, as feminists, women
> should work to transform the institutions of modern society that
> discriminate against women and minorities.[85]

A summer institute on "Ecology and Feminism" at Goddard College
in 1980, a second ecofeminist conference on the West Coast in April
1981, and the appearance of environmental themes at a host of other
feminist gatherings in 1980–1981 signaled an explosion of interest in
the topic.[86]

Ecofeminism drew most heavily from important strands in cultural
feminism, including writers as diverse as theologian Rosemary Radford
Reuther, Mary Daly, Susan Griffin, and Nancy Choderow.[87] What
these held in common was an analysis that linked the patriarchal domi-

nation of women with domination of the earth and claimed for women a special relationship with nature. Whether they viewed the connection between women and nature as a product of history or an essential expression of women's biological capacity for childbearing, they asserted that women had a unique vantage point from which to speak out against both patriarchal domination and ecological devastation. In Susan Griffin's lyrical version, "I know I am made from this earth, as my mother's hands were made from this earth, as her dreams came from this earth . . . all that I know speaks to me through this earth and I long to tell you, you who are earth too, and listen as we speak to each other of what we know: the light is in us."[88] Ynestra King's manifesto in 1981, "The Eco-feminist Imperative," brought the threads together:

> We believe that a culture against nature is a culture against women. We know we must get out from under the feet of men as they go about their projects of violence. In pursuing these projects men deny and dominate both women and nature. It is time to reconstitute our culture in the name of that nature, and of peace and freedom, and it is women who can show the way. We have to be the voice of the invisible, of nature who cannot speak for herself in the political arenas of our society.[89]

Ecofeminism bridged the academy and the cultural feminist community, flourishing especially in the latter, in which there was less discomfort with the dualistic and usually essentialist linking of woman and nature. Ecofeminism flowed naturally into an emerging feminist spirituality movement emphasizing images of Mother Earth and ancient goddess traditions. For many ecofeminists, it was important to evoke an earlier time, only hinted at in the archeological record, when societies were less patriarchal, when divinities were female as well as male, and when human beings coexisted with nature in a more harmonious way than in the modern industrial age. Both women's gatherings and environmental protests in opposition to nuclear power plants, deforestation, acid rain, and toxic waste were increasingly marked by the presence of rituals led by pagan spiritual leaders like Starhawk.[90] And a new round of lifestyle issues came to the fore: vegetarianism, abjuring leather products, using recycled paper, riding bicycles, and otherwise striving to live in a manner congruent with the values of honoring and preserving the earth.[91] The evolution of ecofeminism represented yet another of the boundary-blurring developments within the women's movement.

The emphasis on maternal values also contributed to a revival of feminist peace activism in the tradition of Jane Addams's Women's Peace Party during World War I, the Women's International League for Peace and Freedom in the 1920s, and Women Strike for Peace in the 1960s. In the summer of 1983, a Women's Encampment for a Future of Peace and Justice convened for several months in Seneca County, New York. Modeled after the British women's encampment at Greenham Common, the group framed its opposition to nuclear weapons in the context of "a value system which affirms qualities that have traditionally been considered female: nurturing of life, putting others' well-being before one's own, cooperation, emotional and intuitive sensitivity, attention to detail, the ability to adapt, perseverance." Women provided the backbone of a "nuclear freeze campaign" in 1984, urging a freeze on nuclear weapons. Women Against Military Madness (WAMM) joined feminist and pacifist actions across the world in confronting the horror of global holocaust with a female vision of a humane world. The spirit of Frances Willard's Women's Christian Temperance Union found new focus in a powerful lobby as Mothers Against Drunk Driving (MADD), founded in 1980, made alcohol consumption a political issue again. In the name of protecting innocent loved ones, laws against drunk driving were strengthened across the country.[92]

The fragmentation of the women's movement and the blurring of its boundaries were caused by both internal and external changes. Women's activism lost focus in the 1980s as feminism spread to encompass a far broader range of American women; feminist experiments stabilized and became institutionalized; and women emerged into public life in a dizzying array of roles. This change was exacerbated by the political strength of the opposition (symbolized by the defeat of the ERA) and a loss of government funding, which forced many activist institutions into hard times. For some, cultural events and celebrations became a critical means of feminist persistence. It is an interesting paradox that an essentialist, maternalistic, cultural feminism, which emphasized the difference between women and men, continued to attract a following at the same time that women struggled with deep differences among themselves. Soon a new generation of women would reject the idea that difference meant separation or that one had to choose among identities based on race or class or sexual preference.

The emphasis of cultural feminists on female difference, in turn, was ironically congruent with the popular culture's stress on gender polarization. Maternal values of peacemaking, nurture, and cooperation that informed ecofeminism, goddess spirituality, and peace activism echoed many of the same themes of the "women's leadership" workshops being offered to corporate leaders. By the late 1980s, such notions had become part of the mainstream. A bestseller, *The Chalice and the Blade*, offered a sweeping interpretation of history, contrasting societies based on dominance (the blade) and those based on egalitarianism and partnership (the chalice)—the same ideas that management consultants used in workshops that described "women's leadership" as a style more appropriate to the economy of an information society.[93]

IN THE CONSERVATIVE climate of the 1980s, feminist-driven changes in mainstream institutions provoked growing resistance. Inclusive language revisions of the 1989 Methodist hymnal, carefully calibrated to avoid changing the gender of references to God or the words of especially beloved hymns (e.g., "Onward Christian Soldiers"), were greeted with polls proving that most Methodists preferred male images of God.[94] So were inclusive language translations of the New Testament and Psalms.[95] Protestant denominations also struggled with the ordination of homosexuals.[96]

Multiculturalism joined feminism and homophobia as touchstones for conservatives emboldened by pronouncements of National Endowment for the Humanities (NEH) Chair William Bennett and his successor Lynne V. Cheney.[97] Once again, backlash was a measure of feminist success. Although resources for the humanities were diminishing, feminist scholars were in the vanguard of many disciplines and beginning to

appear in positions of professional prominence. It was their very success, against the grain of official policy, that drove an energetic right-
wing assault on liberal education that by the late 1980s was gathering
considerable momentum.[98] Even as the "culture wars" gathered steam,
however, the feminist spirit of feisty confrontation countered with another round of consciousness-raising activism. In 1985, a group of
women artists, writers, performers, and filmmakers created Guerrilla
Girls to protest discrimination against women in the art world:

> Dubbing ourselves the conscience of culture, we declare ourselves
> feminist counterparts to the mostly male tradition of anonymous
> do-gooders like Robin Hood, Batman, and the Lone Ranger. We
> wear gorilla masks to focus on the issues rather than our personal-
> ities. We use humor to convey information, provoke discussion,
> and show that feminists can be funny.[99]

They called attention to the absence of women artists in shows at
major galleries like New York's Metropolitan Museum of Modern Art
and the fact that art, like popular culture, had taken a strong turn toward
masculine imagery and style. They curated their own exhibitions to
provide women artists with opportunities to exhibit their work, and
they showed up in gorilla suits to demonstrate, hand out leaflets, and
plaster posters all over town.[100] In 1989 Guerrilla Girls posters carried
the following headlines:

- When Sexism & Racism Are No Longer Fashionable, What Will
  Your Art Collection be Worth?
- Get Naked: How Women Get Maximum Exposure in Art Museums
- Relax, Senator Helms, the Art World Is Your Kind of Place
- Are Bus Companies More Enlightened than NYC Art Galleries?[101]

A resurgence of feminist activism was gathering force among young
women just coming of age in a world already transformed by their
mothers' generation.

CHAPTER 7

Resurgence

*This movement never stops. It rises
and subsides, just like waves and, like waves, it erodes what
it cannot smash.*

— BEV MITCHELL
CEDAR RAPIDS, IOWA, 1992[1]

*Women will run the 21st century. . . . this is going to be the
women's century, and young people are going to be its leaders.*

— BELLA ABZUG
APRIL 24, 1997[2]

THE END OF THE COLD WAR in 1989, with the dismantling of the So-
viet empire in Eastern Europe and the overthrow of communist
regimes, changed the dynamics of domestic American politics. Americans watched with amazement as people around the world toppled authoritarian governments on both the Left and the Right. The
international surge toward democracy took place alongside—and perhaps even drew strength from—an increasingly internationalized movement for women's rights. In the summer of 1985 14,000 women from
around the world gathered in Nairobi, Kenya under the sponsorship of
the United Nations. They debated the implications for women of political participation, economic development, human rights, and sexual exploitation. Inspired by the Nairobi meeting, American women joined
the international campaign to place women's rights on the human rights
agenda, creating new institutions and networks linked to women's

213

rights activism across the globe, such as the Center for Global Women's Leadership at Rutgers, directed by Charlotte Bunch, and Arvonne Fraser's Women's Rights Action Watch Project at the University of Minnesota. By 1995, among the 35,000 participants at another United Nations women's conference in Beijing, 7,000 were from the United States.

Yet even as the Berlin Wall crumbled in 1989, young women in the United States were increasingly aware that the rights they had taken for granted could also be ephemeral. Abortion, although legal for more than 15 years, had remained the most severely polarizing issue in American politics, and the violence against abortion clinics that began in the late 1970s had succeeded in shutting down many of them. Supreme Court decisions upholding increasingly restrictive state laws generate fears that *Roe v. Wade* could be overturned. By the spring of 1989, when NOW called a national demonstration for abortion rights, between 300,000 and 600,000 people showed up for one of the largest demonstrations ever held in Washington, D.C. Yet that July, the U.S. Supreme Court again confirmed its willingness to severely restrict abortion, and four of its five justices wrote a minority opinion signaling that they would have preferred to overrule *Roe v. Wade* altogether. In *Webster v. Reproductive Health Services*, the Court upheld a highly restrictive Missouri law, which began with a preamble stating that life begins at conception and went on to prohibit the use of public funds and public facilities for abortions, except to save the life of the mother.

As always, adversity proved a boon to women's organizations. Membership in NOW and NARAL soared. Younger women had found their issue. Paula Kamen found that many young women she interviewed in the late 1980s said that " . . . after *Webster*, they suddenly realized how tenuous their rights were and how seriously they must fight for them."[3]

Glimmers of a new assertiveness among younger women in the late 1980s broadened into the voice of a new, overtly feminist generation by the early 1990s. Feminist publishing had never waned in the 1980s, but it suddenly shifted from the margins to the best-seller lists in 1990 with books like *The Beauty Myth* by 26-year-old Naomi Wolf. This passionate critique of beauty standards reignited conversations (common in consciousness-raising groups two decades before) about women's identities and the commercialization and manipulation of the female body.[4] In 1991, Susan Faludi's *Backlash* exposed in graphic detail the antifeminism of the Reagan era, and Paula Kamen's *Feminist Fatale* explored the ambivalence and ignorance of young women vis-à-vis feminism.[5]

A new sense of solidarity showed up among younger activists. Undergraduates at Mills College initiated a strike on May 3, 1990, when the board announced its decision to admit men for the first time. After 2 weeks, the decision was reversed.[6] By the mid-1990s young feminists labeling themselves the "Third Wave" announced their presence with anthologies like *Listen Up: Voices from the Next Feminist Generation* (1995), *Feminism³ The Third Generation in Fiction* (1996), *To Be Real: Telling the Truth and Changing the Face of Feminism* (1995), and *Third Wave Agenda: Being Feminist, Doing Feminism* (1997).[7] None of these were best-sellers, but they marked a new rhetorical presence within feminist debates matched by the appearance of new organizations, including WHAM (Women's Health Action and Mobilization), FURY (Feminists United to Represent Youth), and YELL (Youth Education Life Line). A reporter for *U.S. News & World Report* found these Third-Wavers to be both confident and angry. "While they have witnessed social change and believe they have the power to affect the status quo, young feminists . . . complain that they are inheriting a ravaged environment and a ruined economy. . . ."[8]

The culture of this emerging generation was assertive, multicultural, and unabashedly sexy. Gone were the rules and the academic theory (mostly). In their place were powerful, sexual women who claimed to have "no limits." Pop star Madonna was one embodiment of the contradictions and ironies of the new feminists. Younger women loved her brilliant manipulation of image and persona, musical talent, and business acumen—her "in-your-face" attitude. Her muscular body, honed with hours of exercise, clothed with sexy underwear, was hers to use or display as she chose. Cultural critic Camille Paglia argued in the *New York Times* in 1990 that "Madonna is the true feminist." Challenging what she saw as the "puritanism" of American feminism, Paglia proclaimed that "Madonna has taught young women to be fully female and sexual while still exercising control over their lives. She shows girls how to be attractive, sensual, energetic, ambitious, aggressive, and funny— all at the same time."⁹ Similarly, for 2 weeks in the summer of 1992, Americans watched the Olympics, mesmerized by images of female physical excellence. Perhaps the greatest of them all, African-American track star Jacqueline Joyner-Kersee, flamboyantly demonstrated the power of an unabashedly sexual body with the discipline, grace, and muscle that had once been presumed masculine.¹⁰

Such sensibilities underlay the success of Riot Grrrls music and *Sassy* magazine, founded in 1988 for girls aged 14–19. *Sassy's* frank articles about sex and birth control provoked a Moral Majority boycott, however, which forced many advertisers to withdraw and the magazine to be sold. It rapidly recovered its readership, and by the early 1990s had a circulation of 650,000, but *Sassy's* coverage of sexual issues had been toned down.¹¹ By 1994 it had become just another "teen magazine."

Riot Grrrls, on the other hand, represented an underground movement of young women in the alternative rock music scene, less vulnerable to mainstream control than *Sassy*. It began in the punk rock scene in Olympia, Washington in 1991, when girls decided to invade the mosh pit, the very crowded space near the stage where members of the audience (mostly men) dance in an often violent crush. Girls would form groups and make their way into the dance pit, protecting each other. The next step was to claim the public space of the stage itself with "angry grrrl" bands like Bratmobile and Bikini Kill. Their movement spread quickly through band tours, fanzines (self-published, ephemeral journals), and word-of-mouth networks. In July 1992, they held a week-long Riot Grrrl Convention in Washington, D.C., where "women gathered together for workshops on topics including sexuality, rape, unlearning racism, domestic violence, and self-defense." Participant Melissa Klein wrote that Riot Grrrl feminism constituted "a new feminism, a new kind of activism emphasizing our generation's cynical and disenfranchised temperament, born of distaste for the reactionary politics and rat-race economics of the 1980s. . . . I see punk, like the antiwar and civil rights movements before it, as a place where young women learned or solidified radical means of analyzing the world and then applied these powers of analysis to their own lives, only to realize that, as girls, they felt disenfranchised within their own supposedly 'alternative' community."[12]

Around the same time, the Native Tongues movement within gangsta rap/hip-hop music challenged the overt misogyny of rap. Rap groups like NWA had splashed into the mainstream in 1989–1990 with powerful rhythms and rage-filled language, offering violent revenge fantasies not only against perpetrators of racial and economic injustice but also against women and feminists: "this so-called women's lib/ I'll retire it./ That's why I'm a walking threat."[13] Especially for young, African-American women, female artists like Queen Latifah and Monie Love and all-male rap groups like A Tribe Called Quest and De La Soul offered a new kind of validation. In her sophomore year at Harvard, Elisa Davis recalled, "when I was introduced to Latifah in 1990, Afrocentric racial consciousness and progressive gender politics joined hands in hip hop. . . ." "Hip Hop gave me a language that made my black womanhood coherent to myself and the world. . . ."[14]

The new feminist upsurge focused primarily on cultural issues. In the world of mainstream art, Guerrilla Girls, formed in 1985, developed chapters in several major cities and continued their poster and public demonstration campaign to expose the exclusion of women and minorities. Their newsletter, *Hot Flashes: "All the Sexism, Racism, and Homophobia that Fits, We Complain About,"* began in 1993 with an evaluation of the *New York Times* coverage of women in art.[15] The second issue, published the following year, carried a banner headline: "Guerrilla Girls Predict That Museums in the East Will Have a White Male Winter. And a White Male Spring, Summer and Fall."[16] At the same time they expanded their poster campaign beyond the world of art to include such issues as homelessness, the environment, and AIDS.[17]

The Women's Action Coalition (WAC) was a direct action group started by artists in the aftermath of the Hill-Thomas hearings but drawing on the experience of other groups, such as Guerrilla Girls, ACT UP (1987–1989), and Queer Nation. Founded in January 1992 in New York City, WAC meetings drew 450–500 by early summer with this mission statement: "WAC is an open alliance of women committed

to DIRECT ACTION on issues affecting the rights of all women. . . .
WAC insists on economic parity and representation for all women, and
an end to homophobia, racism, religious prejudice and violence against
women. We insist on every woman's right to quality health care, child
care and reproductive freedom. We will exercise our full creative power
to launch a visible and remarkable resistance."[18] WAC's success at conducting more than 30 tightly organized actions in its first year sparked
chapters in cities across the country. WAC's slogan to "act now and phi-
losophize later" was clearly energizing to hundreds of women eager to
"do something." Their "WAC Attacks," conducted with consummate
media savvy, generated significant coverage. They developed a logo of a
watching eye and a blue dot evoking the blue dot used by TV newscasts
to hide the identity of rape victims. Dressed in black, backed by a drum
corps, and using posters with clear, frequently ironic messages, they
regularly made prime-time TV news. On Mother's Day 1992, WAC
draped the Grand Central Station train schedule board with a pink banner that said "It's Mother's Day: $30 billion owed in child support."
Similar messages were erected at the 1992 Democratic Convention, "O
say can you see, 10 million more women voters than men," and the 1992
Gay Rights Parade, "WAC is here, some are queer." At demonstrations,
drum corps drummed while WAC members whistled and chanted:
"We're WAC, we won't go back" "Off our backs! On our feet! We
refuse to be discreet!" "We're women, we're angry, we vote!" As one
participant, Anna Blume, said in 1992, "I've done a lot of radical things
in my life, but WAC sometimes gives me nightmares. Hundreds of angry women in a room deciding to fight back is a phenomenon. Women
aren't supposed to do what we've been doing."[19]

The new assertiveness showed up in more traditional venues as well.
Mary Ann Lundy, Associate Director for Churchwide Planning for the
Presbyterian Church, dreamed in 1988 of "a global theological colloquium" to honor the World Council of Churches' Ecumenical Decade:
Churches in Solidarity with Women. By 1990 she had persuaded a
group in Minnesota to host a gathering that would celebrate the feminist theological insights circulating for nearly two decades. "Re-Imagining" they called it. Held in November 1993, the Re-Imagining

Gathering drew a crowd of 2,000 and turned away hundreds more. For several days women—and a few men—absorbed themselves in reimagining ideas about God, incorporating female as well as male metaphors and challenging the patriarchal assumptions embedded in Christian tradition. They listened to feminist theologians and then debated theological ideas at roundtables. They celebrated femaleness by sharing milk and honey and praying to Sophia, the Greek word for wisdom used in several Biblical references to God. Most of those who attended described the conference with words like homecoming, release from isolation, and breaking silence.[20]

Planners of the gathering, however, had never thought of it as "radical." After all, feminist theologians began rethinking the patriarchal images of God in the 1970s. Indeed, compared to feminist New Age spirituality, they were definitely conservative in their insistence on wrestling with rather than rejecting their tradition. So, they were unprepared for the reaction they drew. Conservative religious papers sent reporters who published accounts of the conference. To their minds referring to God as "She" was heresy, goddess worship. Experimental ritual was pagan. That mainstream denominations had provided some support and staff time "ignited the fear and fury of the religious right. Suddenly, what had been a dangerous but marginalized movement was encroaching on home territory—and many conservatives rose up to stop it."[21] Hate mail, death threats, and roiling controversy in the religious press cowed denominational leaders. Several key organizers of the conference, including Mary Ann Lundy, lost their jobs.[22] Shocked and horrified by the intensity of the hostile response, the organizers decided that the only thing to do was to hold more such gatherings, to see themselves as a movement.[23]

Predictably, the emergence of a new feminist assertiveness in the late 1980s and early 1990s coincided with a crescendo of antifeminist attacks. What had started in the mid-1980s as a coordinated and well-funded effort to focus the conservative political agenda on cultural issues exploded in 1990–1991 into a popular media campaign against "political correctness," including multiculturalism, women's studies, ethnic studies, curriculum reform, and affirmative action.[24] In 1990 there were 656 articles on "political correctness" in the print media and 3,989 in 1991.²⁵ They constituted a right-wing assault on ideas flowing from the social movements of the 1960s and policies, like affirmative action, designed to rectify historic inequities. Their target was academia, where such ideas had been able to flourish even in conservative times and where curricula now included women, racial minorities, and attention to the voices and the historical experience of peoples around the world. Certainly there were examples of leftist political purism and efforts to silence other views. By working and reworking a small number of incidents, however, the media blitz generated an impression that all of higher education was consumed with conflict and further that the "politically correct multiculturalists" were in a position to stifle all dissent. President George Bush gave his imprimatur to this perception at a University of Michigan commencement address in May 1991. "Political extremists roam the land," he charged, "abusing the privilege of free speech, setting citizens against one another on the basis of their class or race."²⁶ Leading journals told the same story with headlines like "The Rising Hegemony of the Politically Correct," "The Storm over the University," "The Academy's New Ayatollahs," "High Noon at the PC Corral," and "Upside Down in the Groves of Academe."²⁷ Such hyperbole effectively obscured the reality that 3–10 percent of universities and colleges experienced controversies over "political correctness" concerns regarding classes or invited speakers, but 36 percent of all institutions of higher education reported incidents of intolerance related to race, gender, or sexual preference.²⁸

This was the context into which a new generation of "feminist antifeminists" launched their critique. When Sally Quinn opined that "feminism as we have known it is dead," she laid the cause at the feet of "feminists who felt having babies was not the politically correct thing to do," leaving women to "feel betrayed and lied to because trying to live a politically correct personal life doesn't always work. . . ." In her view, in fact, such a life would be "unnatural."²⁹ Christina Hoff Sommers, characterized in the *Chronicle of Higher Education* as a "key player in the national debates on 'political correctness' and the curriculum" similarly charged that "feminism is relentlessly hostile to the family" and that women's studies programs are like "a powerful cult."[30] "The plain truth is: the feminist leaders have no troops. While the gender gap proved to be a feminist myth, the gap dividing the feminists from the women they claim to speak for is no myth and is worth pondering."[31] Charging that "much of what students learn in women's studies classes is not disciplined scholarship but feminist ideology," Sommers warned her readers that "the New Feminism has been rapidly colonizing and 'transforming' the American university."[32] Camille Paglia, scornful of feminist "whining" about sexual harassment, glass ceilings, and the difficulty of balancing motherhood with a high-powered career, had equal venom for the postmodern turn in feminist literary theory. "Today's academic leftists are strutting wannabes, timorous nerds who missed the 60s while they were grade-grubbing in the library and brown-nosing the senior faculty. Their politics came to them late, secondhand, and special delivery via the Parisian import craze of the 70s."[33]

Sommers, Paglia, and Elizabeth Fox-Genovese tore into the women's movement for its individualism (Fox-Genovese), puritanism (Paglia), and rage (Sommers) with books like *Who Stole Feminism: How Women Have Betrayed Women*. For all their differences, they shared a sharp edge of personal grievance toward what they viewed as a feminist establishment. Each had been embroiled in battles with other feminist scholars. Camille Paglia made no bones about having been " . . . expelled from the feminist movement."[34] Sommers, after describing feminist critiques of Naomi Wolf's book *Fire with Fire* remarked bitterly, "Get used to this, Ms. Wolf. You'll soon be finding out how it feels to be called antifeminist simply because you refuse to regard men as the enemy and women as their hapless victims."[35] It is ironic that they describe an all-powerful cultlike Mafia of feminist scholars when the experience of many students in the 1980s was that their faculty were too worried about being successful in academia to be activists.[36] These critics also touched on a set of ongoing debates *within* feminism that traced back at least to the Barnard Conference in 1980 and probably before that as well. The accusation that feminists were obsessed with women as victims had a kernel of truth. Some were. Rhetorical excesses showed up, as they always had, in the parts of the movement still seeking absolutes.

Feminist activism in the eighties and early nineties, for example, was especially visible around the issue of reproductive choice and violence against women, and key theorists of the latter, such as Catharine MacKinnon and Andrea Dworkin, did indeed emphasize victimization over agency. For them, most if not all heterosexual sex was comparable to rape, and like all charismatic leaders, they inspired followers to proclaim their views as the one true feminism. This had two consequences: on the one hand many activists withdrew from the discussion, choosing to work on specific issues far from the polemical debates.[37] On the other, critics could accept their claims at face value and use the words of a few to characterize feminism as a whole. Katie Roiphe, a graduate student at Princeton, wrote a youthful polemic against "rape crisis feminism," noting that she and her classmates at Princeton had not felt in danger of being raped and dismissing women who claimed to have been raped by acquaintances as failing to accept responsibility for their own safety and sexuality.[38] Critics like Roiphe undermined the many true stories of rape; they also overlooked the simultaneous existence of highly assertive forms of feminist activism, such as Guerrilla Girls, and issues like comparable worth or women's growing electoral power as expressed in Emily's List that did not lend themselves to marches and demonstrations. It is also interesting to note that campus activism in the early 1990s drew attention to the problem of date rape, but by the late 1990s it was equal parts sexual assertiveness and antiviolence. Eve Ensler's play *The Vagina Monologues* has played on hundreds of campuses since 1998. In typical consciousness-raising fashion, this one-woman show consists of interviews with a variety of women about "down there" that range from joyful sexual self-discovery to rape. Paula Kamen observed that "These events typically attract massive sold-out audiences that rival the size of those seen at major sporting events, such as with the attendance of a thousand at Duke University and two thousand at Oregon State in Corvallis in February 2001."[39]

Criticisms of feminism also pointed to the continuing power of identity politics and racial division exemplified in the National Women's Studies Association's self-destruction in 1990. A personnel issue within the national office became the mechanism for an all-out assault on the association at its annual meeting in 1990. A small minority of the Coordinating Council dissented from the decision to fire a black staff member, on the grounds that to do so was racist. They then disrupted the 1990 Annual Conference in Akron, Ohio, taking over the microphone of every plenary session to denounce the racism of NWSA and to make "nonnegotiable" demands that she be reinstated with $75,000 in back pay and damages and that NWSA fire its Executive Director, Karen Musil. When the Delegate Assembly refused to be railroaded, some members of the Women of Color caucus staged a walkout.[40] After that, the association was virtually paralyzed. Rhetorical attacks on the "white leadership" and "white dominated power structure" of NWSA successfully "bleached out" the women of color who were active in leadership positions. Protestors called themselves the Women of Color caucus, yet many women of color objected to their tactics and protested later that they had been "bullied and shouted down."[41] Feminist journals printed both charges and responses but, on the whole, tended to give greater credence to the protesters than to the NWSA leadership.[42] Once again, personalized politics held sway. The claim of victimization, especially on the grounds of race, was deemed unassailable. Unwilling to offer public support to their leadership, the Coordinating Council watched the entire staff resign within months. Soon NWSA was a shadow of its former self and more than 6 years of work evaporated.[43]

The *Women's Review of Books* 8 months later devoted four pages to the June 1990 NWSA Akron conference. The unquestioned assumption of all the articles was that NWSA was in fact unalterably racist, that the employee was a victim pure and simple. Numerous pieces by women of color made it clear that their gut reaction to any such charge was to believe it, to find denials by white women painful and racist, and to turn to the comfort of an association with other women of color. Sociologist Barbara Scott wrote, "Now when I think of NWSA and Akron in 1990, I think not so much about white women and racism but of home. With women of color I feel something very familiar, very nostalgic, very spiritual and something very protective and safe that reminds me of home—a place where I can be me. This feeling of coming home is at most almost orgasmic and at the very least far less painful and masochistic than my previous attempts to 'fit in' to white organizations."[44] The burden of providing a "home," a sisterhood of sameness, was probably too much for any organization to bear but certainly was incompatible with the realities of a professional association. Over the course of the 1980s NWSA had increasingly become two organizations, one bearing the political legacy of its founding as a branch of the women's liberation movement the other drawn increasingly to the powerful possibilities of actually being "at the table" in the world of higher education. For many there was more comfort on the margins than at the center.[45]

The battle within NWSA mirrored numerous others across more than three decades of feminist activism. The forces of disintegration—antileadership, suspicion of structure, personalism, ad hominem attack, and the stresses of diversity—continued to be powerful. The context had also changed by 1990. For one thing, NWSA as an expression of women's culture was increasingly at odds with the institutionalization of women's studies in most colleges and universities, where several generations of women had undergone the rigors of tenure and assumed positions of institutional power and responsibility. Women's studies as a field was not as marginal as it had been when NWSA was founded. Second, the debates over race sounded increasingly anachronistic. The controversy within NWSA about race and racism echoed its roots in identity politics with the claim of one group to speak for all women of color (presuming racial solidarity that was not, in fact, the case) and their insistence on posing the problem as a stark choice between good and evil. Yet many of the very same academics involved were busy teaching and writing about race as a "social construction," a meaning that human beings give to difference rather than something essential or intrinsic. Younger generations of feminists by this time were waxing impatient, insisting, for example, on their right to claim more than one racial heritage, claiming multiculturalism as central, not marginal, to their understanding of feminism, and taking lesbianism and bisexuality for granted in ways that did not necessarily link them to a unique women's culture.

THE REMOBILIZATION of women in the 1990s occurred despite a conservative political climate, driven by the persistence of change and the normalization of perceptions once seen as extreme. The attack on abortion rights energized young women who had begun to take it for granted, and sexual harassment turned out to be another issue about which most women, even the conservatives, had come to agree, although many men remained oblivious to the shift in norms. When these perceptions clashed in the high drama of a congressional hearing, thousands of women were suddenly motivated to make themselves heard.

The fall 1991 Senate confirmation hearings on President Bush's nominee to replace retiring Supreme Court Justice Thurgood Marshall were not expected to provide a flashpoint for feminist resurgence. A civil rights leader who had argued the landmark civil rights cases, Marshall had been the only African-American to serve on the Court. His proposed replacement, Clarence Thomas, was a conservative African-American and former director of the Equal Employment Opportunities Commission. Civil rights and feminist leaders were strongly opposed to Thomas, who had been an outspoken opponent of affirmative action and comparable worth, but they had little expectation that they could do more than place a few objections on the record.

Then on October 6, 1991, Nina Totenberg on National Public Radio and an article in *Newsday* revealed that the committee had suppressed testimony alleging that Thomas had engaged in sexual harassment. The next day Anita Hill, an African-American law professor from Oklahoma, held a press conference to confirm these charges. Suddenly, the fault lines of gender became chasms. Men generally shrugged. African-American men perceived racism in the sensationalism that surrounded the charges. Women, by a substantial proportion but in differing degrees by race, were outraged that the testimony had been covered up. On October 8, Democratic congresswomen marched from the House to the Senate and demanded an investigation. Their angry confrontation was high drama for the media. Airwaves were filled with women calling to say, "They just don't get it, do they?" In short order the Senate Judiciary Committee changed its mind and extended its hearings to incorporate public testimony from Anita Hill.[46]

For 3 days, the nation stopped to watch hearings in which a committee of eight white men grilled a genteel African-American woman lawyer. Anita Hill's quiet dignity contrasted sharply with her interrogators' palpable discomfort and ineptitude. They made light of this "sexual harassment crap" and dwelled on salacious details. Critics of feminism like Camille Paglia showed no mercy: "I'm sick and tired of Anita Hill and women like her being excused for yuppiness. She had a choice of toadying up to the boss or speaking up, and she chose the career track."[47] Many, many women, however, were neither amused nor dismissive. The *Wall Street Journal* predicted in October 1991, shortly after the hearings, that "The seeds of fear and hope planted by Anita Hill's sexual harassment charges against Clarence Thomas will grow in America's offices for years to come."[48] In July 1992 the *New York Times* reported that sexual harassment complaints to the Equal Employment Opportunity Commission had risen sharply, and Congress and the administration "responded to allegations of sexual abuse in the military in ways that would have been unimaginable nine months ago."[49] From private homes to political campaigns, the debate, once ignited, catalyzed a new wave of activism.

The next year, the number of women who ran for national office rose sharply. It was a lucky coincidence that an unusually large number of seats were open as a result of retirements and reapportionment. Twenty-two women ran for the Senate in 1992, compared with only eight 2 years before. The first African-American woman to be elected to the Senate, Carol Moseley-Braun of Illinois, was moved by the hearings to challenge Senator Alan Dixon, a Thomas supporter. In Pennsylvania, Lynn Yeakel gave Senator Arlen Specter a run for his money with ads showing him questioning Anita Hill. In a voiceover, Yeakel asked rhetorically, "Did this make you as angry as it made me?"[50]

Grassroots support for women candidates doubled and tripled. Contributions to the National Women's Political Caucus, the Women's Campaign Fund, and Emily's List grew exponentially. Membership in Emily's List went from 3,000 to 24,000 members in only 1 year, allowing it to contribute $6 million to women candidates, four times what it had raised in 1990. Almost overnight Emily's List had become the most powerful PAC in the Democratic Party.

Suddenly the choices shifted from finding women to run to choosing between more than one feminist candidate. In New York, two heroes of feminist politics announced that they would be candidates in the Democratic primary for U.S. Senate. Elizabeth Holtzman had made a major splash in 1972 as a member of the House Judiciary Committee during the Watergate hearings. She went on to be a founder and key leader of the Congressional Women's Caucus in the 1970s.[51] In 1980 she left Congress to run for the Senate against Republican Al D'Amato, losing by a narrow margin. Having served in elected positions of District Attorney and as New York City Comptroller in the meanwhile, she felt ready to take on D'Amato in 1992 and win. Then Geraldine Ferraro, the 1984 Democratic vice-presidential nominee, announced her candidacy. Feminist political activists in general felt tortured about having to choose. Manhattan Borough President Ruth W. Messinger, who ran for mayor 5 years later, said, "It is making people crazy. They know they want a woman, and they know they want to beat Al D'Amato. But that's all they know." Leaders of New York NOW sent a mass mailing endorsing Holtzman. Unwilling to choose, the National Women's Political Caucus and other feminist PACs endorsed both candidates. Ann Lewis, former political director of the Democratic National Committee, urged women to send money to both.[52]

Emily's List, however, stuck to their strategy of investing in a single candidate and appointed a special committee to evaluate the race and make a recommendation. Ellen Malcolm recalled their process: "We decided that the goal of Emily's List was to add pro-choice Democratic women to high office. When more than one woman is running, our first benchmark decision would be: do we have to choose? We concluded that we would choose if it appeared that by not choosing, neither woman would win. Our goal was to win the general election." Because Robert Abrams was the front-runner, the committee decided that it would be necessary to make a choice. "We then did the evaluation; did our own poll of voters, met with both candidates, talked with their campaigns many times, evaluated their ability to raise money, and concluded that at every level Gerry was the stronger candidate. Polls showed more support for Gerry upstate. Holtzman had a hard time moving outside New York City. Gerry had a national ability to raise money and the kind of political charisma that was going to be necessary to beat D'Amato."[53] She looks back on that decision as a moment of maturation, the kind of dilemma produced by success. In the election, however, Holtzman's negative ads eviscerated Ferraro; both women lost to Abrams and he lost to D'Amato in the general election.

Clearly the grassroots revival did not signal a simple victory. The 1992 election was marked by controversy over "family values," which the Republicans made central to their campaign. Conservative rhetoric reflected not only male anxiety but also the growing marginalization of women who chose traditional roles. As one study of a Midwest city found, many of the women in the antiabortion movement were middle-class housewives who had come of age after the golden years of the feminist breakthrough. Most of their peers, whether by choice or necessity, combined motherhood with paid employment, leaving those who chose motherhood as their primary identity and occupation increasingly isolated and defensive. Some blamed feminism for their marginalization.[54] When Vice President Dan Quayle criticized a popular television character, Murphy Brown, for having a child out of wedlock, he ignited a debate about single motherhood, the stigma of illegitimacy, and abortion. His wife, Marilyn Quayle, told the Republican Convention that "most women do not wish to be liberated from their essential natures as women," a pointed reference to Hillary Clinton's difficulty responding to media criticism of her legal career.[55]

The polarized responses to Hillary Clinton were a measure of both the revival of feminism and the ongoing hostility to women's changing roles. Wellesley graduate in 1970, brilliant lawyer, and activist for children's rights, she struggled during the campaign and after to avoid being labeled a feminist (or as Maureen Dowd referred to it, "the f-word"). Careful to distance herself from aspects of what feminism "has come to mean today"—hostility to maternal values and to men—she was nonetheless tripped up by incessant press questioning about her professional activities while her husband was governor of Arkansas. When she sighed in exasperation that she supposed she could have "stayed home, baked cookies, and had teas," the press exploded with criticism of her for disrespect toward homemakers.[56] Her advisors felt she had little choice but to join a chocolate chip cookie recipe contest with Barbara Bush at the invitation of *Family Circle*. That too invited derision, as did her efforts to adopt a more traditional wardrobe and demeanor. Some derided her for insincerity. She couldn't win. *The Cleveland Plain Dealer* described her as "looking as though she'd just swallowed some castor oil" when she asked a Texas audience to help by sending ballots to *Family Circle*. Anna Quindlen was appalled: "Here was an accomplished professional who had already changed her name, her hair, her clothes, and her comments . . . [now] reduced to hawking her chocolate chip cookie entry. What next? Eleanor Roosevelt fudge?"[57] "Policy making [versus] cookie baking" was a double bind with no way out.[58]   .

Once Bill Clinton was elected, Hillary was both idolized and vilified for assuming a strong public role in debates on health policy and children's issues.[59] The deficits generated during the Reagan years, added to the sheer complexity of health care policy with its many "stakeholders," had made it politically impossible to consider any dramatic expansion of the welfare state, however, and as Hillary Clinton's health care task force's recommendations went down to defeat in Congress, she shifted to a lower profile, more "feminine" image only to face criticism once again on that score as well.[60] First ladies are inherently tricky as role models because their position rests on the husband's election, not their own. Any policy activism on their part tends to arouse fears of a "power behind the throne," easily framed as a failure to be properly subordinate (i.e., failure to be a woman).

The 1994 Republican victory, in which Republicans gained majorities in both houses of Congress, was widely portrayed as a revolt of the "angry white males," whose voices were heard in a profusion of radio talk shows. The most popular talk show host, Rush Limbaugh, led the attack on Hillary Clinton and what he viewed as a liberal takeover. "We have lost control of our major cultural institutions. Liberalism long ago captured the arts, the press, the entertainment industry, the universities, the schools, the libraries, the foundations, etc."[61]

For Limbaugh and others, a galling symbol of this loss was the surrender of the last bastions of an all-male military culture, the Citadel in

South Carolina and Virginia Military Institute (VMI). Shannon Faulkner, who had applied without indicating her gender and then waged a battle in the courts, entered the Citadel in 1995 in the national spotlight. But 2 years of litigation and public scrutiny had taken their toll and she dropped out after 2 weeks, to the cheers of her fellow students.[62] By the next year, however, there were several female students, and the Citadel joined West Point and Annapolis as a coeducational institution. Phyllis Schlafley, in an impassioned letter to VMI, offered a challenge to that final holdout of all-male, military education: "You've lost a major battle. Are you going to be survivors, or are you going to let the enemy wipe you and your kind from the face of the earth, pour salt in the soil that produced you, and drop you down the Memory Hole?"[63]

Schlafley skillfully deployed the threat to manhood articulated throughout American history whenever women moved forcefully into public life. By 1996, however, those changes had reshaped the lives of women and men alike, and the arguments, though virulent, no longer had the same potency. Debates themselves were more public and took place in more varied arenas. The 1994 elections may have been driven by "angry white men," but 2 years later those men no longer dominated the campaign. Instead, the "gender gap" returned in force, and when Bill Clinton was reelected in 1996, a president's margin of victory was clearly based on the votes of women for the first time.

WHEN THE "THIRD WAVE" women appeared in the mid-1990s they set out to claim a place within feminism distinct from that of their literal and figurative mothers. Born between 1965 and 1974, the very years when Second Wave feminism was hurtling across the landscape, they grew up believing they could do anything. Legal barriers to education, work, and athletics, which enraged their mothers, were long gone. They also came of age when feminism was visible primarily as a stereotype, however. Introduced to feminist theory in colleges, the most powerful writers among them were women of color who challenged what they perceived to be a monolithic, white, middle-class "sisterhood." They never experienced feminism as a sisterhood of sameness. Indeed, they stumbled over saying "we."

Multiplicity and contradiction, "lived messiness," these are recurrent terms in the stories of those who name themselves Third Wave. "Third Wavers waver," as one writer put it.[64] "As Gen-Xers we have no utopias," writes another.[65] Like the founders of women's liberation, Third Wavers need to tell their stories (even against an academic culture that now disparages personal storytelling), to articulate the distinguishing aspects of their life stories, the ways in which their generational experience demanded a different feminism.

Third Wavers criticize others of their own generation, including Naomi Wolfe, Rene Denfeld, and Katie Roiphe, who (admittedly in very different ways) castigate Third Wavers as "victim feminists" and advocate a frequently individualistic, assertive "power feminism" or "equity feminism." Sharply critical of the individualism of these writers, they also point out the implicitly white and middle-class assumptions built into their use of the word "woman."[66] Thus, Third Wavers not only differentiate themselves from their feminist elders, they also participate in a public debate with others of their own generation about what feminism might mean and how it needs to change. The good news is that on all sides of this conversation one hears calls for a feminist discourse that can tolerate disagreement.

When Third Wavers meet resistance, unfortunately, is from some Second Wavers unwilling to hear that the world is different. At the Re-Imagining Gathering in November 2000, both Mary Daly (early theorist of women's culture and ecofeminism) and Rebecca Walker (daughter of Alice Walker and one of the originators of the Third Wave) were invited speakers, especially interesting since neither of them considered herself Christian. Daly, in her talk, spoke dismissively of the so-called Third Wave. Walker responded from the audience afterward, defending herself and others in her generation as able to define feminism for themselves. Daly brusquely dismissed any need for redefinition. In the aftermath of that interaction, a group of young women linked to the Re-Imagining community sent out a call via e-mail for others of their generation to meet as a Third Wave group. Soon after, the office received a gruff response: "Well you can take me off this mailing list. I'm not in my 20's or 30's. As usual, I'm just an old bitch not needed anymore. You forget who went ahead of you and paved through this shit."[67]

Feminists who have been active for more than three decades, fighting not only with the world but also with each other, are understandably tired. Younger women are often ignorant about and cavalierly dismissive of the struggles of previous generations. By the same token, older generations have trouble listening to and supporting younger women's effort to claim the movement as their own and assert leadership for struggles that will be no less difficult than those in the past. The early years of women's liberation were marked by a full measure of youthful hubris and intolerance toward elders on the Left (who failed to understand the fundamental nature of the "woman question") and "First Wave" suffragists who "screwed up" because they focused on a single issue.

THE FUTURE OF FEMINISM

Feminism in the twenty-first century inherits all the complexities and contradictions stirred up in the late twentieth century. Personal politics was the wellspring of feminism's power to reshape the landscape legally, institutionally, and personally because it named the realities of power and inequality in the most deeply personal and private aspects of women's lives. As personal politics entered increasingly differentiated public spaces, however, the women's liberation movement found it difficult to be *effectively* radical, to rethink traditional constructions of public and private *as a politics*. In its early years, the dominating model for change was individual conversion, the "click" that consciousness-raising group participants could almost universally recall:

" . . . the sudden comprehension, in one powerful instant, of what sexism exactly meant, how it had colored one's own life, the way all women were in this together. It was that awe-inspiring moment of vision and of commonality, when a woman was instantly and irrevocably transformed from naive to knowing, from innocent to experienced, from apolitical to feminist."[68]

That "vision of commonality" touched deep needs for relatedness, for release from isolation, marginality, and deviance. It was creative and powerful, but at the same time it remained a fundamentally private impulse. Each woman's vision of commonality looked outward from herself and presumed that others only needed the opportunity to "see" their own reality in this new way. It depended, in fact, on an assumption of "sameness"—captured in the language of "sisterhood"—and it faltered in the face of fundamental differences and institutional realities that consciousness alone could not combat. Too quickly, difference became hierarchy (good versus bad) to be erased or suppressed, and the moral privilege to speak from feelings made serious debate extremely difficult.

Soon, of course, activists had begun to address the *theoretical* problem of difference, starting with feminists of color and socialist feminists in the 1970s and broadening to include much of academic feminism in the 1980s. Theorists explored different structures of oppression, different histories, and different subjectivities (i.e., what is the inner experience of being a particular combination of race, gender, sexuality, and so on?). Although the rapid growth of activism among women in all racial, ethnic, and religious groups made coalition politics increasingly possible, the difficulty of creating feminist public spaces in which differences could coexist remained an ongoing source of fragmentation. This is where the perspectives of a new generation may bring about a fundamental and necessary shift. In the early years of women's liberation, the struggle simply to challenge the subordination of women based on their "natural" roles in the privacy of the family called into question cultural definitions of "male" and "female." The consciousness-raising task of naming the realities of power and inequality in personal life required such a radical (in the sense of fundamental) assault on conventional notions of what constituted personal and political, private and public that it led some activists to try to erase those distinctions altogether. At its logical extreme, that side of personal politics established a recurring disintegrative force in the movement.

In a sense, the energy behind feminism will always lie at the intersection of personal and political, public and private, but the force of the tidal wave has also revolutionized those categories. American women in the new millennium confront a rough new terrain shaped by the tumultuous energy of the last half-century. The wave has swept through our labor force, our laws, our language, and even our bedrooms. The contrasts with the past are striking. Women now comprise almost half of the paid labor force and can be found in virtually every field. They occupy positions of public authority that would have been unthinkable even in the 1960s: Supreme Court justices, ministers and rabbis, engineers, generals, and airline pilots. Their political clout is growing, through a sophisticated policy infrastructure and a presence in state and local politics.

Family formation is no longer uniform. Marriage ages are up and marriage rates are down, fertility remains low, divorce is common, and a high proportion of children are born out of wedlock. Indeed, the definition of "family" has been challenged profoundly by single parents, by gay and lesbian couples, and by reproductive technologies that separate biological from social parenthood, sex from conception, and conception from gestation. Laws now provide defenses against not only employment discrimination but also marital rape and sexual harassment. For most men as well as women, the feminist ideal of marriage as a partnership is, according to Paula Kamen, "utterly mainstream." She cites poll data showing that young women's attitudes shifted dramatically toward a "liberal feminist" view of marriage and of women's place in society in the late 1970s and early 1980s. Young men were slower to change, but by the late 1980s their attitudes were close to those of women in the 1970s.[69]

The contradictions of women's lives are likely to continue to fuel their involvement in feminist politics. Women remain caught between a world of work, which assumes that there is someone behind every worker who is available to take care of family needs, and the tenacious presumption that women have primary responsibility for children and household. The process of redefining work through such measures as flextime, shared or part-time jobs with full benefits, parental leave, and on-site child care has proceeded at a glacial pace even as "welfare reform" forces large numbers of single mothers into low-wage jobs with minimal benefits. Through the eighties, women's expectations regarding work and family changed far more rapidly than men's. In the nineties, however, as even middle class men began to expect their wives to work, in some instances they actively opposed wives' taking off time or working part-time while children were young.[70]

It is possible that the shift toward more egalitarian expectations might have a different and less coercive impact if, as seems also to be the case, men are more and more drawn into serious engagement with the daily life of their households. Perhaps they too will see the necessity of policies that affirm the social importance of child care and personal life. For the moment, however, in the political arena fights over child care continue to mark women as a voting bloc, and we can anticipate that women are likely to be at the center of policy initiatives on these issues for the foreseeable future.

The crumbling of legal barriers has also created an illusion of equality, especially in contrast to the earlier, overt forms of discrimination. It is still the case that men comprise 85 percent of all elected officials and 95 percent of corporate executives. Although two-thirds of female attorneys would say that they have experienced discrimination, only one-third of male attorneys have noticed any such thing. Job discrimination is subtle, and the people doing it not only deny it but genuinely believe that they do not discriminate. When an ABC television crew followed a man and a woman with similar qualifications as they applied for jobs and subsequently confronted employers with their very different job offers (management positions for the man, secretarial and receptionist positions for the woman), the employers sputtered that they were not prejudiced. They did believe, however, that women don't "do well" in field management positions, and men really should not be answering phones.[71] Legal scholar Deborah Rhode argues that a widespread pattern of denial makes it difficult to acknowledge the continuing need for fundamental change. "We settle for equality in form rather than equality in fact, for commitment in legal mandates rather than in daily practice."[72]

As a result of longer life expectancies, different generations of women have distinct and sometimes conflicting experiences. Those who fought for access to work and public life face new generations raised with different expectations. Younger women presume that they will combine work outside the home with family responsibilities. The harsh realities of doing so, however, lead some of them to reassert the value of parenting and family, charging that the values of the market-place have overshadowed something for which they not only remain responsible but which gives them pleasure and meaning. This explains some of the political popularity of "family values" among people who do not, in fact, advocate returning to traditional, patriarchal family norms. At the same time, older women are creating a new life stage in their forties, fifties, and sixties. Vital, healthy, energetic, they face yet another round of discriminatory attitudes and practices based on sex and age.

Will it be possible to reconcile the goals of women who wish to make work more hospitable and tolerable for those who bear heavy family responsibilities, those who wish to create a better safety net for impoverished women and children, and those who want to reclaim the importance of parenting and motherhood? Finding common ground among women of different generations and backgrounds will be the key to creating spaces for experimentation and building working relationships that go beyond demonizing stereotypes. Women as a group are more favorable to using government as an instrument of social policy. Furthermore, in our still sex-segregated labor force, women are far more likely than men to work in settings—in the health, education, services, and government sectors—in which they experience government as a positive and necessary force rather than as a burden imposing regulation and taxation.

Despite the current suspicion of government, the new century will probably generate a number of decentralized experiments, led by women, to address community problems related to child care, public safety, and health. In their long struggle for access to public life, women in the United States have often invented new forms of voluntary association that have given this country an unusually rich civil society. Renewing that civic resource, as both a training ground for leaders and an environment for experiments in public problem solving, is certainly one of the keys to the survival of democracy in the twenty-first century. Fortunately, an infrastructure exists from which to build. The tidal wave of feminism created hundreds, even thousands, of organizations and institutions, and many survived and grew through the ebb and flow of the late twentieth century. The Women's Funding Network, for example, was founded in 1985 with 20 member organizations and by 2002 its members included 90 women's and girls' funds and philanthropic organizations.[73]

Finally, feminism, like all aspects of life, has become global and leaders of the United States women's movement have increasingly joined their voices to those of women around the world. After Nairobi, women became a force at every major United Nations conference. In 1990 Bella Abzug and journalist Mim Kelber founded Women's Environment and Development Organization (WEDO), "an international advocacy network that seeks to increase the power of women worldwide as policymakers in governance and in policymaking institutions, forums and processes, at all levels, to achieve economic and social justice, a peaceful and healthy planet and human rights for all."[74] WEDO organized a World Women's Congress for a Healthy Planet at which 1,500 women from 83 countries laid plans for the forthcoming 1992 United Nations environmental summit in Brazil. Their success at the summit led to active women's caucuses at all subsequent major United Nations Conferences to ensure that women's equality remained on the agenda, whatever the topic.[75] Similarly, the Center for Women's Global leadership has, since 1990, sponsored intensive 2 week leadership training institutes. During the 1990s, seven institutes trained 160 women from 77 countries to become effective women's rights policy advocates and leaders. The first leadership institute proposed a campaign against violence against women naming November 25 to December 10 as "16 days of activism against gender violence." Over 800 organizations in at least 90 countries have participated in this campaign since 1991.

When 7,000 American women traveled to Beijing, China for the Fourth World Conference on Women sponsored by the United Nations, they found there "[a] virtual city of female people. Turbans, caftans, saris, abayas, sarongs, kente cloth, blue jeans, T-shirt libraries. Banners, posters, buttons. A twenty-kilometer-long Sisterhood Ribbon initiated by Cambodian women, added to at the forum, later stretched along the Great Wall. Almost four thousand workshops—on soybeans, sexuality, paid and unpaid labor, reproductive freedom, microcredit, caste, solar stoves, networking techniques, inheritance, health, refugee/ displaced women, regional priorities, you name it."[76]

The irreducible realities of difference among women on this global stage have not stood in the way of solidarity largely because of the strong leadership of women from the developing world on issues of concern to them. They in turn cast new light on the dilemmas with which American feminists wrestle. The example of women's horrific plight in Afghanistan, for example, is a reminder that women *are* victims. At the same time, the active intervention of Afghan women through the Revolutionary Association of the Women of Afghanistan (RAWA) shows that even under the most extreme conditions, women can and do act to change their situation, broaden their choices, and demand a place at the table. In the eighties, while American feminists struggled mightily with the dilemmas of multicultural feminism, the international movement shifted leadership from Western feminists to women in the developing world and international women's nongovernmental organizations. As a result women have been central to the initiation of a global civic infrastructure that holds the potential for public problem solving in a world fraught with environmental devastation, murderous violence, and extreme disparities between the wealthy and the poor.[77] American women will continue to play a critical role in that struggle, knowing that massive change is possible but there is no end in sight.

NOTES

Chapter 1

1. See Nancy Cott, *The Grounding of Modern Feminism* (New Haven: Yale University Press, 1987).
2. Dorothy Dunbar Bromley, "Feminist—New Style," *Harper's* 155 (October 1927): 552.
3. *Phyllis Schlafley Report* 5 (February 1972), quoted in Jane J. Mansbridge, *Why We Lost The ERA* (Chicago: University of Chicgo Press, 1996), 104.
4. Gilder quote from *Sexual Suicide* (New York: Quadrangle Books, 1973), p. 238; on daycare see George Gilder, "An Open Letter to Orrin Hatch," *National Review*, vol. 40, no. 9 (May 13, 1988): 32–34.
5. Susan Bolotin, "Voices from the Post-Feminist Generation," *New York Times Magazine*, (October 17, 1982): 28–21, 103, 106–107; quotes on 29, 31.
6. Paula Kammen, *Feminist Fatale: Voices from the "Twentysomething" Generation Explore the Future of the "Women's Movement"* (New York: Donald I. Fine, 1991), pp. 2, 7.
7. Two or three others of us changed our names in subsequent years when we were no longer in the group. I reclaimed my birth name in 1974.
8. The first three books, all published in 1970, were Sara Evans Boyte, *Jenny's Secret Place*; Paula Goldsmid, *Did You Ever?*; and Margrit Eichler, *Martin's Father*. At that time Margrit was a graduate student in sociology. She and her then husband were members of the child care cooperative. Today she is Professor of Sociology and Equity Studies in Education at the Ontario Institute for Studies in Education (OISE) at the University of Toronto and Director of the Institute for Women's Studies and Gender Studies (IWSGS) at the University of Toronto. Paula Goldsmid was at that time an assistant professor at the UNC School of Social Work. Subsequently she was Associate Dean of Arts and Sciences (in charge of women's studies) and Associate Professor of Sociology & Anthropology at Oberlin College from 1974 to 1981, Dean of Faculty at Scripps College (Claremont, CA) from 1981 to 1989, where she also taught gender role courses, and Director of the Center for Women and Gender Education at University of California, Irvine, from 1990 to 2000, as well as lecturer in women's studies during some of that time. Her current title is Graduate Fellowships/Medical Sciences Coordinator at Pomona College.

9. Lee Rainwater, Richard P. Coleman, and Gerald Handel, *Workingman's Wife: Her Personality, World and Life Style* (New York: Oceana Publications, 1959); Mirra Komarovsky, "Cultural Contradictions and Sex Roles," *American Journal of Sociology* 52 (November 1946): 182–189); Komarovsky, *Blue-collar Marriage* (New York: Random House, 1964); and Komarovsky, *Women in the Modern World: Their Education and Their Dilemmas* (Boston: Little, Brown, 1953).

10. My own work in 1968–1969 as a community organizer in the poor white community of Durham, North Carolina, was a constant reminder of such difference. My pregnancy was an immediate link to the women I worked with, but they were astounded that this was my *first* child at age 25—some of them were already grandmothers in their mid-thirties. Their complicated familial and work histories involved work in textile and tobacco factories, welfare, and frequent household moves in response to divorce and changing economics.

11. New York: Knopf, 1979.

12. The publication of *Sisterhood Is Powerful* (New York: Random House, 1970), a collection of early feminist writings edited by Robin Morgan, contained several articles articulating this viewpoint, notably Marge Piercy, "Grand Coolie Damn" and Robin Morgan, "Goodbye to All That." Neither actually intended to be a story of origins, although each constituted a jeremiad against the sexism of the left. Together, however, they shaped a narrative that continues to predominate.

13. This effort to come to terms with the history of the "second wave" dates at least from the work of Jo Freeman, *The Politics of Women's Liberation* (New York: Longman, 1975) and Edith Hole and Ellen Levine, *Rebirth of Feminism* (New York: Quadrangle Books, 1971) in the mid-1970s. By the 1980s, there were a growing number of journal articles as well as social scientific studies, such as Myra Marx Ferree and Beth B. Hess, *Controversy and Coalition [CITE]*, Flora Davis' encyclopedic *Moving the Mountain: The Women's Movement in America Since 1960* (New York: Simon and Schuster, 1991), and Alice Echols, *Daring to Be Bad: Radical Feminism in America 1967–1975* (Minneapolis: University of Minnesota Press, 1989). For the most recent works see Nancy Whittier, *Feminist Generations: The Persistence of the Radical Women's Movement* (Philadelphia: Temple University Press, 1995); Sheila Tobias, *Faces of Feminism: An Activist's Reflections on the Women's Movement* (Boulder: Westview Press, 1997); Susan Brownmiller, *In Our Time: Memoir of a Revolution* (New York: Dial Press, 1999); Ruth Rosen, *The World Split Open: How the Modern Women's Movement Changed America* (New York: Viking, 2000). In many ways, this book builds on what they have already done, adding the interpretation described in this introduction and argued more fully throughout the book and also extending the story of the movement beyond the early 1980s, when most other accounts end.

Chapter 2

1. *Bread and Roses Newsletter* (November 1970): 5.

2. See Elaine Tyler May, *Homeward Bound: American Families in the Cold War Era* (New York: Basic Books, 1988) and Wini Breines, *Young, White, and Miserable* (Boston: Beacon Press, 1992); Sara M. Evans, *Born for Liberty: A History of Women in America* (New York: Free Press, 1989), chapter 11.

3. Betty Friedan, *The Feminine Mystique* (New York: Dell Publishing, 1963).

4. See Susan Chira, "Standing out in the Crowd," *New York Times* (August 10 1993): A1, 16. Madeline Kunin's autobiography offers a wonderful account of her life. See *Living a Political Life: One of America's First Women Governors Tells Her Story* (New York: Knopf, 1994).

5. Sara Ruddick, "A Work of One's Own," in Sara Ruddick and Pamela Daniels, eds., *Working It Out: 23 Women Writers, Artists, Scientists, and Scholars Talk About Their Lives and Work* (New York: Pantheon, 1977), p. 129.

6. Marilyn Young, "Contradictions," in Ruddick and Daniels, eds., *Working It Out*, p. 215.

7. Ruddick, "A Work of One's Own," p. 145.

8. Jane O'Reilly, "The Housewife's Moment of Truth," *Ms.*, vol. 1, no. 1 (Spring 1972): 54–55, 57–59.

9. See Sara Evans, *Personal Politics: The Roots of Women's Liberation in the Civil Rights Movement and the New Left* (New York: Knopf, 1979); Edith Hole and Ellen Levine, *Rebirth of Feminism* (New York: Quadrangle Books, 1971), and Jo Freeman, *The Politics of Women's Liberation: A Case Study of an Emerging Social Movement and Its Relation to the Policy Process* (New York: Longman, 1975); Flora Davis, *Moving the Mountain* (New York: Simon and Schuster, 1991).

10. On the concept of "free space" and the origins of feminism, see Evans, *Personal Politics*, and Sara M. Evans and Harry C. Boyte, *Free Spaces: Sources of Democratic Change in America* (New York: Harper and Row, 1986).

11. Seven state commissions were established in 1962 and 1963 while the Kennedy Commission prepared its report. "By February 1976, commissions had been set up in all fifty states and the District of Columbia." Catherine East, "Newer Commissions," in Irene Tinker, ed., *Women in Washington: Advocates for Public Policy* (Beverly Hills: Sage Publications, Inc., 1983), pp. 35–36.

12. See Evans, *Personal Politics*, pp. 50–53, quotes on pp. 51–52.

13. One of the best accounts of the traumatic events of 1968 is William Chafe, *1968: The Unfinished Journey* (New York: Oxford University Press, 1999), chapter 12. For other sources on the sixties see Todd Gitlin, *The Sixties: Years of Hope, Days of Rage* (New York: Bantam, 1993); Terry Anderson, *The Movement and the Sixties* (New York: Oxford University Press, 1996); Alexander Bloom, ed., *Takin' It to the Streets: A 60s Reader* (New York: Oxford University Press, 2001).

14. See, for example, Marge Piercy, "Grand Coolie Damn" and Robin Morgan, "Introduction: The Women's Revolution," in Robin Morgan, ed., *Sisterhood Is Powerful* (New York: Random House, 1970), pp. xiii–xl, 421–437.

15. Jo Freeman was one of the first to point out the similarities between the two "branches" of the second wave and to differentiate them primarily in terms of age and structure. Others have agreed with her. See Jo Freeman, *The Politics of Women's Liberation;* Jo Freeman, "Resource Mobilization and Strategy: A Model for Analyzing Social Movement Organization Actions," in Mayer N. Zald and John D. McCarthy, eds., *The Dynamics of Social Movements: Resource Mobilization, Social Control, and Tactics* (Cambridge, MA: Winthrop, 1979), pp. 57–189. See also Maren Lockwood Carden, *Feminism in the Mid-1970s: The Non-establishment, the Establishment and the Future: A Report to the Ford Foundation* (New York: Ford Foundation, 1977); Barbara Ryan, *Feminism and the Women's Movement: Dynamics of Change in Social Movement, Ideology and Activism* (New York: Routledge, 1992); and Flora Davis, *Moving the Mountain: The Women's Movement in America Since 1960* (New York: Simon and Schuster, 1991).

16. Quoted in Hole and Levine, *Rebirth of Feminism,* p. 84.

17. Hole and Levine, *Rebirth of Feminism,* pp. 81–87; Davis, *Moving the Mountain,* pp. 56–61; and Freeman, *The Politics of Women's Liberation,* pp. 73–79.

18. Hole and Levine, *Rebirth,* pp. 95–98; Davis, *Moving the Mountain,* pp. 67–68; Marguerite Rawalt, "The Equal Rights Amendment," in Irene Tinker, ed., *Women in Washington: Advocates for Public Policy* (Beverly Hills: Sage Publications, 1983), pp. 60–62.

19. Florynce Kennedy, *Color Me Flo: My Hard Life and Good Times* (Englewood Cliffs, NJ: Prentice-Hall, 1976), pp. 39, 54. See also Gloria Steinem, "The Verbal Karate of Florynce R. Kennedy," *Ms.,* vol. 1, no. 9 (March 1973): 54–55, 89.

20. Amy Swerdlow, "Ladies Day at the Capitol: Women Strike for Peace Versus HUAC," *Feminist Studies,* vol. 8 (Fall 1982): 493–520; Amy Swerdlow, *Women Strike for Peace: Traditional Motherhood and Radical Politics in the 1960s* (Chicago: University of Chicago Press, 1993), pp. 10, 135–141. SWP had begun with a "strike" on November 1, 1961, when an estimated 50,000 women left jobs and kitchens to lobby to "End the Arms Race—Not the Human Race" while a radioactive cloud from a Russian nuclear test floated across the U.S. In 1962 the organization was called before the House Un-American Activities Committee where they employed the symbols and language of middle-class domesticity to make hash of the committee's efforts to intimidate them.

21. The description of this meeting in Chicago is based on my own memory of that event, at which I was present.

22. Kathie Amatniek, "Funeral Oration for the Burial of Traditional Womanhood," in *Notes from the First Year: Women's Liberation* (New York: New York

Radical Women, 1968), Documents from the Women's Liberation Movement, an On-Line Archival Collection, Special Collections Library, Duke University.

23. The breakaway meeting was chaotic because it was huge, beyond anyone's imagining, and the radicals proclaiming "Sisterhood Is Powerful" had no program or plan of action. About 50 women from New York, Chicago, and Washington continued to meet over 2 days, laying plans for future women's liberation gatherings, but there, too, the tensions over what New Yorkers began to call "feminists" and "politicos" remained strong. For accounts of the Jeanette Rankin Brigade, see Echols, *Daring to Be Bad*, pp. 54–59; Rosen, *The World Split Open*, pp. 201–203; Brownmiller, *In Our Time*, pp. 21–23; Davis, *Moving the Mountain*, pp. 78–79.

24. Ellen Willis, "Radical Feminism and Feminist Radicalism," in Sonya Sayres, Anders Stephanson, Stanley Aronowitz, and Fredric Jameson, eds., *The '60's Without Apology* (Minneapolis: University of Minnesota Press, 1984), p. 94. See also Marge Piercy, "Grand Coolie Damn," in Robin Morgan, ed., *Sisterhood Is Powerful* (New York: Random House, 1970), pp. 473–492; and Robin Morgan, "Goodbye to All That," in Leslie Tanner, *Voices of Women's Liberation* (New York: New American Library, 1970), pp. 268–277.

25. The process of speaking bitterness was described in William Hinton, *Fanshen: A Documentary of Revolution in a Chinese Village* (New York: Vintage Books, 1966), pp. 157–158.

26. "Redstockings Manifesto," *Notes from the Second Year* (1970), p. 113.

27. Judith Herman, "Dear Kathie," December 3, 1972, letter quoted in Ann Hunter Popkin, "Bread and Roses: An Early Moment in the Development of Socialist-Feminism" (unpublished Ph.D. Dissertation, Sociology, Brandeis University, 1978), p. 59.

28. Linda Gordon, quoted in Popkin, "Bread and Roses," p. 98.

29. Quoted in Flora Davis, *Moving the Mountain*, p. 143.

30. Shirley Geok-Lin Lim, "'Ain't I a Feminist: Re-forming the Circle," in Rachel Blau DuPlessis and Ann Snitow, eds., *The Feminist Memoir Project: Voices from Women's Liberation* (New York: Three Rivers Press, 1998), p. 453.

31. Elaine Brown, *A Taste of Power: A Black Woman's Story* (New York: Pantheon Books, 1992); and Kathleen Cleaver and George Katsiaficas, eds., *Liberation, Imagination, and the Black Panther Party: A New Look at the Panthers and Their Legacy* (New York: Routledge, 2001).

32. Transcript of Sandy Springs Meeting, p. 37. Also Alice Echols, *Daring to Be Bad: Radical Feminism in America, 1967–1975* (Minneapolis: University of Minnesota Press, 1989), pp. 105–107.

33. Patricia Haden, Donna Middleton, and Patricia Robinson, Rosalyn Baxandall and Linda Gordon, eds., *Dear Sisters: Dispatches from the Women's Liberation Movement* (New York: Basic Books, 2000), pp. 93–95, quote on p. 95.

34. Inez Smith Reid, *"Together" Black Women* (New York: Third Press, 1975), pp.

35–54, quote on p. 40. See also Bell Hooks, *Ain't I a Woman: Black Women and Feminism* (Boston: South End Press, 1981), p. 189.

35. Anna Nieto-Gomez, "La Femenista," *Encuentro femenil*, vol. 1, no. 2 (1974): 36.

36. Mirta Vidal, "New Voice of LaRaza: Chicanas Speak Out," *International Socialist Review,* vol. 32, no. 9 (1971): 8; see also Francisca Flores, "Comision Femenil Mexicana," *Regeneracion*, vol. II, no. 1 (1971): 6–8; "Chicana Regional Conference," *La Raza*, vol. 1, no. 6 (1071): 43–44.

37. Flores, "Comision Femenil Mexicana," *Regeneracion*, vol. II, no. 1 (1971): 6–8, quote on 6.

38. Mirta Vidal, "New Voice of LaRaza: Chicanas Speak Out," *International Socialist Review*, vol. 32, no. 9 (1971): 7–9, 31–33.

39. Jennie V. Chavez, "Women of the Mexican-American Movement: An Opinion," *Mademoiselle* (April 1972): 82, 150.

40. Anna Nieto-Gomez, "La Femenista," *Encuentro Femenil*, vol. 1, no. 2 (1974): 34–47, quotes on 38.

41. "Introduction: This Isn't One of Those Blondes You Can Pick up in the Supermarket," *Asian Women*, Berkeley, 1971, p. 4. Christina Adachi, "Nisei Women Speak!" *Women: A Journal of Liberation*, vol. 3, no. 4 (1974): 30–31.

42. Esther Ngan-Ling Chow, "The Development of Feminist Consciousness Among Asian American Women," *Gender & Society*, vol. 1, no. 3 (September 1987): 284–299; Merilynne Hamano Quon, "Individually We Contributed, Together We Made a Difference," in Steve Louie and Glenn K. Omatsu, eds., *Asian Americans: The Movement and the Moment* (Los Angeles: UCLA Asian American Studies Center Press, 2001) pp. 207–219; Asian Women United of California, eds., *Making Waves: An Anthology of Writings by and About Asian American Women* (Boston: Beacon Press, 1989).

43. "Indian Women's Groups Span a Broad Spectrum," *Indian Truth* (publication of the Indian Rights Association), no. 239 (May–June 1981): 8.

44. Shirley Geok-Lin Lim, "Ain't I A Feminist: Re-forming the Circle," in Du-Plessis and Snitow, eds., *The Feminist Memoir Project*, p. 453.

45. Barbara Grizzuti Harrison, "Unlearning the Lie: How One Group of Parents Dealt with Sexism and Racism in Their School and Among Themselves," *Ms.*, vol. 2, no. 5 (November 1973): 81–83, 110. Quotes on pp. 81 and 82. See also Bell Hooks, *Ain't I a Woman*, chapter 5.

46. Harrison, "Unlearning the Lie," 83, 110, 82. Similar attitudes were expressed by a number of authors. For example, Linda La Rue wrote, "It is not that women ought not to be liberated from the shackles of their present unfulfillment, but the depth, the extent, the intensity, the importance—indeed, the suffering and depravity of the *real* oppression blacks have experienced—can only be minimized in an alliance with women who heretofore have suffered little more than boredom, genteel repression and dishpan hands." "Blacks are *oppressed*. . . . White women, on the other hand, are only *suppressed*. . . ." See "The

Black Movement and Women's Liberation," in Robert Chrisman and Nathan Hare, eds., *Contemporary Black Thought: The Best from the Black Scholar.* (New York: Bobbs-Merrill, 1973), pp. 116–125, quotes on pp. 117, 119.

47. Harrison, "Unlearning the Lie," p. 110.

48. Frances M. Beale, "Sisterhood Is Still Powerful: Speaking up When Others Can't." *CrossRoads,* no. 29 (March 1993): 4–5, quotes on 4.

49. Ida Sloan Snyder, "Convention 1970: A Gentle Revolution," *YWCA Magazine,* 64 (June 1970): 5–7, quote on 5; ISS, "One Imperative for All," *YWCA Magazine,* 64 (June 1970), 8–11; quote on 8; Renetia Martin, in Sara M. Evans, ed., *Faithful Journeys: Women, the Student Christian Movement, and Social Justice Activism 1955–1975* (New Brunswick, NJ: Rutgers University Press, forthcoming 2004).

50. Renetia Martin in Evans, ed., *Faithful Journeys.* (New Brunswick, NJ: Rutgers University Press, forthcoming 2004).

51. See, for example, "Second Printing! The Black Woman in the Black Struggle," *Black Scholar,* vol. 2, no. 3–4 (January-February 1970); Linda LaRue, "The Black Movement and Women's Liberation," *Black Scholar* vol. 1, no. 7 (May 1970): 36–42; "The Black Woman," *Black Scholar,* vol. 3, no. 4 (December 1971); and Panther Women, "Panther Sisters on Women's Liberation," *The Movement* (September 1969).

52. See Ruth Bordin, *Women and Temperance: The Quest for Power and Liberty, 1873–1900* (New Brunswick, NJ: Rutgers University Press, 1990).

53. Eleanor Smeal, February 1978, quoted in *The Decade of Women: A Ms. History of the Seventies in Words and Pictures,* edited and produced by Suzanne Levine and Harriet Lyons (New York: Putnam, 1980), p. 188.

54. Interview with Jan Schakowsky by Harry C. Boyte, Evanston, Illinois, April 30, 1977. Also quoted in *Personal Politics,* pp. 227–228.

55. Jo Freeman, *The Politics of Women's Liberation* (New York: David McKay, 1975), p. 148; F. Cancian and B. Ross, "Mass Media and the Women's Movement: 1900–1977," *Journal of Applied Behavioral Science* 17 (1981): 9–26; Myra Marx Ferree and Beth B. Hess, *Controversy and Coalition: The New Feminist Movement* (Boston: Twayne Publishers, 1985), pp. 74–77.

56. "Take her off the stage . . ." quote was leveled at Marilyn Webb, who spoke at an antiwar rally in January 1969 in Washington, D.C. While she retained some loyalty to the left and the antiwar movements, others at the rally defined the reaction to her speech as a turning point in their relationship with the left. See Alice Echols, *Daring to Be Bad,* pp. 117–120; Rosen, *The World Split Open,* p. 134; Susan Douglas, *Where the Girls Are: Growing up Female with the Mass Media* (New York: Random House, 1994), p. 164.

57. "The New Feminists: Revolt Against Sexism," *Time* (November 21, 1969): 56; "Woman-power," *Time* (March 30): 1970, 59.

58. *New York Times* (August 12, 1970): 40. Both quoted in Davis, *Moving the Mountain,* p. 127.

59. *The Reader's Guide to Periodical Literature* first listed "women's liberation" as a subtopic under "women" in volume 29, March 1969–February 1970, with three entries. The next year there were more than 75 entries under "women's liberation."

60. Susan Brownmiller, *Against Our Will: Men, Women, and Rape* (New York: Simon and Schuster, 1975), p. 27.

61. Personal communication from Ros Baxandall, Fall 2000; Ruth Rosen, *The World Split Open: How the Modern Women's Movement Changed America* (New York: Viking, 2000), p. 160.

62. Susan Suthein, "Radical Women Protest Ugly Pageant," *National Guardian,* September 14, 1968; "No Miss America!" leaflet in Jo Freeman's files; Beverly Grant to Pam Allen, personal letter, September 9, 1968, Pam Allen's files; Maren Lockwood Carden, *The New Feminist Movement* (New York: Russell Sage Foundation, 1974), p. 32; and Echols, *Daring to Be Bad,* pp. 92–96.

63. Sheila D. Collins, "Women and the Church: Poor Psychology, Worse Theology," *Christian Century* (December 30, 1970): 1557–1559, quotes on 1557, 1559.

64. See Charlotte Bunch, *Passionate Politics: Feminist Theory in Action; Essays, 1968–1982* (New York: St. Martin's Press, 1989), p. 7.

65. *Life,* vol. 69, no. 10 (September 4, 1970): 16B.

66. See coverage in *Time* (September 7, 1970): 12–13; *New Yorker,* vol. 46, no. 4 (September 5, 1970): 26–29; *Life,* vol. 69, no. 10 (September 4, 1970): 16B. See also Betty Friedan, *It Changed My Life* (New York: Random House, 1976), pp. 180–202.

67. Sandie North, "Reporting the Movement," *Atlantic* 235 (March 1970): 106; Freeman, *The Politics of Women's Liberation,* p. 150.

68. Sophy Burnham, "Women's Lib: The Idea You Can't Ignore," *Redbook,* vol. 135 (September 1970): 188, 191.

69. "Bev Mitchell," in Louise Rosenfield Noun, ed., *More Strong-Minded Women: Iowa Feminists Tell Their Stories* (Ames, IA: Iowa State University Press, 1992), pp. 75, 76.

70. "Bev Mitchell," in Noun, ed., *More Strong-Minded Women,* pp. 77, 78, 82.

71. See Naomi Weisstein and Virginia Blaisdell, "Feminist Rock: No More Balls and Chains," *Ms.,* vol. 1, no. 6 (December 1972): 25–27, quote on 26.

72. Judy Chicago quoted in "Forum: What Is Female Imagery?" *Ms.,* vol. 3, no. 11 (May 1975): 34.

73. Announcement is reproduced in Lucy R. Lippard, "Transformation Art," *Ms.,* vol. 4, no. 4 (October 1975): 34.

74. See, for example, Lise Vogel, "Women, Art, and Feminism" in Deborah Rosenfeldt, ed., *Female Studies VII, Going strong: New Courses/New Programs* (Old Westbury, N.Y.: The Feminist Press, 1973), pp. 42–53; Pat Mainardi, "A Feminine Sensibility?" *Feminist Art Journal,* Vol. 1, No. 1 (April 1972): 4+; and Marjorie Kramer, "Some Thoughts on Feminist Art," *Women and Art*

(Winter 1971): 3. By the early seventies there were several new journals in this area including *Feminist Art Journal, Women and Art,* and *Womanspace Journal.*

75. Nancy Anzara, "Artists in Their Own Image," *Ms.,* vol. 1, no. 7 (January 1973): 56; Lippard, "Transformation Art," 33–38.

76. Lippard, "Transformation Art," 33.

77. Wilson quoted in Lippard, "Transformation Art," 36.

78. For example, Day Piercy in the Chicago Women's Liberation Union worked closely with NOW in founding Women Employed, a pioneering organization of clerical workers (flyers announcing meetings and convention on October 20, 1974 sponsored by Women Employed, NOW, and other organizations, Women Employed: Rights & Roses, Gender Collection, Social Welfare History Archives, University of Minnesota); Sherrie Holmes, a socialist-feminist, founded a NOW chapter in Dayton and created a Task Force on Working Women to initiate Dayton Women Working, modeled on Women Employed. See Judith Sealander and Dorothy Smith, "The Rise and Fall of Feminist Organizations in the 1970s: Dayton as a Case Study," *Feminist Studies* vol. 12, no. 2 (Summer 1986): 325; and Judith Ezekiel, "Feminism in the Heartland: The Women's Movement in Dayton, Ohio in the 1970s," unpublished manuscript, 1999, pp. 182–183, 219–221 forthcoming Ohio State University Press, August 2002. New York Radical Feminists also experimented with organizing clerical workers in the late 1960s. Personal communication, Rosalyn Baxandall, Fall 2000.

79. Hole and Levine, *Rebirth of Feminism,* pp. 136–157; Echols, *Daring to Be Bad,* chapter 4, "Varieties of Feminism"; Susan Brownmiller, *In Our Time: Memoir of a Revolution* (New York: Dial Press, 1999), pp. 59–68; Jo Freeman, "The Tyranny of Structurelessness," *Berkeley Journal of Sociology,* vol. 17 (1972–1973): 151–164, reprinted in Baxandall and Gordon, eds., *Dear Sisters,* pp. 73–75.

80. See Ellen Willis, "Up from Radicalism: A Feminist Journal," *US* (October 1969): 5; also see Rosalind Pollack Petchesky, *Abortion and Woman's Choice: The State, Sexuality and Reproductive Freedom,* (Boston: Northeastern University Press, 1990), p. 129; Hole and Levine, *Rebirth of Feminism,* pp. 296–299; and Diane Schulder and Florynce Kennedy, *Abortion Rap* (New York: McGraw-Hill Book Company, 1971), pp. 3–4.

81. Gloria Steinem, "Introduction," edited and produced by Suzanne Levine and Harriet Lyons with Joanne Edgar, Ellen Sweet, and Mary Thom, *The Decade of Women: A Ms. History of the Seventies in Words and Pictures* (New York: Putnam, 1980), p. 9.

82. "Shock troops" is Rosalind Petchesky's term. See Petchesky, *Abortion and Woman's Choice,* p. 127.

83. Laura Kaplan, *The Story of Jane: The Legendary Underground Feminist Abortion Service* (New York: Pantheon Books, 1995), pp. 9, 12, 44–46, 102, 280; Petch-

esky, *Abortion and Woman's Choice*, p. 128. These sources are somewhat confusing about the meaning of the number of abortions performed. It may be that the number 11,000 includes all abortions carried out at their underground clinic both before and after they began, in the fall of 1970, to perform the operations themselves.

84. Sarah Weddington, *A Question of Choice* (New York: Putnam, 1992), chapters 3–7. See also David Garrow, *Liberty and Sexuality: The Right to Privacy and the Making of Roe v. Wade* (New York: Lisa Drew, 1994), chapters 7 and 8.

85. Popkin, "Bread and Roses," p. 175; author's interview with Nancy Hawley, Cambridge, Massachusetts, August 7, 1973. See also Wendy Coppedge Sanford, "Working Together, Growing Together: a Brief History of the Boston Women's Health Book Collective," *Heresies*, vol. 2, no. 3 (1979): 83–92.

86. Anita Shreve, *Women Together, Women Alone: The Legacy of the Consciousness-Raising Movement* (New York: Viking, 1989), pp. 83–86. Anne Koedt, "The Myth of the Vaginal Orgasm," *Notes from the First Year* (1968), reprinted in Anne Koedt, Ellen Levine, and Anita Rapone, eds., *Radical Feminism* (New York: Quadrangle Books, 1973), pp. 198–207.

87. Meredith Tax, "Woman and Her Mind: The Story of Everyday Life," *Notes from the Second Year* (1970): pp. 10–16.

88. Susan Griffin, "Rape—The All-American Crime," *Ramparts*, vol. 10, no. 3 (September 1971): 26, 35. This analysis was spelled out more fully in Brownmiller, *Against Our Will*.

89. Susan Schecter, *Women and Male Violence: The Visions and Struggles of the Battered Women's Movement* (Boston: South End Press, 1982), pp. 35–38.

90. Schecter, *ibid.*, pp. 33, 58–65; Women's Advocates, *Women's Advocates: The Story of a Shelter* (St. Paul, MN: The Advocates, 1980). Author's interview with Sharon Rice Vaughan, St. Paul, Minnesota, May 1, 1998. See also Susan Brownmiller, *In Our Time*, pp. 263–264.

91. Anne Koedt, "The Myth of the Vaginal Orgasm."

92. Sidney Abbott and Barbara Love, *Sappho Was a Right-on Woman: A Liberated View of Lesbianism* (New York: Stein and Day, 1972), p. 135.

93. Davis, *Moving the Mountain*, pp. 262–264. For Brown's version see Rita Mae Brown, "Take a Lesbian to Lunch," in Karla Jay and Allen Young, eds., *Out of the Closets: Voices of Gay Liberation* (New York: New York University Press, 1972, 1992), pp. 185–195.

94. Susan Brownmiller quotes Friedan as cautioning against the "lavender menace" whereas Brownmiller herself saw it only as a "lavender herring." Friedan recalls fearing a lesbian takeover and only gradually coming to realize that "some of the best, most hard-working women in NOW were in fact lesbian." Betty Friedan, *It Changed My Life: Writings on the Women's Movement* (New York: Random House, 1976), p. 141. Certainly the movement grapevine associated the term "lavender menace" with Friedan, and the Lavender Menace zap action was intended to refer to her.

95. Quoted in Abbott and Love, *Sappho Was*, p. 134.

96. Radicalesbians, "The Woman-Identified Woman," in Anne Koedt, Anita Rapone, and Ellen Levine, eds., *Notes from the Third Year: Women's Liberation* (New York: New York Radical Feminists, 1971), pp. 81–87; see also Echols, *Daring to Be Bad*, pp. 210–241; and Kate Millett, *Flying* (New York: Alfred Knopf, 1974), pp. 14–19.

97. Karla Jay, *Tales of the Lavender Menace: A Memoir of Liberation* (New York: Basic Books, 1999), chapter 9, quote on p. 137. See also Brownmiller, *In Our Time*, pp. 96–100; Davis, *Moving the Mountain*, pp. 264–266.

98. Popkin, "Bread and Roses," p. 180.

99. "A Letter From Mary," in Jay and Young, eds., *Out of the Closets*, p. 182. For a discussion of the sexual tensions and the gay-straight split within Bread and Roses, see Popkin, "Bread and Roses," pp. 180–184.

100. Susan Griffin, "Reverberations," in Karol Hope and Nancy Young, eds., *Out of the Frying Pan . . . A Decade of Change in Women's Lives* (Garden City, NY: Anchor Books, 1979), p. 247.

101. *Time* (December 14, 1970): 50.

102. Sidney Abbott and Barbara Love, *Sappho Was A Right-on Woman: A Liberated View of Lesbianism* (New York: Stein and Day, 1972), pp. 123–125; Brownmiller, *In Our Time*, pp. 148–151.

103. Alice S. Rossi, "Equality Between the Sexes: An Immodest Proposal," *Daedalus*, vol. 93, no. 2 (Spring 1964): 607–652; Popkin, "Bread and Roses," 77; Kate Millett, "Sexual Politics: A Manifesto for Revolution," in Shulamith Firestone and Anne Koedt, eds., *Notes from the Second Year: Women's Liberation; Major Writings of the Radical Feminists* (New York: Radical Feminism, 1970), pp. 111–112. Radical feminists, indeed, defined their goal as the abolition of sex roles. See Anne Koedt, "The Myth of the Vaginal Orgasm," in Anne Koedt, Ellen Levine, and Anita Rapone, eds., *Radical Feminism* (New York: Quadrangle Books, 1973), pp. 198–207.

104. Pat Mainardi, "The Politics of Housework," in *Notes from the Second Year* (1970), pp. 28–31, quotes on p. 29; Jane O'Reilly, "The Housewife's Moment of Truth," *Ms.*, vol. 1, no. 1 (Spring 1972): 54–55, 57–59.

105. Anita Shreve, *Women Together, Women Alone: The Legacy of the Consciousness-Raising Movement* (New York: Viking, 1989), p. 139.

106. Popkin, "Bread and Roses," p. 77.

107. Popkin, "Bread and Roses," pp. 23–30; Shreve, *Women Together*, pp. 40–43, 51–52.

108. Popkin, "Bread and Roses," p. 78.

109. Interview with Alice Kessler-Harris, New York City, December 13, 1997.

110. "The Feminists: A Political Organization to Annihilate Sex Roles," in Firestone and Koedt, eds., *Notes from the Second Year* (New York: Radical Feminism, 1970), p. 117.

111. The plummeting birthrate cannot be overstated. The number of births per

1000 women ages 15–44 had fallen by the mid-1970s to nearly half the rate in 1957 at the peak of the baby boom. See Cynthia Taeuber, *Statistical Handbook on Women in America* (Phoenix, AZ: Oryx Press, 1991), p. 20.

112. Falk-Dickler quoted in Davis, *Moving the Mountain*, p. 281; Friedan, *It Changed My Life*, p. 175.

113. Author's interview with Day Piercy, Chicago, July 16, 1981.

114. Davis, *Moving the Mountain*, p. 283; Edward F. Zigler and Jody Goodman, "The Battle for Day Care in America: A View from the Trenches," in Edward F. Zigler and Edmund W. Gordon, eds., *Day Care: Scientific and Social Policy Issues* (Boston, MA.: Auburn House Publishing, 1982), pp. 343–345.

115. I attended this meeting in Baltimore and remember meeting Alix Kates Shulman there. The first book published by the Feminist Press was a children's book designed for young readers, *The Dragon and the Doctor*, by Barbara Danish.

116. Author's telephone interview with Cheri Register, August 21, 1993.

117. *Ibid.*; letter to Howard Casmey, Commissioner of Education, April 16, 1971, Emma Willard Task Force on Education Packet (Minneapolis, MN: February 23, 1972; December 8, 1971).

118. *Ibid.*; Emma Willard Task Force on Education Packet. The packet included a biography of Emma Willard, articles and position papers regarding women's liberation and girls and sports, consciousness-raising exercises for classroom use, and a 38 page bibliography.

119. The following, for example, can be found in the Emma Willard Task Force Bibliography: Janice Law Trecker, "Women in U.S. History High School Textbooks," *Social Education* (March 1971), 249–260, 338; *Little Miss Muffet Fights back: A Bibliography of Recommended Non-sexist Books About Girls for Young Readers* (New York: Feminists on Children's Media, 1974); Marcia Federbush, *Let Them Aspire: A Plea and Proposal for Equality of Opportunity for Males and Females in the Ann Arbor Public Schools* (May 1971); Anne Grant West, *Report on Sex Bias in the Public Schools* (New York: New York City Chapter of NOW, n.d.); Women on Words and Images, *Dick and Jane as Victims: Sex Stereotyping in Children's Readers* (Princeton, NJ: Women on Words and Images, 1975).

120. Connie Dvorkin, "High School Women: The Suburban Scene," Emma Willard Task Force on Education Packet.

121. Cynthi Ellen Harrison, *Women's Movement Media: A Source Guide* (New York: R.R. Bowker Company, 1975), based on 2000 questionnaires sent out in 1973 or 1974, lists several national and local radio sources. The Pacifica Program Service, for example, serving four stations (KPFA in Northern California, KPFK in southern California, KPFT in Houston, and WBAI in New York) and distributing programs to nonprofit or educational radio stations located principally on school, college, and university campuses, listed more than 60 taped programs of interest to feminists. Similarly, Radio Free People and Ra-

dio Free Women of Washington, D.C. listed numerous tapes and interviews available for rebroadcast. What Harrison's questionnaire did not capture, apparently, was the existence of locally produced feminist "women's shows" on nonprofit, usually campus-based, radio stations across the country.

122. See, for example, "Human Potential: The Revolution in Feeling," *Time* 96 (November 9, 1970): 54–58.

Chapter 3

1. "Never Underestimate . . ." *Newsweek*, July 26, 1971, 29.
2. "Never Underestimate . . ." *Newsweek*, July 26, 1971, 29–30, quotes on 29; Rona F. Feit, "Organizing for Political Power: The National Women's Political Caucus," in Bernice Cummings and Victoria Schuck, eds., *Women Organizing: An Anthology* (Metuchen, NJ: Scarecrow Press, 1979), p. 185; Sheila Tobias, *Faces of Feminism: An Activist's Reflections on the Women's Movement* (Boulder, CO: Westview Press, 1997), pp. 246–247; Winifred Wandersee, *On the Move: American Women in the 1970s* (Boston: Twayne Publishers, 1988), pp. 22–23.
3. Political scientists Joyce Gelb and Marian Lief Palley, in *Women and Public Policies: Reassessing Gender Politics* (Charlottesville and London: University Press of Virginia, 1996), pp. 5–6, argue similarly that the issues that provoked least controversy were issues of equity that did not—on the surface at least—threaten role changes. One of their primary examples of a reform that fit this requirement was the Equal Credit Opportunity Act. See also Zillah R. Eisenstein, *The Radical Future of Liberal Feminism* (New York: Longman, 1981).
4. *Boston Globe* quoted in *NWPC Newsletter IV*, vol. II, no. IV (June 1973): 5.
5. Dennis A. Deslippe, *"Rights, Not Roses": Unions and the Rise of Working-Class Feminism, 1945–80* (Urbana: University of Illinois Press, 2000), p. 120; Catherine East, "Remarks for Veterans of Feminist American Meeting," May 26, 1993 (typescript); Hole and Levine, *Rebirth of Feminism*, pp. 82–83, 85; Davis, *Moving the Mountain*, pp. 53–54, 57.
6. Susan M. Hartmann, "Allies of the Women's Movement: Origins and Strategies of Feminist Activists in Male Dominated Organizations in the 1970s: The Case of the International Union of Electrical Workers," Paper presented at the 1993 Berkshire Conference on the History of Women, Poughkeepsie, New York, June 1993, and *The Other Feminists: Activists in the Liberal Establishment* (New Haven: Yale University Press, 1998).
7. In *Rosenfeld v. Southern Pacific Co.* (1968) a district court invalidated a California weight-lifting law for women. The court held that state protective laws didn't constitute a bfoq and that such laws were superseded by Title VII. This case is often cited as "the catalyst for the eventual demise of state protective laws." See Karen J. Maschke, *Litigation, Courts and Women Workers* (New

York: Praeger, 1989), p. 45. See also Sally J. Kenney, *For whose protection? Reproductive Hazards and Exclusionary Policies in the United States and Britain* (Ann Arbor: University of Michigan Press, 1992).

8. Davis, *Moving the Mountain*, pp. 62–64; Hole and Levine, *Rebirth of Feminism*, pp. 36–37; *Weeks v. Southern Tel. & Tel. Co.* (CA-5, 3-4-69) 408 F. 2d, rev. & rem. S.D. Ga 277 F. supp. 117.

9. Author's interviews with Olga Madar in Detroit on December 10, 1982, Dorothy Haener in Detroit on January 21, 1983, and Mildred Jeffrey, January 21, 1983.

10. See Flora Davis, *Moving the Mountain*, chapter 7; "The Senate: Woman Power," *Newsweek* (April 3, 1972): 28.

11. Catherine East, "Remarks for Veteran Feminists of America Meeting," May 26, 1993 (typescript in author's possession); Hole and Levine, *Rebirth of Feminism*, p. 55.

12. Arvonne Fraser, "Notes from 50th Anniversary Conference of Women's Bureau," 948-1978, Minnesota Historical Society, St. Paul, MN, Box 2.

13. Margurite Rawalt, "The Equal Rights Amendment," in Irene Tinker, ed., *Women in Washington: Advocates for Public Policy* (Beverly Hills, CA: Sage Publications, 1983), pp. 49–78; Davis, *Moving the Mountain*, pp. 121–127; Hole and Levine, *Rebirth of Feminism*, p. 56; Gelb and Palley, *Women and Public Policies*, pp. 50–51; Catherine East, "Remarks," p. 4.

14. See Women in the DFL, "Present but Powerless? A Preliminary Report," (St. Paul, Minnesota), May 1971. Copy in Arvonne Fraser Papers, Box 2, Minnesota Historical Society. The acknowledgments especially note Koryn Horbal and Arvonne Fraser as key sources of information. This became the founding document of the DFL Feminist Caucus that was a major force in state politics for several decades.

15. Mary Ann Milsap, "Sex Equity in Education," in Tinker, ed., *Women in Washington*, pp. 93–94 (quote on p. 94). See also Ethel Klein, *Gender Politics: From Consciousness to Mass Politics* (Cambridge, MA: Harvard University Press, 1984), pp. 25–26.

16. According to Rosalyn Baxandall, both Susan Brownmiller and Jan Goodman, early activists in New York Radical Women, were rejected for membership in NOW with letters stating that NOW was a membership organization for professional women [Susan Brownmiller, *In Our Time: Memoir of a Revolution* (New York: Dial Press, 1999), p. 3].

17. Arvonne Fraser, "Insiders and Outsiders," in Irene Tinker, ed., *Women in Washington*, p. 123.

18. Arlene Horowitz, "Education—Female Fact or Fiction," *NWPC Newsletter VI*, vol. II, no. VI (August 1973): 2–4, quote on 4.

19. Fraser, "Insiders and Outsiders," p. 131.

20. *Ibid.*, p. 131.

21. Davis, *Moving the Mountain*, p. 148; see also U.S. Congress, Hearings, Joint

Economic Committee, *Economic Problems of Women*, 93rd Congress, 1st Session, 12 July 1973, pp. 152–153, 202–210. See also Sheila Tobias, *Faces of Feminism: An Activist's Reflections on the Women's Movement* (Boulder CO: Westview Press, 1997), pp. 106–108.

22. Jane Roberts Chapman, "Policy Centers: An Essential Resource," in Irene Tinker, ed., *Women in Washington*, p. 179.

23. Davis, *Moving the Mountain*, pp. 148–152; Gelb and Palley, chapter 4, in Emily Card, ed., *Staying Solvent: A Comprehensive Guide to Equal Credit for Women* (New York: Holt, Rinehart, 1985); Jane Roberts Chapman, "Policy Centers: An Essential Resource," in Irene Tinker, ed., *Women in Washington*, pp. 177–185.

24. J. McKowan to Anne Truax, Pittsburgh, PA, June 20, 1971. This was an individually addressed, photocopied letter sent out to recruit women in colleges and universities into the NWPC. Other individuals were responsible for constituencies that included welfare rights, ethnic groups, students, peace and religious groups, political parties, trade unions, arts, professionals, civil rights, civil liberties, and women's groups. Gender Issues Collection, NWPC Newsletter Box, Social Welfare History Archives, University of Minnesota, Minneapolis, MN.

25. The Initiating Committee, National Women's Political Caucus to "Dear Friend," Washington, D.C., June 1971, photocopy of letter with attached registration form for July 10–11, 1971, Organizing Conference, Gender Issues Collection, NWPC Newsletter Box, Social Welfare History Archives, University of Minnesota, Minneapolis, MN.

26. *Ibid.*

27. Rona F. Feit, "Organizing for Political Power: The National Women's Political Caucus," in Bernice Cummings and Victoria Schuck, eds., *Women Organizing: An Anthology* (Metuchen, NJ: Scarecrow Press, 1979), p. 191.

28. *Ibid.*, p. 188.

29. *NWPC Newsletter I*, Washington, D.C., December 10, 1971.

30. See M. Kent Jennings, "Women in Party Politics," in Louise A. Tilly and Patricia Gurin, eds., *Women, Politics, and Change* (New York: Russell Sage Foundation, 1990), pp. 223–226.

31. Mary Ziegenhagen, "To Members of the Minnesota Women's Political Caucus: A Convention Report," Burnsville, Minnesota, February 20, 1973, 2. SWHA; Shirley Chisholm subsequently observed, "The whole convention had been a bitter disappointment to many delegates from the women's movement point of view; it had been organized from the start by the McGovern people to make sure that no group could upset the plan to nominate the South Dakota Senator." Shirley Chisholm, *The Good Fight* (New York: Harper & Row, 1973), p. 128.

32. *NWPC Newsletter I: Convention Report*, vol. II, no. 1 (February–March, 1973): 2, 3.

33. Rona F. Feit, "Organizing for Political Power: The National Women's Political Caucus," in Bernice Cummings and Victoria Schuck, eds., *Women Organizing: An Anthology* (Metuchen, NJ: Scarecrow Press, 1979), p. 190; Mary Ziegenhagen, "To Members of the Minnesota Women's Political Caucus."

34. *Ibid.*, p. 2.

35. Avis Foley, "Report from Black Caucus, NWPC Conference—Houston," Minnesota Women's Political Caucus Newsletter (March 1973): 1–2.

36. Ziegenhagen, "To Members of the Minnesota Women's Political Caucus."

37. Toni Morrison, "What the Black Woman Thinks About Women's Lib," *New York Times Magazine* (August 22, 1971).

38. Author's interview with Lael Stegall, Washington, D.C., February 19, 1998.

39. Bernette Golden, "Black Women's Liberation," *Essence*, vol. 4, no. 10 (February 1974): 36–37ff., quote on 36.

40. National Black Feminist Organization, "Statement of Purpose," *Ms.*, vol. 2, no. 11 (May 1974): 99; see also "Black Feminism: A New Mandate" in the same issue of *Ms.*, 97.

41. Caroline Handy interviewed in "Beating the System Together: Interview with a Black Feminist," *off our backs*, vol. 3, no. 11 (October 1973): 2–3, quotes on 2.

42. Quoted in "Input and Outreach: Day by Day at the NBFO," *Ms.*, vol. 2, no. 11 (May 1974): 100.

43. Letter to the editor, *Ms.*, vol. 3, no. 2 (August 1974): 4.

44. Letter to the editor, *Ms.*, vol. 3, no. 2 (August 1974): 4–6, quote on 6. Reprinted in Alice Walker, *In Search of Our Mother's Gardens: Womanist Prose* (New York: Harcourt, Brace, Jovanovich, 1983), pp. 273–277.

45. Telephone interview with Lourdes R. Miranda by author, February 23, 1998. See also Lourdes Miranda King, "Puertorriquenos in the United States: The Impact of Double Discrimination," *Civil Rights Digest*, vol. 6, no. 3 (Spring 1974): 20–27; Lourdes R. Miranda, *Hispanic Women in the United States: A Puerto Rican Women's Perspective* (Washington, DC: Miranda Associates, 1986).

46. For example, *Salt of the Earth* was the centerpiece for the 1968 Chicago Women's Liberation International Women's Day event on March 8. For the story of the strike, see Vicki Ruiz, *From out of the Shadows: Mexican Women in Twentieth-Century America* (New York: Oxford University Press, 1998), p. 85.

47. Interview with Eliza Sanchez, Washington, D.C., February 19, 1998.

48. Author's interview with Carol Bonasarro, Washington, D.C., December 16, 1997. "National Coalition Against Domestic Violence—Organizational Background," 1994 (document available online via *FirstSearch*, Contemporary Women's Issues Database).

49. *Ibid.*

50. *Civil Rights Digest*, vol. 6, no. 3 (Spring 1974).

51. National Council of Negro Women, "Women and Housing: Information

Sheet (1974), in Arvonne S. Fraser papers, 1948–1978, Box 13, Minnesota Historical Scoiety, St. Paul, MN.

52. Dorothy I. Height to Arvonne S. Fraser, Washington, D.C., August 13, 1974, Arvonne S. Fraser papers, 1948–1978, Box 13, Minnesota Historical Society, St. Paul, MN.

53. Perhaps the most common concern of consciousness-raising groups among middle-class women was the problem of work, career, and identity. See Shreve, *Women Together, Women Alone*, p. 103.

54. Author's interview with Dorothy Nelms, Washington, D.C., February 29, 1968.

55. *Ibid.*

56. Among the earliest were the Women's Caucus for Political Science (1968), the Coordinating Committee for Women in the Historical Profession (1969), the Society for Women in Philosophy (1970), and the Committee on Women in Physics (1971). The American Association for University Professors also reactivated its "Committee W" on women at a national level in 1970. Catharine R. Stimpson with Nina Kressner Cobb, *Women's Studies in the United States: A Report to the Ford Foundation* (New York: Ford Foundation, 1986), p. 5.

57. See Kay Klotzberger, "Political Action by Academic Women," in Alice Rossi and Ann Calderwood, eds., *Academic Women on the Move* (New York: Russell Sage Foundation, 1973), pp. 359–391; "Women's Groups in Professional Associations," in Mariam K. Chamberlain, ed., *Women in Academe: Progress and Prospects* (New York: Russell Sage Foundation, 1988), pp. 275–298.

58. See Florence Howe and Paul Lauter, *The Impact of Women's Studies on the Campus and the Disciplines* (Washington, D.C.: U.S. Department of Health, Education, and Welfare, National Institute of Education, 1980); and Catharine R. Stimpson, "The New Scholarship About Women: The State of the Art," *Annals of Scholarship* I (Spring 1980): 2–14. This new generation, of course, built on the work of pioneering scholars who had begun their work in the fifties and before. Among the most important of these were sociologists Jessie Bernard and Alice Rossi and historians Gerda Lerner and Anne Firor Scott.

59. Just the previous year the AHA had appointed a Commission on the Status of Women in the Historical Profession headed by Professor Willie Lee Rose. Rose's report resulted in the establishment of a standing committee on the status of women. See Kay Klotzburger, "Political Action by Academic Women," in Alice S. Rossi and Ann Calderwood, eds., *Academic Women on the Move* (New York: Russell Sage Foundation, 1973), pp. 364–365, 389.

60. Bernice Sandler, "A Little Help from Our Government: WEAL and Contract Compliance," in Alice S. Rossi and Ann Calderwood, eds. *Academic Women on the Move* (New York: Russell Sage Foundation, 1973), pp. 440–441; and Mary Ann Millsap, "Sex Equity in Education," in Irene Tinker, ed., *Women in Washington: Advocates for Public Policy* (Beverly Hills: Sage Publications, 1983), pp. 92–93.

61. By contrast, the total number of applicants tripled in that same time. See Donna Fossum, "A Lawyer-Sociologist's View on Women's Progress in the Profession," in Emily Couric, ed., *Women Lawyers: Perspectives on Success* (New York: Law and Business, 1984), p. 257.

62. Lei Etta Robinson, ed., *AAMC Data Book: Statistical Information Related to Medical Schools and Teaching Hospitals, January 2001* (Washington, D.C.: Association of American Medical 'Colleges, 2001), p. 23.

63. This story about harassment of chemistry graduate students is one I heard on several occasions from colleagues in the sciences soon after my arrival at the University of Minnesota in 1976. It had been presented as part of the evidence in a class action suit brought by a chemistry professor, Shamala Rajender, in 1974.

64. Author's interview with Kathleen Graham, St. Paul, Minnesota, September 18, 2001. I had a similar experience in 1969, when my first advisor in graduate school outlined a course of study and said, "Here is when you will take your exams, unless you decide to have a baby and leave school" (my son was 6 months old at the time). In the 7 years of my graduate training, the composition of the profession palpably changed, leaving my doctoral advisor to reminisce nostalgically about the days when the American Historical Society meeting was a "stag affair."

65. Sandra Hughes Boyd, "A Woman's Journey Toward Priesthood: An Autobiographical Study from the 1950s through the 1980s," in Catherine M. Prelinger, ed., *Episcopal Women: Gender, Spirituality and Commitment in an American Mainline Denomination* (New York: Oxford University Press, 1992), p. 273. See also reports in *The Christian Century* (November 18, 1970): 1391; (July 1, 1970): 827; (December 2, 1970): 1443; (September 2, 1970), 1047; Suzanne R. Hiatt, "How We Brought the Good News from Graymoor to Minneapolis: An Episcopal Paradigm," *Journal of Ecumenical Studies*, 20 (1983): 576–584.

66. See Heather Ann Huyck, "To Celebrate a Whole Priesthood: The History of Women's Ordination in the Episcopal Church" (Ph.D. Dissertation, University of Minnesota, 1981); Catherine M. Prelinger, "Ordained Women in the Episcopal Church: Their Impact on the Work and Structure of the Clergy," in Prelinger, ed., *Episcopal Women*, pp. 285–309.

67. Author's interview with Day Piercy, Chicago, Illinois, July 16, 1981.

68. Author's interviews with Ellen Cassedy, Bryn Mawr College, Bryn Mawr, PA, July 11, 1981; Heather Booth, Chicago, Illinois, July 15, 1981; Day Piercy, July 16, 1981.

69. Interview with Darlene Stille by Harry C. Boyte, Chicago, Illinois, April 28, 1977. Also quoted in Evans, *Personal Politics*, pp. 229–230.

70. *Chicago Sun-Times*, "Irate at Firing: Secretaries Boil, Try Coffee Coup" (February 4, 1977): 1; *Chicago Tribune*, "Coffee Case—Grounds for Protest" (February 4, 1977, sec. 1): 3; *Chicago Daily News* (February 3, 1977): 3. Piercy interview. Quotes from *Sun-Times*.

71. See Ellen Cassedy and Karen Nussbaum, *9 to 5: The Working Woman's Guide to Office Survival* (New York: Penguin Books, 1983), and Ellen Bravo and Ellen Cassedy, *9 to 5 Guide to Combating Sexual Harassment* (New York: John Wiley and Sons, 1992).

72. See Bravo and Cassedy, *9 to 5 Guide to Combating Sexual Harassment*, p. 7.

73. A number of women's liberation activists also became involved in the organizing process once plans were off the ground. Rosalyn Baxandall recalls, for example, Meredith Tax, Barb Winslow, and herself. Personal communication, Fall 2000.

74. Author's interviews with Olga Madar, Detroit, December 10, 1982; Addie Wyatt, Chicago, June 15, 1983; Joyce Miller, New York City, February 7, 1983. See also Susan Hartmann, *The Other Feminists: Activists in the Liberal Establishment* (New Haven: Yale University Press, 1998).

75. Susan M. Hartmann, *The Other Feminists*, pp. 25–26.

76. Author's interviews with Olga Madar, Detroit, December 10, 1982; Dorothy Haener, Detroit, January 21, 1983; Addie Wyatt, Chicago, June 15, 1983; Joyce Miller, New York City, February 7, 1983; CLUW Papers, ca. 1970–1975; Dorothy Haener Papers, UAW Women's Department Papers; Marjorie Stern Papers 1967–1975, Wayne State University, Archives of Labor and Urban Affairs, Walter P. Reuther Library, Detroit; *New York Times* (March 25, 1974): 27. See also Sarah Slavin, ed., *Women's Interest Groups; Institutional Profiles* (Westport, CT: Greenwood Press, 1985), pp. 124–128.

77. Joan M. Goodin, "Working Women: The Pros and Cons of Unions," in Tinker, ed., *Women in Washington*, pp. 141–142.

78. Quoted in Goodin, *Ibid.*, p. 143.

79. Author's interview with Joyce Miller, New York City, February 7, 1983.

80. *New York Times* (August 22, 1980): A1.

81. Author's interview with Anne Ladky, Chicago, Illinois, April 18, 1983.

82. Similar grammatical constructions (e.g., black lawyer, Asian-American doctor) signal the perception that minorities are also "exceptional" in public, professional, and political roles.

83. "'Man!' Memo from a Publisher," *New York Times Magazine* (October 20, 1974): 38, 104–108.

84. Cynthia Ellen Harrison, *Women's Movement Media: A Source Guide* (New York: R.R. Bowker, 1975), lists 190 periodicals and 39 "publishers," many of which published one book, catalogue, or journal. Anne Mathas claims that more than 560 feminist publications appeared in the United States between March 1968 and August 1973. "A History of Feminist Periodicals, Part I," *Journalism History*, vol. 1, no. 3 (Autumn 1974): 82.

85. Amy Erdman Farrell, *Yours in Sisterhood: Ms. Magazine and the Promise of Popular Feminism* (Chapel Hill: University of North Carolina Press, 1998), pp. 27–28, 45, 141.

86. *Ms.*, preview edition (Spring 1972). Amy Farrell describes this cover as a refusal "to construct a definitive image of the '*Ms.*' woman" by combining "the

accouterments of a housewife—the role primarily of a white, middle-class Western woman—[while] the woman herself suggested a Hindu goddess, indicating that this magazine intended to speak to all women, to transcend differences created by race or class." Farrell, *Yours in Sisterhood*, pp. 31–32, 141.

87. *Ms.*, preview edition (Spring 1972).
88. Amy Farrell, *Yours in Sisterhood*, pp. 29–30.
89. See Carolyn G. Heilbrun, *The Education of a Woman: The Life of Gloria Steinem* (New York: Dial Press, 1995); Sydney Ladensohn Stern, *Gloria Steinem: Her Passions, Politics, and Mystique* (Secaucus, NJ: Carol Publishing Group, 1997); and Jennifer Scanlon, ed., *Significant Contemporary American Feminists: A Biographical Sourcebook* (Westport, CT: Greenwood Press, 1999).
90. *Ms.*, vol. 1, no. 1 (Spring 1972): 113.
91. Author's interviews with Naomi Weisstein, New Providence, New Jersey, July 30, 1975, and Heather Booth, Chicago, Illinois, July 9, 1973, and July 15, 1981. Note that one of the earliest of these was in Chicago in 1966. In 1970, for example, in addition to the multiplication of journals, newletters, and mimeographed essays, major publishers issued *Sisterhood Is Powerful*, edited by Robin Morgan (New York: Random House), *Sexual Politics* by Kate Millett, and *The Dialectic of Sex* by Shulamith Firestone.
92. Friedan, *It Changed My Life*, p. 139; Tobias, *Faces of Feminism*, pp. 191–192.
93. Sheila Tobias, ed., *Feminist Studies I* (Pittsburgh, PA: Know, Inc., ca. 1970); Florence Howe, ed., *Female Studies II* (Pittsburgh, PA: Know, Inc., 1972).
94. Rosalyn Baxandall, personal communication, September 2000.
95. Author's interview with Karen McTighe Musil, Washington, D.C., November 11, 1997.
96. A look at the vitae of a number of eminent feminist historians (Linda Kerber, Joan Scott, Linda Gordon, and Jane DeHart) would reveal that their first books (based on dissertations) were utterly unrelated to women's history. Slightly younger scholars, such as Karen Musil and Deborah Rosenfeldt, describe the struggle to complete a traditional dissertation even as they were beginning to read and teach the new feminist scholarship. Interviews with Linda Gordon, New York City, December 13, 1997; Karen Musil, Washington, D.C., December 15, 1997, and Deborah Rosenfeldt, College Park, Maryland, December 15, 1997.
97. Kate Millett, *Sexual Politics* (New York: Doubleday, 1970).
98. Stimpson and Cobb, *Women's Studies in the United States*, p. 21.
99. Susan Cahn, *Coming on Strong: Gender and Sexuality in Twentieth-Century Women's Sport* (New York: Free Press, 1984), pp. 250–252.
100. Bud Collins, "Billie Jean King Evens the Score," *Ms.* (July 1973): 37–43; "There She Is, Ms. America," *Sports Illustrated* 39 (October 1, 1973): 30–32ff.; and Wandersee, *On the Move*, 150–154.

Chapter 4

1. Dana Densmore, "A Year of Living Dangerously: 1968," in Rachel Blau Du-Plessis and Ann Snitow, eds., *The Feminist Memoir Project: Voices from Women's Liberation* (New York: Three Rivers Press, 1998), p. 81.

2. Charlotte Bunch with Linda, Elinore, Marlene, Sharon, and Joan, "Ourstory: Herstory and Development of the D.C. Women's Liberation Movement," Washington, D.C.: mimeograph in author's possession, n.d. (ca. 1971). The dating for this document is clear from the first draft: Charlotte Bunch, "Ourstory: D.C. Herstory," compiled for a women's retreat on May 21, 1971. Mimeo in Bunch's files and in author's possession.

3. Bunch, "Ourstory," p. 6ff.

4. Charlotte Bunch notes that these groups formed at a time when the movement had suddenly grown too large for continuing, face-to-face conversation. Most were neither groups that lived together nor specifically project or issue oriented. Rather, they were an effort to create environments in which women could move beyond the initial stages of consciousness-raising and develop analyses and strategies for future work. Conversation with Charlotte Bunch, April 19, 2002.

5. Bunch, et al., "Ourstory."

6. Bunch et al., "Ourstory."

7. Bunch et al., "Ourstory."

8. Bunch et al, "Ourstory"; see also Echols, *Daring to Be Bad*, pp. 222–223.

9. Bunch, "Lesbians in Revolt," in Bunch and Myron, eds., *Lesbianism and the Women's Movement* (Baltimore: Diana Press, 1975), p. 33, quoted in Echols, *Daring to Be Bad*, p. 232.

10. See Echols, *Daring to Be Bad*, pp. 228–230.

11. Rita Mae Brown, "Living with Other Women," *Radical Therapist* (April/May 1971): 14.

12. Author's interview with Charlotte Bunch, New York City, December 14, 1997.

13. Author's interview with Charlotte Bunch, New York City, December 14, 1997. For an excellent discussion of the totalizing nature of the new left in the late sixties and early seventies, see Jack Whalen and Richard Flacks, *Beyond the Barricades: The Sixties Generation Grow up* (Philadelphia: Temple University Press, 1989).

14. Beverly Jones and Judith Brown, "Toward a Female Liberation Movement," Gainesville, FL, 1968. Mimeographed pamphlet.

15. Bernadine Dohrn in New Left Notes, quoted in Kathy McAfee and Myrna Wood, "Bread and Roses," *Leviathan* (June 1979): 8.

16. Marge Piercy, "Grand Coolie Damn," in Robin Morgan, ed., *Sisterhood is Powerful* (New York: Random House, 1970), pp. 434, 429.

17. Maureen Davidica, "Women and the Radical Movement," *No More Fun and Games*, vol. 1 (August 1968).

18. Author's interview with Linda Gordon. Shulamith Firestone responded in *Notes from the First Year* that a separate movement had first to allow women to break away from old categories before it could begin to agitate for specific reforms. Consciousness-raising, in her view, was the pathway to a correct consciousness, a perspective from which to make political decisions.

19. Author's interview with Charlotte Bunch. See also Alice Echols, *Daring to Be Bad: Radical Feminism in America 1967–1975* (Minneapolis: University of Minnesota Press, 1989), pp. 108–114.

20. For detailed accounts of the early women's liberation movement in New York, see Alice Echols, *Daring to Be Bad*, and Susan Brownmiller, *In Our Time*.

21. Charlotte Bunch with Linda, Elinore, Marlene, Sharon, and Joan, "Ourstory: Herstory and Development of the D.C. Women's Liberation Movement," Washington, D.C.: mimeograph in author's possession, (ca. 1971), p. 2.

22. Alice Echols, *Daring to Be Bad*. Although I am indebted to Echols' scholarship, my own interpretation is different. She argues that "radical feminism" was a highly distinctive strand of women's liberation and that "by 1975 radical feminism virtually ceased to exist as a movement. Once radical feminism was superseded by cultural feminism, activism became largely the province of liberal feminists" (p. 5). By contrast, I maintain that the "movement" cannot be confined to a single group; it did not decline in the early 1970s, and those who called themselves "radical feminists" were not as unique as they believed themselves to be at the time.

23. Robin Morgan, *Going Too Far: The Personal Chronicle of a Feminist* (New York: Random House, 1977), pp. 119–120.

24. Naomi Weisstein, "Days of Celebration and Resistance: The Chicago Women's Liberation Rock Band, 1970–1973," in DuPlessis and Snitow, eds., *The Feminist Memoir Project*, p. 358.

25. Quoted in Mary Thom, *Inside Ms.: 25 Years of the Magazine and the Feminist Movement* (New York: Henry Holt and Company, 1997), p. 81.

26. Redstockings, "Press Release," May 9, 1975, in Redstockings, Inc. *The Feminist Revolution*, New Paltz, N.Y.: Redstockings, 1975.

27. On surveillance see Rosen, *The World Split Open*, chapter 7. For detailed narratives of the attack on Steinem and the conflict at Sagaris, see Rosen, pp. 254–260; Brownmiller, *In Our Time*, pp. 233–243; and Mary Thom, *Inside Ms.*, pp. 74–49. Redstockings rested their case against Steinem on the fact that in the late 1950s and early 1960s she had worked for the Independent Research Service, a foundation that sponsored American youth to attend international youth festivals in the Communist world. Partially funded by the CIA, the foundation was clearly linked to a liberal Cold War agenda. When this information was first made public in 1967, Steinem had explained her work as the product of her youthful and naive Cold War liberalism, when there was no public knowledge of the violent and disruptive role of the CIA throughout the world.

NOTES   *261*

28. Ti-Grace Atkinson quoted in Rosen, *The World Split Open*, p. 256.
29. Lucinda Franks, "Dissention Among Feminists," *New York Times* (August 29, 1975): 32.
30. See Rosen, *The World Split Open*, p. 236; Brownmiller, *In Our Time*, pp. 237–238.
31. The Redstockings/Betty Friedan/Gloria Steinem fracas was the most prominent of several public splits within the movement at this time. These have been described in some detail in Susan Brownmiller, *In Our Time*; Ruth Rosen, *The World Split Open*; Alice Echols, *Daring to Be Bad*; Caroline Heilbrun *The Education of a Woman: The Life of Gloria Steinem* and others.
32. See Enid Nemy, "13 NOW Leaders Form a Dissident Network," *New York Times*, November 15, 1975, Pp., 1, 12, quote by Mary Jean Tully, President, NOW Legal Defense Education Fund, on p. 12; Joan Zyda, "Internal Struggle Jeopardizes NOW," *Chicago Tribune*, November 20, 1975, sec. 3, p.:3; Beth Gillin Pombiero, "NOW Takes a Turn Toward All Women, Not Just Members," *Philadelphia Inquirer*, October 28, 1975, A:3.
33. Barbara Ryan, *Feminism and the Women's Movement: Dynamics of Change in Social Movement Ideology and Activism* (New York: Routledge, 1992), pp. 71–73; Toni Carabillo and Judith Meuli, "Chronology of 'The Split,'" 1991, Schlesinger Library, Radcliffe College.
34. National Women's Education Fund, "What is the N.W.E.F.?" n.d., Leaflet in Arvonne Fraser Papers, Box 1, Minnesota Historical Society.
35. On the seventies economy, see Charles B. Reeder, *The Sobering Seventies: A Month-by-Month Analysis of Significant Developments in the U.S. Economy During the 1970s* (Wilmington, DE: Reeder, 1980), unemployment figures on pp. 131, 160, 172; and Harry Magdoff and Paul M. Sweezy, *The End of Prosperity: The American Economy in the 1970s* (New York: Monthly Review Press, 1977).
36. See, for example, "The Furor over 'Reverse Discrimination,'" *Newsweek* 90 (September 26, 1977): 52–55ff.
37. On the number of Americans killed in Vietnam, see Stanley Karnow, *Vietnam: A History* (New York: Viking, 1983), pp. 9, 11.
38. On the origins of NARAL, see Lawrence Lader, *Abortion II: Making the Revolution* (Boston: Beacon Press, 1973). See also Rosalind P. Petchesky, *Abortion and Woman's Choice: The State, Sexuality, and Reproductive Freedom* (New York: Longman, 1984).
39. On right-wing women, see Andrea Dworkin, *Right Wing Women* (New York: Perigee Books, 1983); Phyllis Schlafley, *The Power of the Positive Woman* (New Rochelle, NY: Arlington House, 1977); Carol Virginia Pohli, "Church Closets and Back Doors: A Feminist View of Moral Majority Women," *Feminist Studies* 9 (Fall 1983): 529–558.
40. See Jane Sherron Dehart and Donald Mathews, *Sex, Gender, and the Politics of ERA: A State and the Nation* (New York: Oxford University Press, 1990).
41. See Elaine Brown, *A Taste of Power: A Black Woman's Story* (New York: Pantheon Books, 1992).

42. Flora Davis, *Moving the Mountain*, pp. 138–141, describes the Socialist Worker's Party's efforts to take over women's centers and other feminist groups. International Socialists (IS) made a similar effort to take over the New American Movement, which provided substantial leadership in the socialist feminist movement. There were numerous other sectarian groups: October League (a descendant of the RYM II faction of SDS), which based its analysis of race as the "primary contradiction," the Revolutionary Union, the Communist Labor Party, and others.

43. Doug Rossinow has argued persuasively that the search for authenticity was a hallmark of the New Left. "From the new left's viewpoint, revolutionary agency and authenticity were yoked together so that those who possessed one of these automatically possessed both." *The Politics of Authenticity: Liberalism, Christianity, and the New Left in America* (New York: Columbia University Press, 1998), p. 164. Similarly, Doug McAdam finds the origins of "the personal is political" in the Mississippi Freedom Summers of 1964 and 1965, when hundreds of northern white students joined the civil rights movement in the Deep South. The summer projects were "suffused" with a "general emphasis on self-discovery and personal liberation." *Freedom Summer* (New York: Oxford University Press, 1988), p. 183.

44. This begins, of course, with the Moynihan Report, authored by a white male sociologist. See also Ruth Feldstein, *Motherhood in Black and White: Race and Sex in American Liberalism, 1930–1965* (Ithaca, NY: Cornell University Press, 2000); and Albert Murray, "White Norms, Black Deviation," in Joyce Ladner, ed., *The Death of White Sociology* (Baltimore: Black Classic Press, 1998), pp. 96–113.

45. Quote from Toni Morrison, "What the Black Woman Thinks About Women's Lib," *New York Times Magazine* (August 22, 1971).

46. Charlotte Bunch with Linda, Elinore, Marlene, Sharon, and Joan, "Herstory and Development of the D.C. Women's Liberation Movement," Washington, D.C.: mimeograph in author's possession, (ca. 1971), p. 2.

47. Frances Beale, "Speaking up When Others Can't," *Crossroads* (March 1993): 4.

48. Nathan Hare, "Will the Real Black Man Please Stand up?" *Black Scholar*, vol. 2, no. 10 (June 1971): 32–35, quotes on 32, 33.

49. Kay Lindsey, "The Black Woman as a Woman," in Toni Cade, ed., *The Black Woman: An Anthology* (New York: New American Library, 1970), p. 85.

50. See, for example, Mitsuye Yamada, "Asian Pacific American Women and Feminism," in Cherrie Moraga and Gloria Anzaldua, eds., *This Bridge Called My Back: Writings by Radical Women of Color* (New York: Kitchen Table Press, 1981), pp. 71–75.

51. See, for example, Consuelo Nieto, "The Chicana and the Women's Rights Movement," *Civil Rights Digest*, special issue on "Sexism and Racism: Feminist Perspectives" vol. 6, no. 3 (Spring 1974): 36–42.

52. Paula Giddings, *When and Where I Enter: The Impact of Black Women on Race and Sex in America* (New York: William Morrow, 1984), pp. 193–195.

53. Quoted in Miriam Lynnell Harris, *"*From Kennedy to Combahee: Black Feminist Activism from 1960 to 1980," unpublished Ph.D. Dissertation, American Studies, University of Minnesota, 1997, p. 102.

54. *Ibid.*, p. 104.

55. *Ibid.*

56. Cherrie Moraga and Gloria Anzaldua, eds., *This Bridge Called My Back: Writings by Radical Women of Color,* 1st ed. (Watertown, MA: Persephone Press, 1981), 2nd ed. (New York: Kitchen Table Women of Color Press, 1983); Gloria T. Hull, Patricia Bell Scott, and Barbara Smith, *All the Women Are White, All the Blacks Are Men, but Some of Us Are Brave: Black Women's Studies* (Old Westbury, NY: Feminist Press, 1981); Bell Hooks, *Feminist Theory from Margin to Center* (Boston, MA: South End Press, 1984).

57. See Alice Echols, *Daring to Be Bad,* for a detailed history of radical feminism. Of the four radical feminist groups she describes in some detail, three (New York Radical Women, Redstockings, and the Feminists) were in New York and one, Cell 16, was in Boston. Several key position papers, however, were written by women outside the Northeast: Beverly Jones and Judith Brown, "Towards a Female Liberation Movement (Gainesville, FL, 1968, reprinted in Leslie Tanner, ed., *Voices from Women's Liberation*), and Barbara Burris, "The Fourth World Manifesto" (Detroit, MI, 1971; reprinted in Anne Koedt, ed., *Radical Feminism,* pp. 322–357). For ideological positions of New York groups see the "manifestos" printed in Anne Koedt and Shulamith Firestone, eds., *Notes from the Second Year.*

58. Quoted in Popkin, *Bread and Roses,* p. 102.

59. Popkin, *Bread and Roses,* chapter 3 passim, quotes on p. 63.

60. Barbara Ryan makes a similar point regarding the primacy of identity in *Feminism and the Women's Movement: Dynamics of Change in Social Movement Ideology and Activism* (New York: Routledge, 1992), p. 63.

61. Author's interview with Ellen Cassidy.

62. Rita Mae Brown quoted in Charlotte Bunch, "Forum: Learning from Lesbian Separatism," *Ms.,* vol. 5 no. 5 (November 1976): 61.

63. Sidney Abbott and Barbara Love, *Sappho Was a Right-on Woman: A Liberated View of Lesbianism* (New York: Stein & Day, 1978), pp. 136–137.

64. Jo Freeman, "The Tyranny of Structurelessness," in Anne Koedt, Ellen Levine, and Anita Rapone, eds., *Radical Feminism* (New York: Quadrangle, 1973), pp. 285–299. The article was first published in 1970.

65. Alice Echols offers numerous examples from New York, where these struggles began very early and set a pattern of strident discord. See *Daring to Be Bad,* pp. 88–89, 99–100, 191–192, 204–210.

66. Amy Kesselman with Heather Booth, Vivian Rothstein, and Naomi Weisstein, "Our Gang of Four: Friendship and Women's Liberation," in Rachel

Blau DuPlessis and Ann Snitow, eds., *The Feminist Memoir Project: Voices from Women's Liberation* (New York: Three Rivers Press, 1998), p. 47; Evans, *Personal Politics*, p. 223.

67. Weisstein, "Days of Celebration and Resistance: The Chicago Women's Liberation Rock Band," in Rachel Blau DuPlessis and Ann Snitow, eds., *The Feminist Memoir Project: Voices from Women's Liberation* (New York: Three Rivers Press, 1998), p. 359.

68. Quoted in Amy Kesselman with Heather Booth, Vivian Rothstein, and Naomi Weisstein, "Our Gang of Four," in DuPlessis and Snitow, eds., *The Feminist Memoir Project*, p. 51.

69. Elinor Langer, "Confessing," *Ms.*, vol. 3, no. 6 (December 1974): 69–71, 108, quote on 70.

70. Quoted in Anita Shreve, *Women Together, Women Alone*, p. 58.

71. The women's movement established patterns that affected other progressive movements as well. Similar conflicts can be found in efforts around racial justice, peace, and the environment, all of which had overlapping memberships with the women's movement and were deeply influenced by its visionary language and organizing methods.

72. Examples of declension articles: Victoria Geng, "Requiem for the Women's Movement, *Harper's*, vol. 253 (November 1976): 49–68; Naomi Weisstein and Heather Booth, "Will the Women's Movement Survive?" *Lesbian Tide* (Fall 1976): 28–33; Carmen Kerr, "The Corruption of Feminism," *Issues in Radical Therapy* III, 4 (Fall 1976): 3–8; Charlotte Bunch, "Beyond Either/Or: Feminist Options," *Quest: A Feminist Quarterly*, IV, 1 (Summer 1977): 88–96.

Chapter 5

1. Anita Buzick II, Killeen, Texas, Letter to *Ms.* (June 1975), reprinted in *Ms.*, XII, 1 (December 2001/January 2002): 95.

2. Byllye Y. Avery, "Breathing Life into Ourselves: The Evolution of the National Black Women's Health Project," in Evelyn C. White ed. *The Black Women's Health Book: Speaking for Ourselves* (Seattle: Seal Press, 1990), pp. 4–5.

3. Regarding women's health networks in the 1970s, see Sheryl Burt Ruzek, *The Women's Health Movement: Feminist Alternatives to Medical Control* (New York: Praeger, 1978).

4. Author's interview with Carol Bonasarro, Washington, D.C., December 16, 1997; author's interview with Sharon Vaughan, May 1, 1998.

5. Jan Griesinger, "Out of Right Field," manuscript in author's possession, 2001, p. 14.

6. See, for example, *Engage/Social Action* (a United Church of Christ/United Methodist magazine), vol. 3, no. 4 (March 1975) and *The Christian Ministry*

(May 1975). Both were cited in *Daughters of Sarah*, vol. 1, no. 7 (November 1975).

7. Mary Fainsod Katzenstein, "Discursive Politics and Feminist Activism in the Catholic Church," in Ferree and Martin, eds., *Feminist Organizations*, p. 37. Among the most important opening salvos of feminist religious activism was Mary Daly's devastating *Critique of Sexism within the Catholic Church: The Church and the Second Sex* (New York: Harper & Row, 1968) and her critique of male imagery in Christian theology in *Beyond God the Father: Toward a Philosophy of Women's Liberation* (Boston: Beacon Press, 1973). By the mid-1970s, however, Daly had rejected Christianity as irredeemably patriarchal.

8. *Daughters of Sarah*, volumes 1–5 (1974–1979), at the Social Welfare History Archives, University of Minnesota, Minneapolis. Quotes from vol. 1, no. 1 (November 1974): 1, and vol. 2, no. 1 (January 1976): 9.

9. Author's interview with Lael Stegall, Washington, D.C., February 19, 1998.

10. The ACLU Women's Rights Project was a major innovator in reproductive rights and employment law. Spurred into being in 1970 by long-time feminists Pauli Murray, Dorothy Kenyan, and Harriet Pilpel, the project galvanized the energies of a younger generation, most notably Ruth Bader Ginsburg (later Supreme Court Justice). There was considerable cross-fertilization between the Women's Rights Project and NOW. Through a newsletter, a quarterly docket of pending sex discrimination cases, and a conference on feminist litigation in 1973, the Women's Rights Project, according to historian Susan Hartmann, "brought considerable order and focus to feminist litigation." Susan M. Hartmann, *The Other Feminists: Activists in the Liberal Establishment* (New Haven: Yale University Press, 1998), chapter 3, quote on p. 85.

11. Author's interview with Kathleen Graham, St. Paul, Minnesota, September 18, 2001.

12. Author's interview with Carolyn Chalmers, Minneapolis, Minnesota, September 19, 2001.

13. Brownmiller, *In Our Time*, pp. 279–294; Enid Nemy, "Women Begin to Speak out Against Sexual Harassment at Work," *New York Times* (August 19, 1975): 38. See also Laura W. Stein, *Sexual Harassment in America: A Documentary History* (Westport, CT: Greenwood Press, 1999); Lin Farley, *Sexual Shakedown: The Sexual Harassment of Women on the Job* (New York: McGraw-Hill, 1978); Catharine A. MacKinnon, *Sexual Harassment of Working Women* (New Haven: Yale University Press, 1979). In the 1980s, MacKinnon was probably the leading legal theorist on this issue, but she cannot be credited with initiating it.

14. Susan Cahn, *Coming on Strong: Gender and Sexuality in Twentieth Century Women's Sport* (New York: Free Press, 1994), p. 254.

15. "Comes the Revolution: Joining the Game at Last, Women Are Transforming American Athletics," *Time* 111 (June 26, 1978): 54–60, quoted in Susan

Cahn, *Coming on Strong: Gender and Sexuality in Twentieth Century Women's Sport* (New York: Free Press, 1994), p. 253.

16. Cahn, Coming on Strong, pp. 254–256.

17. Dorothy I. Height to Arvonne S. Fraser, Washington, D.C., August 13, 1974. Arvonne S. Fraser Papers 1948–1978, Minnesota Historical Society, St. Paul, MN, Box 8.

18. Women's Action Alliance, "Respondents to our Invitation to Join in the Creation of the National Women's Agenda," May 21, 1975, in Arvonne S. Fraser Papers, Box 23. The 61 organizations include: ACLU Women's Rights Project; AFTRA National Women's Committee, Alliance of Media Women, SSUW, American Business Women's Association, AFSCME Commission on Sex Discrimination; Association of American Colleges Project on Status and Education of Women; Junior League, Camp Fire Girls, Catalyst, Center for American Women and Politics, Center for a Woman's Own Name, Center for Law and Social Policy, Center for Women Policy Studies, Church Women United, Connecticut Women's Education and Legal Fund, Federation of Organizations of Professional Women, the Feminist Press, Future Homemakers of America Girls Clubs, Girl Scouts of America, Gray Panthers, Hadassah, Healthright, Inc., Institute of Women's Wrongs, La Leche League, Leadership Conference of Women Religious, League of Women Voters, Lesbian Mothers National Defense Fund, MOMMA, Muher Integrate Ahora (MIA), National League of Pen Women, National Gay Task Force, National Association of Commissions on Women, National Association of Women Lawyers, National Association for Women in Criminal Justice, National Black Feminist Organization, National Committee on Household Employment, National Conference of Puerto Rican Women, Inc., National Conference of Jewish Women, National Education Association, Resource Center on Sex Roles and Education; National Federation of BPW Clubs, National Institute of Spanish Speaking Women, National Resource Center on Women Offenders, National Women's Education Fund, NWPC, NOW LDEF, Phi Delta Gamma, Saint Joan's International Alliance, UAW Women's Committee, Women in Communication, Women on Words and Images, Women's Caucus for Art, WEAL, Women's Institute for Freedom of the Press, WILPF, Women's Law Project, Women's Legal Defense Fund, Women's Strike for Peace, and YWCA.

19. Paquita Vivo, "Puerto Rican Viewpoint," *Women's Agenda*, vol. 1, no. 1 (February 1976): 7

20. Interview with Leslie Wolfe, Washington, D.C., November 12, 1997. Weddington describes her appointment and her responsibilities in *A Question of Choice*, p. 193.

21. Interview with Betty Dooley, Washington, D.C., November 12, 1997.

22. See Irwin N. Gertzog, *Congressional Women: Their Recruitment, Integration, and Behavior*, 2nd ed., revised and updated (Westport, CT: Praeger, 1995), chapter 10.

23. See Women's Bureau, U.S. Department of Labor, *Time of Change: 1983 Handbook on Women Workers*, Bulletin 298 (Washington, D.C.: U.S. Government Printing Office, 1983), pp. 81–84, especially tables III-1 and III-2. The ratio did not reach 60 percent until 1981.

24. See Jane J. Mansbridge, *Why We Lost the ERA* (Chicago: University of Chicago Press, 1986), chapter 5.

25. Evans and Nelson, *Wage Justice*, p. 37. See also *Lemons v. City and County of Denver* 620F. 2d 228 (10th Cir. 1980).

26. See Janet A. Flammang, "The Implementation of Comparable Worth in San Jose," in Rita Mae Kelly and Jane Bayes, eds., *Comparable Worth, Pay Equity, and Public Policy* (Westport, CT: Greenwood Press, 1988), pp. 159–190.

27. See Evans and Nelson, *Wage Justice*; Dennis A. Deslippe, *Rights, not Roses: Unions and the Rise of Working-Class Feminism, 1945–80* (Urbana: University of Illinois Press, 2000); and Susan Hartmann, *The Other Feminists: Activists in the Liberal Establishment* (New Haven: Yale University Press, 1998), chapter 2. The NAS study was published in 1981. See Donald Treiman and Heidi Hartmann, eds., *Women, Work, and Wages: Equal Pay for Jobs of Equal Value* (Washington, D.C.: National Academy Press, 1981). The establishment of "comparability" based on measurements of skill, effort, responsibility, and working conditions requires the use of highly technical job evaluation systems (Evans and Nelson 1989, chapters 2–3).

28. Interview with Leslie Wolfe, Washington, D.C., November 12, 1997.

29. Title IX reads as follows: "No person in the United States shall, on the basis of sex, be excluded from participation in, be denied the benefits of, or be subjected to discrimination under any education program or activity receiving federal financial assistance. . . ." *United States Statutes at Large: Containing the Laws and Concurrent Resolutions Enacted During the Second Session of the Ninety-Second Congress of the United States of America, 1972, and Proposed Amendment to the Constitution and Proclamations*, Vol. 86 (Washington, D.C.: U.S. Government Printing Office, 1973), p. 373.

30. "Women's Educational Equity Act Program, Office of Education, Department of Health, Education, and Welfare," *Federal Register: Rules and Regulations*, vol. 45, no. 66 (Thursday, April 3, 1980): C1–C11, quotes on C2. Mary Ann Millsap and Leslie R. Wolfe, "A Feminist Perspective in Law and Practice: The Women's Educational Equity Act," *Readings in Equal Education* (March 8, 1985): 221–230. See also NCPRW Conference report in *off our backs*, vol. 10, no. 6 (June 1980): 6.

31. Ruth Abram, Executive Director, Women's Action Alliance, to "Friends," New York, July 25, 1975. In Arvonne S. Fraser Papers, Box 13.

32. Tanya Melich, *The Republican War Against Women: An Insider's Report from Behind the Lines* (New York: Bantam Books, 1996).

33. Alice S. Rossi, *Feminists in Politics: A Panel Analysis of the First National Women's Conference* (New York: Academic Press, 1982).

34. Bella Abzug with Mim Kelber, *Gender Gap: Bella Abzug's Guide to Political Power for American Women* (Boston: Houghton Mifflin, 1984), p. 58.

35. Author's interview with Charlotte Bunch, New York City, December 14, 1997. On Steinem's role see Carolyn G. Heilbrun, *The Education of a Woman: The Life of Gloria Steinem* (New York: Ballantine Books, 1995), pp. 310–324. In 1974 Bunch had been appointed to the National Gay and Lesbian Task Force, signaling her strong belief in the importance of moving away from separatism and building coalitions.

36. Rossi, *Feminists in Politics*, p. 178.

37. Tanya Melich, *The Republican War Against Women: An Insider's Report from Behind the Lines* (New York: Bantam Books, 1996), quote on p. 87.

38. Melich, *The Republican War Against Women*, quotes on pp. 84, 87–88.

39. Beverly Jones, Saturday morning presentation, Transcript of the Sandy Springs Conference, August 12, 1968, copy in author's possession, p. 5. See also Alice Echols, *Daring to Be Bad* (Minneapolis: University of Minnesota Press 1989), Appendix A.

40. Judy Brown, Saturday morning presentation, Transcript of the Sandy Springs Conference, August 1968, p. 8.

41. Transcript of the Sandy Springs Conference, August 1968.

42. The New York women, who had coined the term, insisted that consciousness-raising had nothing to do with therapy. Rather it was a method of developing theory and defining a political position. Others found the expression of feelings so powerful that they resisted any rigid imposition of either method or goals.

43. Helen Kritzler, Marilyn Salzman Webb, Charlotte Bunch Weeks, and Laya Firestone, "Conference Summary and Impressions of Workshops," mimeograph, Washington, D.C., December 20, 1968. Copy in author's possession. The workshop on sex presaged the lesbian themes that would soon be so divisive and that, in turn, lay at the center of cultural feminism. Shulamith Firestone argued that pregnancy was inherently oppressive to women and that artificial reproduction was essential to liberation (a view she expounded in greater detail in her book, *The Dialectics of Sex*). This was one of the most far-reaching efforts to explore the implications of a radical feminist commitment to the elimination of sex roles. Firestone's workshop coleader, Anne Koedt, presented her pathbreaking article, "The Myth of the Vaginal Orgasm," which proved, eventually, to be a foundational piece for the emergence of lesbian feminism. At that workshop, however, as participants moved into a consciousness-raising mode, exploring personal experiences and fantasies, they recognized that lesbianism was a prominent source of anxiety. Probing the sources of this fear, they reported a tentative conclusion that their erotic fantasies were a product of the sexualization of the female body in American culture while their anxieties expressed a reluctance to be identified with an oppressed group (lesbians).

44. "Impressions of Workshops: Alternative Lifestyles," *ibid.*

45. "Impressions of Workshops: Human Expression—Play Workshop," *ibid.*
46. Popkin, *Bread and Roses*, pp. 46–47. Such events proliferated rapidly, marked by a joyful aura of self-discovery. A reporter for *off our backs* marveled about an Atlanta Women's Festival in October 1970 that made her feel "good about being a woman" and "positive about the things we do." Just "knowing that there is a festival going on which is created by, for and about me and my sisters cause we think so much of each other that we want to work and celebrate with each other," left her with a warm afterglow. Jan, "Women's Festival," *off our backs*, vol. 1, no. 13 (November 8, 1970): 12.
47. Maryse Holder, "Another Cuntree: At Last, a Mainstream Female Art Movement," *off our backs*, vol. 3, no. 10 (September 1973): 11–17, quote on 11. Judy Chicago argued that there were "four patterns in women's art," including repeating forms, circular or breast-like forms, organic forms (plants, genitalia, and gardens), and a central aperture (heart of a flower, tunnel, portals, chasms, rifts, and cracks). See Judy Chicago and Edward Lucie-Smith, *Women and Art: Contested Territory* (New York: Watson-Guptill, 1999).
48. "Female Culture/Lesbian Nation," *Ain't I a Woman?* vol. 1, no. 16 (June 4, 1971): 9.
49. Barbara Burris with Kathy Barry, Joann Parent, Terry Moon, Joann DeLor, and Cate Stadelman, "The Fourth World manifesto: An Angry Response to an Imperialist Venture Against the Women's Liberation Movement," mimeograph, Detroit, January 13, 1971, p. 15. This paper was written in criticism of the "anti-imperialist women" who organized a meeting between Indo-Chinese women and Women's Liberation. The authors claimed that "anti-imperialist women" were using the autonomous women's movement and preventing the Vietnamese women from full access to the burgeoning movement. It was the clash at this meeting in Toronto that also precipitated the formation of the Charlotte Perkins Gilman chapter of NAAM when members of a Durham CR group felt criticized from both sides.
50. *Ibid.*, p. 27.
51. The claim that women were a "colony" had been employed at least since 1966, when a women's caucus in SDS made a similar assertion. In this instance, the definition of women as a "Fourth World" suggested that they were even more oppressed than the colonized, non-Western "Third World." The further step, however, of identifying that Fourth World with a "female culture" based on "the female principle" led the authors farther than they may have realized from the radical feminist emphasis on abolishing sex roles.
52. Adrienne Rich, "The Anti-Feminist Woman," *New York Review of Books* (November 30, 1972), reprinted in Adrienne Rich, *Open Lies, Secrets, and Silence: Selected Prose 1966–1978* (New York: W.W. Norton & Company, 1979), pp. 67–88, quotes on pp. 71, 83–84. In the article, Rich concludes the latter quote with "(and with the ghostly woman in all men)," a sentiment she questioned in 1979.
53. Elizabeth Gould Davis, *The First Sex* (New York: Putnam, 1971). This theory of a "golden age" has not been supported by subsequent scholarship.

54. Rich, "The Anti-Feminist Woman," 76.

55. Adrienne Rich, "Trying to Talk with a Man," *Diving into the Wreck: Poems 1971–1972* (New York: W.W. Norton & Company, 1973), p. 3.

56. Rita Mae Brown, "Living with Other Women," *Radical Therapist* (April/May 1971): 14.

57. Ginny Berson quoted in "The Muses of Olivia: Our Own Economy, Our Own Song," *off our backs*, vol. 4, no. 9 (August/September 1974): 2.

58. Rita Mae Brown, *Plain Brown Rapper*, pp. 20–21, and Charlotte Bunch, *Passionate Politics*, p. 191.

59. Women's Action Collective, "Statement of Philosophy," adopted by consensus May 21, 1974, quoted in Nancy Whittier, "Turning It Over: Personnel Change in the Columbus, Ohio, Women's Movement 1969–1984," in Myra Marx Ferree and Patricia Yancey Martin, eds., *Feminist Organizations: Harvest of the New Women's Movement* (Philadelphia: Temple University Press, 1995), pp. 180–198, quote on p. 190.

60. Adrienne Rich, "Conditions for Work," in Rich, *On Lies, Secrets, and Silence*, p. 208.

61. Echols, *Daring to Be Bad*, pp. 243–245. On the emergence of new kinds of public space, see Anne Enke, "Locating Feminist Activism: Women's Movement and Public Geographies, Minneapolis–St. Paul, 1968–1980," unpublished Ph.D. Dissertation, University of Minnesota, 1999.

62. "Female Culture/Lesbian Nation," *Ain't I a Woman?*, vol. 1, no. 16 (June 4, 1971): 8.

63. See Adrienne Rich, *Of Woman Born: Motherhood as Experience and Institution* (New York: Norton, 1976).

64. See feminist journals, such as *off our backs*, *Ain't I a Woman?*, *Plexus*, *Lesbian Tide*, and *So's Your Old Woman*, for detailed accounts of conferences, workshops, and cultural events.

65. Marlene Schmitz and Carol Edelson, "National Music Festival," *off our backs*, vol. 5, no. 6 (July 1975): 1.

66. Ginny Berson, "First National Women's Music Festival," *off our backs*, vol. 4, no. 8 (July 1974): 2.

67. Dorothy Dean, "A Growing Sense of Breaking New Ground," *off our backs*, vol. 4, no. 8 (July 1974): 3. See also Mary Spottswood Pou, "Giving Music Back to Its Muses," *off our backs*, vol. 4, no. 8 (July 1974): 3.

68. Schmitz and Edelson, "National Music Festival," *off our backs*, vol. 5, no. 6 (July 1975): 1, 18–21. Schmitz repeated the point the following year with a note indicating that she was no longer surprised. "National Music Festival's Third Refrain," *off our backs*, vol. 6, no. 5 (July–August 1976): 14.

69. Georgia Christgau, "Does the Women's Movement Have a Sense of Rhythm?" *Ms.*, vol. 4, no. 6 (December 1975): 39–43, quote on 42.

70. Nancy Stix, "Southwest Feminist Festival," *Big Mama Rag*, vol. 1, no. 4 (ca. April 1973): 15.

71. Debbie Squires, "Southwest Feminist Festival," *Big Mama Rag*, vol. 1, no. 4 (ca. April 1973): 15.

72. Natalie Reuss, "Redwoods, Lovely Women, New Culture," *off our backs*, vol. 4, no. 10 (October 1974): 25.

73. Judith Niemi, "Woman's Music and Free Living," *So's Your Old Lady*, no. 15 (December 1976): 10.

74. Lee Garlington, "Making Music in Michigan Mud," *off our backs*, vol. 7, no. 8 (October 1977): 22.

75. Shirley Hargrove, " . . .'Sweet Honey in the Rock,'" *Big Mama Rag*, vol. 5, no. 7 (August–September 1977): 13–14.

76. For a discussion of feminism and transgendered people, including debates at the Women's Music Festival, see Leslie Feinberg, *Transgender Liberation: Beyond Pink or Blue* (Boston: Beacon Press, 1998).

77. *Off our backs'* fulsome coverage of the festival is a window onto these various debates, their resolutions, and the decisions of the festival organizers. See Niemi, "Woman's Music and Free Living," Lee Garlinton, "Making Music in Michigan Mud," and Mary Fridley, "Commentary: Women's Culture or Mass Culture," *off our backs*, vol. 7, no. 9 (November 1977): 14; The womyn of We Want the Music Collective, "Dear Sisters," *off our backs*, vol. 8, no. 1 (January 1978): 17; Tacie Dejanikus, "Michigan Festival: Music, Matriarchy, Malelessness," *off our backs*, vol. 10, no. 9 (October 1980): 12–13, 17.

78. Sue Dove Gambill, "Letter to the editor," *off our backs*, vol. 10, no. 10 (November 1980): 23.

79. Dejanikus, "Michigan Festival," 17.

80. Nancy Matthews, "Feminist Clash with the State: Tactical Choices by State-Funded Rape Crisis Centers," in Myra Marx Ferree and Patricia Yancey Martin, eds., *Feminist Organizations: Harvest of the New Women's Movement* (Philadelphia: Temple University Press, 1995), p. 299.

81. Women's Advocates, *Newsletter*, vol. v, no. 3 (July 1987): p. 3.

82. Interview with Sharon Vaughan, May 1, 1998.

83. Carol Lease, Sandia, Janet Sergei, and Jackie St. Joan, "Discussion: Dissolution in the Women's Movement," *Big Mama Rag*, vol. 7, no. 5 (June 1979): 9.

84. Jill Zahnheiser, "Feminist Collectives: The Transformation of Women's Businesses in the Counterculture of the 1970s and 1980s," Ph.D. dissertation, University of Iowa, 1985.

85. Pat Wagner, "Effecting Change Through Choice," *Big Mama Rag*, vol. 7, no. 5 (June 1979): 10.

86. Sandia, "Why Does Everything Seem to Fall Apart?" *Big Mama Rag*, vol. 7, no. 5 (June 1979): 11.

87. Quoted in Ann Hunter Popkin, "Bread and Roses: An Early Moment in the Development of Socialist-Feminism," unpublished Ph.D. Dissertation, Sociology, Brandeis University, 1978, p. 102.

88. *Ibid.*, Chapter IV, pp. 89–138.

89. Margaret Strobel, "Organizational Learning in the Chicago Women's Liberation Union," in Myra Marx Ferree and Patricia Yancey Martin, eds., *Feminist Organizations: Harvest of the New Women's Movement* (Philadelphia: Temple University Press, 1995), pp. 146–148, 162. Many original documents from the CWLU may be found at the following website: http://scriptorium.lib.duke.edu/wlm/.

90. Leadership of CWLU included Heather Booth, Amy Kesselman, Vivian Rothstein, and Day Piercy (Creamer), all of whom had extensive organizing experience in the civil rights movement and SDS community organizing projects.

91. Chicago Women's Liberation Union, "Socialist Feminism: A Strategy for the Women's Movement" (Hyde Park Chapter, Chicago Women's Liberation Union, 1972), quotes on p. 1. This document may be found in the Women's Liberation Collection at the Duke University Rare Book, Manuscript, and Special Collections Library and online at http://scriptorium.lib.duke.edu/wlm/socialist.

92. "Signal of a New Harmony: Women's Conference," *New American Movement*, vol. 2, no. 4 (January 1973): 5. This conference was called by the New American Movement, which was founded in 1971 by former student activists wanting an "adult" organization that could provide an ongoing vehicle for political activism even as the student movement disintegrated. From the outset, feminism was one agenda of NAM.

93. Barbara Ehrenreich, "Speech," *Socialist Revolution*, no. 26 (October–December 1975): 92.

94. See Karen V. Hansen, "The Women's Unions and the Search for a Political Identity," *Socialist Review*, vol. 16, no. 2 (March–April 1986): 67–95.

95. "Socialist-Feminist Conference—San Diego, 3/24," *Berkeley/Oakland Women's Union Newsletter*, vol. 2, no. 3 (April 26, 1974): 9, quoted in Hansen, "The Women's Unions," 81.

96. Hansen, "The Women's Unions," 77. See, for example, Bernice, "Chicago News: c.w.l.u.," *off our backs*, vol. 5, no. 1 (January 1975): 20.

97. Perhaps the most important of these was a paper by Peggy Somers and Kathryn Johnson that challenged the place of "reproduction" in classical Marxism, arguing that reproduction was coequal with the sphere of production in shaping human societies and the dynamics of historical change. Their work anticipated the later influential theoretical work of Joan Kelly-Gadol, Heidi Hartmann, Alice Kessler-Harris, Zillah Eisenstein, and others.

98. Barbara Dudley, "Report on the Conference," *Socialist Revolution*, no. 26 (October–December 1975): 90.

99. Quoted in Hansen, 90. According to Barbara Dudley, one of the keynote speakers, "The anti-imperialist caucus, the Marxist-Leninist caucus, the third-world women's caucus, the lesbian caucus, the older women's caucus, etc. presented statements that were not always consistent with socialist-feminism and

were sometimes openly contradictory even to the basic principles of unity of the conference, and yet neither the planning committee nor any other groups systematically responded to these statements. The result was a growing confusion . . . about what socialist-feminism is." Barbara Dudley, "Report on the Conference," *Socialist Revolution*, no. 26 (October–December 1975): 109.

100. Author's interview with Linda Gordon.

101. Author's interview with Alice Kessler-Harris, December 13, 1997.

102. Author's interview with Deborah Rosenfeldt, December 15, 1997, College Park, Maryland.

103. Author's Interview with Alice Kessler-Harris.

104. Rosalyn Baxandall points out that MF1, at least, was so heavily academic that those who were not felt isolated.

105. See, for example, Joan Kelly-Gadol, "The Social Relation of the Sexes: Methodological Implications of Women's History," *Signs*, vol. 1, no. 4 (1976): 809–823. Renate Bridenthal, "The Dialectics of Production and Reproduction in History," *Radical America*, vol. 10, no. 2 (1976): 3–11; Renate Bridenthal and Claudia Koonz, eds., *Becoming Visible: Women in European History* (Boston: Houghton Mifflin, 1977); Linda Gordon, *Woman's Body, Woman's Right: A Social History of Birth Control in America* (New York: Grossman, 1976); "What Should Women's Historians Do?: Politics, Social Theory, and Women's History," *Marxist Perspectives*, vol. 1, no. 3 (1978): 128–137; *The New Feminist Scholarship on the Welfare State* (Madison: University of Wisconsin–Madison, Institute for Research on Poverty, 1989); Alice Kessler-Harris, *Out to Work: A History of Wage-Earning Women in the United States* (New York: Oxford University Press, 1982).

106. See Blanche Weisen Cook, *Dwight David Eisenhower: Antimilitarist in the White House* (St. Charles, MO: Forum Press, 1974); *Eleanor Roosevelt* (New York: Viking, 1992/1999); Donna Haraway, *Primate Visions: Gender, Race, and Nature in the World of Modern Science* (New York: Routledge, 1989); *Simians, Cyborgs, and Women: The Reinvention of Nature* (New York: Routledge, 1991).

107. See Heidi I. Hartmann, ed., *Comparable Worth: New Directions for Research* (Washington, D.C.: National Academy Press, 1985); Robert T. Michael, Heidi I. Hartmann, and Brigid O'Farrell, eds., *Pay Equity: Empirical Enquiries* (Washington, D.C.: National Academy Press, 1989); Barbara F. Reskin and Heidi I. Hartmann, eds., *Women's Work, Men's Work: Sex Segregation on the Job* (Washington, D.C.: National Academy Press, 1986); and Donald J. Treiman and Heidi I. Hartmann, eds., *Women, Work, and Wages: Equal Pay for Jobs of Equal Value* (Washington, D.C.: National Academy Press, 1981).

108. Miriam Lynnell Harris, "From Kennedy to Combahee: Black Feminist Activism from 1960 to 1980," unpublished Ph.D. Dissertation, American Studies, University of Minnesota, 1997), pp. 113–118.

109. Barbara Smith, "Dear Sisters," *off our backs*, vol. 9, no. 10 (November 1979): 13.

110. See Claudia Dreifus, "Sterilizing the Poor," in Claudia Dreifus, ed., *Seizing Our Bodies: The Politics of Women's Health* (New York: Vintage, 1977), pp. 105–120.

111. See Rosalind P. Petchesky, *Abortion and Woman's Choice: The State, Sexuality, and Reproductive Freedom* (New York: Longman, 1984). On the origins of CARASA, see Meredith Tax, "'Bread and Roses! Bread and Roses!" in Rachel Blau DuPlessis and Ann Snitow, eds., *The Feminist Memoir Project: Voices from Women's Liberation* (New York: Three Rivers Press, 1998), pp. 312–324, and Davis, *Moving the Mountain*, pp. 249–251.

112. Hope Landrine, "Culture, Feminist Racism and Feminist Classism: Blaming the Victim: commentary," *off our backs*, vol. 9, no. 10 (November 1979): 2–3.

113. See Harry C. Boyte, Heather Booth, and Steve Max, *Citizen Action and the New American Populism* (Philadelphia: Temple University Press, 1986).

114. See the IWPR website for a list of their publications: www.iwpr.org.

115. Interview with Deborah Rosenfeldt, College Park, Maryland, December 15, 1997.

116. Deborah Rosenfeldt, "The Founding Convention," typed manuscript in author's possession, June 23, 1977, p. 1.

117. Rosenfeldt, "The Founding Convention," p. 5. See also Robin Leidner, "Stretching the Boundaries of Liberalism: Democratic Innovation in a Feminist Organization," *Signs: Journal of Women in Culture and Society*, vol. 16, no. 2 (Winter 1991): 263–289.

118. Quoted in Catharine R. Stimpson with Nina Kressner Cobb, *Women's Studies in the United States: A Report to the Ford Foundation* (New York: Ford Foundation, 1986), p. 27.

119. P.M., "First National Women's Studies Conference: A Lesbian Perspective," *off our backs* (August–September 1979): 33.

120. Toni White, "Lesbian Studies Flourish at National Women's Studies Conference," *off our backs*, vol. 10, no. 7 (July 1980): 16.

121. White, "Lesbian Studies Flourish at National Women's Studies Conference," 18; and Nancy Polikoff, "Addressing Racism," *off our backs*, vol. 10, no. 7 (July 1980): 18.

122. Author's interview with Caryn McTighe Musil, Washington, D.C., November 11, 1997.

123. Donald Mathews and Jane Sherron De Hart, *Sex, Gender, and the Politics of ERA* (New York: Oxford University Press, 1990), quote on p. 173.

124. See Faye Ginzburg, *Contested Lives: The Abortion Debate in an American Community*. (Berkeley: University of California Press, 1989).

125. Quoted in Melich, p. 87.

126. Davis, *Moving the Mountain*, pp. 149–151.

127. Interview with Millie Jeffry by Ruth Pollak, June 24, 1997.

128. Sonia Johnson, *From Housewife to Heretic: One Woman's Spiritual Awakening and Her Excommunication from the Mormon Church* (Garden City, NY: Doubleday Books, 1981), p. 105.

129. See August 5, 1978, editions of *Los Angeles Times*, I:18; *Washington Post*, A5; *San Francisco Chronicle*, 5; *St. Paul Pioneer Press/Dispatch*, 10.

130. Johnson, *From Housewife to Heretic*, p. 165.

131. Johnson, *From Housewife to Heretic*, pp. 157–158.

132. Gloria Steinem, 1978 article (July *Ms.*) quoted in Thom, p. 147.

133. Ann Kolker, "Women Lobbyists," in Irene Tinker, ed., *Women in Washington*, p. 217.

134. See, for example, Diane K. Lewis, "A Response to Inequality: Black Women, Racism, and Sexism," *Signs*, vol. 3, no. 2 (Winter 1977): 339–361; Margaret A. Simons, "Racism and Feminism: A Schism in the Sisterhood," *Feminist Studies*, vol. 5, no. 2 (Summer 1979): 389–410. On the more visible emergence of black feminist groups, see Barbara Smith, "Dear Sisters," *off our backs*, vol. 9, no. 10 (November 1979): 13; MANA, which had been an active lobbying group in the early and middle 1970s, decided around 1977 to encourage local chapters around the country. Interview with Eliza Sanchez, Washington, D.C., February 19, 1998.

135. Rusty Cramer, "Bunch on Feminism: Another Closet," *Plexus*, vol. 6, no. 1 (March 1979): 1. For another thoughtful reassessment see Nancy C. M. Hartsock, "Feminism, Power, and Change: A Theoretical Analysis," in Bernice Cummings and Victoria Schuck, eds., *Women Organizing: An Anthology* (Methuen, NJ: Scarecrow Press, 1979), pp. 2–24.

Chapter 6

1. Interview with Leslie Wolfe, Washington, D.C., December 12, 1997.

2. These themes became political issues subject to policy-oriented debate as a result of feminist activism, but it is worth noting that in the early Cold War years following the Second World War, American propaganda had frequently linked family life and domesticity to the superiority of the United States. See Elaine Tyler May, *Homeward Bound: American Families in the Cold War Era* (Chicago: University of Chicago Press, 1980). On the so-called "epidemic" of teen pregnancy, see Maris Vinovskis, *An Epidemic of Adolescent Pregnancy? Some Historical and Policy Considerations* (New York: Oxford University Press, 1988). Vinovskis shows that there were far more teen pregnancies in the 1950s than in the 1970s. The difference was that in the 1950s, pregnant teens got married.

3. See John L. Palmer and Isabel V. Sawhill, eds., *The Reagan Record: An Assessment of America's Changing Domestic Priorities* (Cambridge, MA.: Ballinger Publishing Company, 1984); Michael Schaller, *Reckoning with Reagan: America and Its President in the 1980s* (New York: Oxford University Press, 1992).

4. See Barbara Ryan, *Feminism and the Women's Movement: Dynamics of Change in Social Movement, Ideology and Activism* (New York: Routledge, 1992), pp. 76–77; Davis, *Moving the Mountain*, p. 384; Jane J. Mansbridge, *Why We Lost*

the ERA (Chicago: University of Chicago Press, 1986), pp. 153–154, 166. For an example of media coverage, see "As Time Runs Out for the E.R.A., Eight Women Stage an Ordeal by Hunger in the Illinois Capitol," *People*, vol. 17 (June 28, 1982): 93–94.

5. Mansbridge, *Why We Lost the ERA*; Mary Berry, *Why ERA Failed: Politics, Women's Rights, and the Amending Process of the Constitution* (Bloomington: Indiana University Press, 1986); Donald Mathews and Jane De Hart, *Sex, Gender and the Politics of ERA: A State and the Nation* (New York: Oxford University Press, 1990).

6. For example, Sonia Johnson, the Mormon housewife who suffered excommunication for challenging her church's opposition to the ERA, by 1988 had renounced the use of "the tolls of patriarchy to free ourselves from it. . . . Now instead of patching up and reforming the system men have made, now instead of trying to persuade the men—either by kindness or threats—to give me what I desire, I want to be among the women who independently create the world that women want and need. Such a world would benefit every living thing." Sonia Johnson, "Preface to the Fourth Edition," *From Housewife to Heretic: One Woman's Spiritual Awakening and Her Excommunication from the Mormon Church*, 4th ed. (Albuquerque, NM: Wildfire Books, 1989).

7. Charles L. Heatherly, ed., *Mandate for Leadership: Policy Management in a Conservative Administration* (Washington, D.C.: Heritage Foundation, 1981).

8. Ronald F. Docksai, "The Department of Education," in Heatherly, ed., *Mandate for Leadership*, pp. 179–180.

9. Heritage Foundation, "A Brief Look at the Women's Educational Equity Act (WEEA)," Washington D.C. (1984), copy in the files of Leslie Wolfe.

10. Interview with Leslie Wolfe, Washington, D.C., December 12, 1997.

11. Heritage Foundation, "A Brief Look," p. 14.

12. Interview with Leslie Wolfe.

13. Wolfe interview. Article in *Tulsa World* (May 20, 1982), quoted in Theresa Cusic, "A Clash of Ideologies: The Reagan Administration Versus the Women's Educational Equity Act," Washington D.C.: Project on Equal Education Rights, Summer 1983. Additional accounts of these events include Susan Faludi, *Backlash*, pp. 259–263; Judith Paterson, "Equity in Exile: The Reagan War on Equality," *Ms.* (November 1984): 18–20; Joy R. Dimonson and Jeffrey A. Menzer, "Catching up: A Review of the Women's Educational Equity Act Program," Washington, D.C.: Citizens Council on Women's Education, A Project of the National Coalition for Women and Girls in Education, February 1984.

14. Interview with Wolfe.

15. Interview with Wolfe.

16. Leslie R. Wolfe to WEEA Project Directors, Washington, D.C., September 16, 1983. The letter begins, "I am writing to you for the last time as Director of the Women's Educational Equity Act (WEEA) Program."

17. See Faludi, *Backlash*, pp. 259-263.

18. *New York Times* (January 22, 1984): Section I, 1. For a detailed discussion of the arguments for and against comparable worth, see Sara M. Evans and Barbara J. Nelson, *Wage Justice: Comparable Worth and the Paradox of Technocratic Reform* (Chicago: University of Chicago Press: 1989), especially chapter 3, "What Is At Stake?"

19. "Concept of Pay Based on Worth Is the 'Looniest,' Rights Chief Says," *New York Times*, (November 17, 1984): 15.

20. Julie Hairston, "Killing Kittens, Bombing Clinics," *Southern Exposure*, vol. 18, no. 2 (1990): 14-18.

21. "Facts on Reproductive Rights: A Resource Manual," NOW Legal Defense and Education Fund, Fact Sheet no. 11, 1989.

22. Sandra Morgen, "'It was the Best of Times, It Was the Worst of Times': Emotional Discourse in the Work Cultures of Feminist Health Clinics," in Myra Marx Ferree and Patricia Yancey Martin, eds., *Feminist Organizations: Harvest of the New Women's Movement* (Philadelphia: Temple University Press, 1995), pp. 234-247.

23. Between 1980 and 1989, total funding for higher education fell 24.3 percent (measured in constant dollars) while costs rose 33.6 percent for public colleges and 44.7 percent for 4 year private colleges. National Education Association, *The 1992 Almanac of Higher Education* (Washington, D.C.: National Education Association, 1992), p. 161.

24. Howard J. Erlich, *Campus Ethnoviolence and the Policy Options* (Baltimore: National Institute Against Prejudice and Violence, 1990), pp. 41-72.

25. Stimpson and Cobb, *Women's Studies in the United States*, p. 50. See also *Chronicle of Higher Education* (May 19, 1982): 8; *Feminist Studies*, vol. 9, no. 1 (Spring 1983): 603.

26. See Susan Faludi, *Backlash: The Undeclared War Against American Women* (New York: Crown Publishers, 1991).

27. Alex Taylor III, "Why Women Managers Are Bailing out," *Fortune* (August 18, 1986): 16-23.

28. Felice N. Schwartz, "Management Women and the New Facts of Life," *Harvard Business Review* 67(January/February 1989): 65-76; Barbara Kantrowitz, "Advocating a 'Mommy Track': An Expert on Career Woman Stirs up a Controversy," *Newsweek*, vol. 113, no. 11 (March 13, 1989): 45(1).

29. Jolie Solomon, "The Invisible Barrier Is Crystal Clear to Many," *Wall Street Journal* (April 20, 1990): B1.

30. Harry Waters, "Games Singles Play," *Newsweek* 82(July 16, 1973): 52-58.

31. Quoted in Faludi, *Backlash*, p.99.

32. Nancy Rubin, "Women vs. Women," *Ladies Home Journal*, vol. XCIX, no. 4 (August 1982): 94-96, 100-103.

33. Carrie Rickey, "Twilight of the Reaganauts," *Tikkun*, vol. 4, no. 6 (November/December 1989): 49-52.

34. Susan Brownmiller, *Femininity* (New York: Fawcett Columbine, 1985), p. 17.

35. Nancy Whittier, *Feminist Generations: The Persistence of the Radical Women's Movement* (Philadelphia: Temple University Press, 1995), p. 198; Ryan, *Feminism and the Women's Movement*, pp. 140–144.

36. See Susan Bolotin, "Voices from the Post-Feminist Generation." *New York Times Magazine*, (October 17, 1982); Eloise Salholz, "Feminism's Identity Crisis," *Newsweek*, 107(March 31, 1986): 58–59.

37. Faludi, *Backlash*, p. 111.

38. For analyses of the history of *Ms.*, see Amy Erdman Farrell, *Yours in Sisterhood: Ms. Magazine and the Promise of Popular Feminism* (Chapel Hill: University of North Carolina Press, 1998); and Mary Thom, *Inside Ms: 25 Years of the Magazine and the Women's Movement* (New York: Henry Holt, 1997).

39. George Gilder, "An Open Letter to Orrin Hatch," *National Review*, vol. 40, no. 9 (May 13, 1988): 33–34.

40. E. J. Dionne, Jr., *Why Americans Hate Politics* (New York: Simon and Schuster, 1991), pp. 105–106.

41. Paula Kamen, *Feminist Fatale: Voices from the "Twentysomething" Generation Explore the Future of the Women's Movement* (New York: Donald I. Fine, 1991), quotes on pp. 1, 6, 2.

42. Amy E. Schwartz, "A Decade of Unlearning," *Tikkun*, vol. 4, no. 6 (November/December 1989): 56.

43. Author's interview with Arrington Chambliss, Minneapolis, Minnesota, September 6, 1993.

44. Jesse Donahue, "Movement Scholarship and Feminism in the 1980s," *Women & Politics*, vol. 61, no. 2 (1996): 61–80; on NOW see also Paula Kamen, *Feminist Fatale*, pp. 99–100.

45. Jeannine Delombard, "Femmenism," in Rebecca Walker, ed., *To Be Real: Telling the Truth and Changing the Face of Feminism* (New York: Anchor Books, 1995), pp. 24–25.

46. Ethel Klein, *Gender Politics: From Consciousness to Mass Politics* (Cambridge, MA: Harvard University Press, 1984), p. 30; R. Darcy, Susan Welch, and Janet Clark, *Women, Elections, & Representation* (Lincoln: University of Nebraska Press, 1994).

47. Byllye Y. Avery, "Breathing Life into Ourselves: The Evolution of the National Black Women's Health Project," in Evelyn C. White, ed., *The Black Women's Health Book: Speaking for Ourselves* (Seattle, WA: Seal Press, 1990), pp. 4–11, quotes on pp. 7, 8.

48. Susan Cahn, *Coming on Strong: Gender and Sexuality in Twentieth Century Women's Sport* (New York: Free Press, 1994), pp. 258–260.

49. William P. Lawrence, "Clearing the Legal Way for Women in Combat," *Washington Post*, (July 28, 1991, C): 7; Eric Schmitt, "War Puts U.S. Service Women Closer than Ever to Combat," *New York Times* (January 22, 1991, A): 1, 12, table 6–15; Paula Ries and Anne T. Stone, eds., *The American Woman, 1992–93: A Status Report* (New York: W. W. Norton, 1992), pp. 344–345.

50. 578 F supp. 846 (W.D. Wash, 1983).

51. Evans and Nelson, *Wage Justice*, Chapter 4, Quote on p. 81.

52. Evans and Nelson, *Wage Justice*, pp. 40–41.

53. Patricia Aburdene and John Naisbitt, *Megatrends for Women* (New York: Villard Books, 1992).

54. Aburdene and Naisbitt, *Megatrends for Women*; Judy B. Rosener, "Ways Women Lead," *Harvard Business Review*, 68(November/December 1990): 119–125; Sally Helgeson, "The Pyramid and the Web," *New York Times* (May 27, 1990): III:13.

55. "More Hymn Changes," *Christian Century*, 104(April 15, 1987): 352; "Avoiding Sexism," *Christian Century*, 104(April 22, 1987): 376.

56. Mary Fainsod Katzenstein, "Feminism Within American Institutions: Unobtrusive Mobilization in the 1980s," *Signs: Journals of Women in Culture and Society*, vol. 16 no. 11 (Autumn 1990): 40.

57. Mary Fainsod Katzenstein, "Discursive Politics and Feminist Activism in the Catholic Church." In Ferree, Myra Marx, and Patricia Yancey Martin, eds., *Feminist Organizations: Harvest of the New Women's Movement* (Philadelphia: Temple University Press, 1995), pp. 39–40. See also Rosemary Radford Ruether, *Womanguides: Readings Toward a Feminist Theology* (Boston: Beacon Press, 1985); Mary Fainsod Katzenstein, *Faithful and Fearless: Moving Feminist Protest Inside the Church and Military* (Princeton, NJ: Princeton University Press, 1998); Gretchen E. Zeigenhals, "Meeting the Women of Women-Church." *Christian Century* (May 10, 1989): 492–94.

58. Barbara Moral and Karen Schwarz, "Living on the Edge: Women and Catholic," *Probe*, vol. 15, no. 4 (September/October 1987): 3.

59. Katzenstein, *Feminism Within American Institutions*, pp. 42–43.

60. See *Daughters of Sarah*, volumes 6–16, 1980–1990, Social Welfare History Archives, University of Minnesota, Minneapolis.

61. Author's interview with Lael Stegall, Washington, D.C., February 19, 1998.

62. We should note that this "loophole" has been a target of campaign finance reformers who point out that until the advent of Emily's List it was primarily used by corporate executives who would "expect" hefty checks from their administrative staff and then send them, bundled, to the party or candidate they wished to influence.

63. Author's telephone interview with Ellen Malcolm, August 31, 2000.

64. Joan E. McLean, "Emily's List," in Sarah Slavin, ed., *U.S. Women's Interest Groups* (Westport, CT: Greenwood Press, 1995), pp. 175–176.

65. Margaret M. Keenan, "The Controversy over Women's Studies," *Princeton Alumni Weekly*, vol. 80, no. 16 (April 21, 1980): 12–18, quote on 15.

66. Mariam K. Chamberlain, *Women in Academe: Progress and Prospects* (New York: Russell Sage Foundation, 1988).

67. Academic feminist journals began in the 1970s with *Signs* and *Feminist Studies*, both of which were interdisciplinary. By the late 1980s there were journals of feminist sociology, literary criticism, history, political science, philosophy, and numerous other specialties.

68. Barbara Findlen, *Listen up: Voices from the Next Feminist Generation* (Seattle, WA: Seal Press, 1995); and Rebecca Walker, ed., *To Be Real: Telling the Truth and Changing the Face of Feminism* (New York: Anchor Books, 1995).

69. See Virginia Cyrus, "Report from the Chair of the Steering Committee," *National Women's Studies Association Newsletter I* (Spring 1983). The coordinating council accepted the resignation of the last in a series of national coordinators and dissolved a costly relationship with the Feminist Press to attain some control of its budget. Each such decision was, of course, a subject of debate and conflict.

70. Interview with Musil; Catharine R. Stimpson, with Nina Kressner Cobb, *Women's Studies in the United States* (New York: Ford Foundation, 1986); and Robin Leidner, "Stretching the Boundaries of Liberalism: Democratic Innovation in a Feminist Organization," *Signs: Journal of Women in Culture and Society*, vol. 16, no. 2: 263–289.

71. Sara M. Evans and Barbara J. Nelson, *Wage Justice: Comparable Worth and the Paradox of Technocratic Reform* (Chicago: University of Chicago Press, 1989).

72. See Adele M. Stan, *Debating Sexual Correctness*; Mary Kay Blakely, "Is One Woman's Sexuality Another Woman's Pornography?" *Ms.*, vol. 13, no. 10 (April 1985); *Feminist Studies*, vol. 9, no. 1 (Spring 1983): 177–182 and vol. 9, no. 3 (Fall 1983): 589–602.

73. Mary Kay Blakely, "Is One Woman's Sexuality Another Woman's Pornography?" *Ms.*, vol. 13, no. 10 (April 1985): 37–47, 120–123; and Barbara Ehrenreich, Elizabeth Hess, and Gloria Jacobs, "A Report on the Sex Crisis," *Ms.*, vol. 10, no. 9 (March 1982): 61–64, 87–88. See Carole S. Vance, *Pleasure and Danger: Exploring Female Sexuality* (Boston: Routledge & K. Paul, 1984); Ann Snitow, Christine Stansell, and Sharon Thompson, *Powers of Desire: The Politics of Sexuality* (New York: Monthly Review Press, 1983); and Estelle B. Freedman and Barrie Thorne, "Introduction to 'The Feminist Sexuality Debates,'" *Signs: Journal of Women in Culture and Society*, vol. 10, no. 1 (Autumn 1984): 102–105. The latter argue that hostility around this issue is "more charged than that of the gay-straight split of the early 1970s."

74. Audre Lorde, "The Role of Difference."

75. Seventh Annual the Scholar and the Feminist Conference at Barnard, New York City, April 12, 1980. Topic: "Class, Race and Sex—Exploring Contradictions, Affirming Connection," *off our backs*, vol. 10, no. 6 (June 1980): 10.

76. See, for example, Jane Gallop, *Around 1981: Academic Feminist Literary Theory* (London and New York: Routledge, 1992).

77. For an excellent anthology of theoretical writings from the U.S., Britain, and France, see Sandra Kemp and Judith Squires, eds., *Feminisms* (Oxford and New York: Oxford University Press, 1997); quotes from Introduction, p. 7.

78. For one of the strongest assertions that the category "women" carries an underlying, and dangerous, essentialism, see Denise Riley, *Am I that Name? Feminism and the Category of "Women" in History* (New York: Macmillan, 1988).

79. See Bonnie Thornton Dill, "Race, Class, and Gender: Prospects for an All Inclusive Sisterhood," *Feminist Studies*, vol. 9, no. 1 (Spring 1983): 131–150; Maria C. Lugones and Elizabeth V. Spelman, "Have We Got a Theory for You! Feminist Theory, Cultural Imperialism, and the Demand for 'The Woman's Voice,'" *Women's Studies International Forum*, vol. 6, no. 6 (1983): 573–581; Audre Lorde, *Sister Outsider* (Trumansburg, NY: Crossing Press, 1984); Gloria T. Hull, Patricia Bell Scott, and Barbara Smith, eds., *All The Women Are White, All the Blacks Are Men, but Some of Us Are Brave* (Old Westbury, CT: Feminist Press, 1982); *Conditions: Five, the Black Women's Issue*, vol. 2, no. 2 (Autumn 1979); Beverly Smith with Judith Stein and Priscilla Golding, "The Possibility of Life Between Us: A Dialogue Between Black and Jewish Women," *Conditions: Seven*, vol. 3, no. 1 (Spring 1981): 25–46; Bell Hooks, *Feminist Theory: From Margin to Center* (Boston: South End Press, 1984); Cherrie Moraga and Gloria Anzaldua, eds., *This Bridge Called My Back: Writings by Radical Women of Color* (Watertown, NY: Persephone Press, 1981); Elly Bulkin, Minnie Bruce Pratt, and Barbara Smith, *Yours in Struggle: Three Feminist Perspectives on Anti-Semitism and Racism* (Brooklyn: Long Haul Press, 1984); Marilyn Frye, *The Politics of Reality: Essays in Feminist Theory* (Trumansburg, NY: Crossing Press, 1983).
80. Moraga and Anzaldua, *This Bridge Called My Back*.
81. Bernice Johnson Reagon, "Coalition Politics: Turning the Century," in Barbara Smith, ed., *Home Girls: A Black Feminist Anthology* (New York: Kitchen Table Press, 1983), p. 357.
82. Cherrie Moraga quoted in "This Bridge Moves Feminists," *oob*, vol. 12, no. 4 (April 1982): 5.
83. Suzanne Staggenborg, "Can Feminist Organizations Be Effective?" in Myra Marx Ferree and Patricia Yancey Martin, eds., *Feminist Organizations: Harvest of the New Women's Movement* (Philadelphia: Temple University Press, 1995), pp. 339–355.
84. See Kath Weston, *Families We Choose: Lesbians, Gays, Kinship* (New York: Columbia University Press, 1991), and *Render Me, Gender Me: Lesbians Talk Sex, Class, Color, Nation, Studmuffins* (New York: Columbia University Press, 1996).
85. Carolyn Merchant, "Earthcare," *Environment*, vol. 23, no. 5 (June 1981): 11.
86. *Ibid.*
87. See Rosemary Radford Reuther, *New Woman? New Earth: Sexist Ideologies and Human Liberation* (New York: Seabury Press, 1975); Mary Daly, *Gyn/Ecology: The Metaethics of Radical Feminism* (Boston: Beacon Press, 1978); Susan Griffin, *Woman and Nature: The Roaring Inside Her* (New York: Harper & Row, 1978); Nancy Choderow, *The Reproduction of Mothering: Psychoanalysis and the Sociology of Gender* (Berkeley: University of California Press, 1978). For this analysis of the origins and evolution of ecofeminism I am indebted to Catronia Sandilands, *The Good-Natured Feminist: Ecofeminism and the Quest for*

Democracy (Minneapolis: University of Minnesota Press, 1999), chapter 1, "A Genealogy of Ecofeminism," pp. 3–27. See also Carolyn Merchant, *Earthcare: Women and the Environment* (New York: Routledge, 1995).

88. Susan Griffin, *Woman and Nature*, p. 227.

89. Ynestra King, "The Eco-feminist Imperative (May 1981)," in Leonie Caldecott and Stephanie Leland, eds., *Reclaim the Earth: Women Speak out for Life on Earth* (London: Women's Press, 1993), quoted in Sandilands, *The Good-Natured Feminist*, p. 15.

90. See, for example, Charlene Spretnak, ed., *The Politics of Women's Spirituality* (Garden City, NY: Doubleday/Anchor, 1982); Starhawk, *Truth or Dare: Encounters with Power, Authority and Mystery* (New York: Harper & Row, 1987).

91. See Lindsy Van Gelder, "It's Not Nice to Mess with Mother Nature," *Ms.*, vol. 17, nos. 7, 8 (January/February, 1989): 60–63.

92. Louise Krasniewicz, *Nuclear Summer: The Clash of Communities at Seneca Women's Peace Encampment* (New York: Cornell University Press, 1992).

93. Riane Tennenhaus Eisler, *The Chalice and the Blade: Our History, Our Future* (Cambridge, MA: Harper & Row, 1987).

94. "In Worship, Methodists Want Tradition," *Washington Post*, June 18, 1990, G–7.

95. The Vatican refused to allow these translations to be used in Catholic liturgies in the United States (see Fox, 1994). Newspapers editorialized against the "PC Bible" as well (See, for example, "PC Bible" *Wall Street Journal*, September 5, 1995, p. A:14).

96. Steinfels, 1991; "World-Wide: A Lesbian Minister," *Wall Street Journal*, November 5, 1992, p. A:1.

97. See William J. Bennett, "The Chattered Humanities," *Wall Street Journal*, 31 (December 1982): 10; and *To Reclaim a Legacy: A Report on the Humanities in Higher Education* (Washington, D.C.: National Endowment for the Humanities, 1984) and Lynne V. Cheney, *The Humanities and the American Promise: A Report of the Colloquium on the Humanities and the American People* (Charlottesville, VA: Colloquium on the Humanities and the American People, 1987); *Humanities in America: A Report to the President, the Congress, and the American People* (Washington, D.C.: National Endowment for the Humanities, 1988).

98. Ellen Messer-Davidow notes that "in 1987, when Cheney's first report was published, mass-market books attacking liberalized higher education began to appear at the impressive rate of two per year." Ellen Messer-Davidow, "Manufacturing the Attack on Liberalized Higher Education," *Social Text* 36(Fall 1993): 40. For example, Allan Bloom, *The Closing of the American Mind* (New York: Simon & Schuster, 1987); Charles Sykes, *Profscam: Professors and the Demise of Higher Education* (Washington, D.C.: Regnery Gateway, 1988); Page Smith, *Killing the Spirit: Higher Education in America* (New York: Viking, 1990); Roger Kimball, *Tenured Radicals: How Politics Has Corrupted Our Higher*

Education (New York: Harper & Row, 1990); and Dinesh D'Souza, *Illiberal Education: The Politics of Race and Sex on Campus* (New York: Free Press, 1991).

99. Statement on Guerrilla Girls Website: http://www.guerrillagirls.com.

100. See *Confessions of the Guerrilla Girls* (New York: HarperPerennial Library, 1995).

101. From Guerrilla Girls website.

Chapter 7

1. "Bev Mitchell," in Louise R. Noun, *More Strong-Minded Women: Iowa Feminists Tell Their Stories* (Ames: Iowa State University Press, 1992), p. 84.

2. Interview with Bella Abzug, April 24, 1997, http://www.netaxs.com/((;td)) gem/interview_with_bella_abzug.html.

3. Paula Kamen, *Feminist Fatale: Voices from the "Twentysomething" Generation Explore the Future of the Women's Movement* (New York: Donald I. Fine, 1991), p. 212.

4. Naomi Wolf, *The Beauty Myth* (London: Chatto & Windus, 1990).

5. Susan Faludi, *Backlash: The Undeclared War Against American Women* (New York: Crown, 1991); Kamen, *Feminist Fatale*.

6. Katherine Bishop, "Women's College Rescinds Its Decision to Admit Men," *New York Times* (May 19, 1990, Section A): 7.

7. Barbara Findlen, ed., *Listen up: The Next Feminist Generation* (Seattle: Seal Press, 1995); Irene Zahava, ed., *Feminism 3: The Third Generation in Fiction* (Boulder, CO: Westview Press, 1996); Rebecca Walker, ed., *To Be Real: Telling the Truth and Changing the Face of Feminism* (New York: Anchor Books, 1995); and Leslie Heywood and Jennifer Drake, eds., *Third Wave Agenda: Being Feminist, Doing Feminism* (Minneapolis: University of Minnesota Press, 1997).

8. Joannie M. Schrof, "Feminism's Daughters," *U.S. News and World Report* (September 27, 1993): 70–71, quoted in Tobias, *Faces of Feminism*, p. 252.

9. Camille Paglia, "Madonna I: Animality and Artifice," *New York Times* (December 14, 1990, A): 39.

10. Her gender and her race, however, will no doubt prevent her from profiting at the same level as world-class male athletes. See Greta L. Cohen, *Women in Sport: Issues and Controversies*, with foreword by Jackie Joyner-Kersee (Newbury Park: Sage Publications, 1993); and Susan K. Cahn, *Coming on Strong: Gender and Sexuality in Twentieth-Century Women's Sport* (New York: Free Press, 1994), pp. 269–271.

11. Kamen, *Feminist Fatale*, pp. 89–92.

12. Melissa Klein, "Duality and Redefinition: Young Feminism and the Alternative Music Community," in Heywood and Drake, eds., *Third Wave Agenda*, pp. 207–225, quotes on pp. 214, 208, 211.

13. Jeff Niesel, "Hip-Hop Matters: Rewriting the Sexual Politics of Rap Music," in Heywood and Drake, eds., *Third Wave Agenda*, pp. 239–253, quote on p. 241.

14. Elisa Davis, "Sexism and the Art of Feminist Hop-Hop Maintenance," in Walker, ed., *To Be Real*, pp. 127–141, quotes on pp. 131, 127.

15. *Hot Flashes*, vol. 1, no. 1 (1993).

16. *Hot Flashes*, vol. 1, no. 2, 3 (1994).

17. See Roberta Smith, "Waging Guerilla Warfare Against the Art World, *New York Times* (June 17, 1990, C1): 31; Catherine S. Manegold, "No More Nice Girls," *New York Times* (July 12, 1992, L25): 1, 31; Jessica Seigel, "In Your Face: A New Generation Takes up the Feminist Struggle," *Chicago Tribune* (August 3, 1992: Section 5, Tempo): 1–2; Josephine Withers, "The Guerrilla Girls," *Feminist Studies*, vol. 14, no. 2 (Summer 1988): 284–300; *Confessions of the Guerrilla Girls/by the Guerrilla Girls Themselves (Whoever They Really Are); With an Essay by Whitney Chadwick* (New York: HarperPerennial, 1995).

18. "WAC is watching: Women's Action Coalition on the Streets of Chicago," *oob*, vol. 24, no. 2 (February 1994): 6–7, 16, quote on 6–7. See also Degen Pener, "Blue Dots, a Drum Corps and Great Production Values," *New York Times* (May 3, 1992, Section 9): 4; Karen Houppert, "WAC Attack," *Village Voice* (June 9, 1992): 33–38; and "Guggenheim in a New Light," *New York Times* (June 27, 1992): L13.

19. Quoted by Houppert in *Village Voice* (1992): 34. See also Catherine S. Manegold, "No More Nice Girls," *New York Times* (July 12, 1992, L25); Jessica Seigel, "In Your Face: A New Generation Takes up the Feminist Struggle," *Chicago Tribune* (August 3, 1992, 5): 1–2.

20. Ninety-five participants reflected on their experience in Nancy J. Berneking and Pamela Carter Joern, eds., *Re-Membering and Re-Imagining* (Cleveland: Pilgrim Press, 1995).

21. Pamela Carter Joern, "Introduction," in Berneking and Joern, eds., *Re-Membering and Re-Imagining*, p. xvii.

22. Gayle White, "Reacting to Re-Imagining," *Atlanta Journal Constitution* (May 21, 1994); Peter Steinfels, "Presbyterians Try to Resolve Long Dispute," *New York Times* (June 17, 1994, A): 24; Catherine Keller, "Inventing the Goddess: A Study in Ecclesiastical Backlash," *Christian Century* (April 6, 1994): 340; Bill Broadway, "Re-imagining Foments Uproar among Presbyterians," *Washington Post* (June 4, 1994): C:7.

23. See Nancy J. Berneking and Pamela Carter Joern, eds., *Re-Membering and Re-Imagining* (Cleveland: Pilgrim Press, 1995), Part Five, "Going On," pp. 179–234, and "Afterword," pp. 235–237.

24. A series of books trace the evolution of the right-wing attack on higher education beginning with NEH Chair William Bennett, *To Reclaim a Legacy: A Report on the Humanities in Higher Education* (Washington, D.C.: National Endowment for the Humanities, 1984). Subsequent books included Allan Bloom, *The Closing of the American Mind: How Higher Education Has Failed Democracy and Impoverished the Souls of Today's Students* (New York: Simon &

Schuster, 1987); Charles J. Sykes, *Profscam: Professors and the Demise of Higher Education* (Washington, D.C.: Regnery Gateway; New York, NY: Distributed to the trade by Kampmann & Co., 1988); Roger Kimball, *Tenured Radicals: How Politics Has Corrupted Higher Education* (New York: Harper & Row, 1990); and Dinesh D'Souza, *Illiberal Education: The Politics of Race and Class on Campus* (New York: Free Press, 1991).

25. National Council for Research on Women, *To Reclaim a Legacy of Diversity: Analyzing the "Political Correctness" Debates in Higher Education* (New York: National Council for Research on Women, 1993), p. 8.

26. Quoted in Patricia Aufderheide, ed., *Beyond PC: Toward a Politics of Understanding* (Saint Paul, MN: Graywolf Press, 1992), p. 227.

27. Richard Bernstein, "The Rising Hegemony of the Politically Correct," *New York Times* (October 28, 1990, Section 4): 1, 4; John Searle, "The Storm over the University," *New York Review of Books* (December 6, 1990): 34–42; John Leo, "The Academy's New Ayatollahs," *U.S. News & World Report* (December 10, 1990): 22; Amanda Foreman, "High Noon at the PC Corral," *New York Times*, Op-Ed. (March 20, 1991): A29; "Upside Down in the Groves of Academe," *Time* (April 1, 1991). For a fuller listing of related articles see the National Council for Research on Women, *To Reclaim a Legacy of Diversity*, pp. 45–47.

28. El-Khawas 1991, cited in NCROW, p. 9.

29. Sally Quinn, "The Death of Feminism," *Washington Post* (January 19, 1992, C): 1:4.

30. Scott Jaschik, "Philosophy Professor Portrays Her Feminist Colleagues as out of Touch and Relentlessly Hostile to the Family," *Chronicle of Higher Education* (January 15, 1992): 1, 16, 18.

31. Christina Hoff Sommers, "Hard-Line Feminists Guilty of Ms-Representation," *Wall Street Journal* (November 7, 1991): A14.

32. Christina Hoff Sommers, *Who Stole Feminism: How Women Have Betrayed Women* (New York: Simon & Schuster, 1994), pp. 51, 134.

33. "Camille Paglia and Suzanne Gordon Meet Face to Face," *Working Woman*, vol. 17, no. 2 (March 1992): 76–79, 106; Camille Paglia, "Ninnies, Pedants, Tyrants and Other Academics," *New York Times Book Review* (May 5, 1991): 29.

34. "Camille Paglia and Suzanne Gordon Meet Face to Face," *Working Woman*, vol. 17, no. 2 (March 1992).

35. Sommers, *Who Stole Feminism*, p. 245.

36. See Jesse Donahue, "Movement Scholarship and Feminism in the 1980s," *Women & Politics*, vol. 61, no. 2 (1996): 61–80.

37. See for example, Susan Brownmiller, *In Our Time*, Chapters 11 and 13, pp. 259–278, 295–325.

38. Katie Roiphe, *The Morning After: Sex, Fear, and Feminism on Campus* (Boston, MA.: Little, Brown, 1993). For an example of other generational voices, see Emilie Morgan, "Don't Call Me a Survivor," in Findlen, ed., *Listen up: Voices from the Next Feminist Generation*, pp. 177–184.

39. Paula Kamen, *Her Way: Young Women Remake the Sexual Revolution* (New York: Broadway Books, 2002).

40. For a detailed description of the Akron Conference from the point of view of participants who were unaware of the conflict before their arrival, see Ruby Jennie et al., "NWSA—Troubles Surface at Conference," *off our backs*, vol. 20 (August–September 1990): 1ff. The same issue printed "A Letter from Ruby Sales" spelling out her charges of racism and demand for restitution [*off our backs*, vol. 20 (August–September 1990): 25].

41. Patsy Schweickart, "Reflections on NWSA '90," *NWSAction* 3 (Fall 1990): 3–4ff., quotes on 4.

42. The debate on what had happened continued in feminist publications for some months. See Marlene Longenecker et al., "NWSA Conference: M. Longenecker Responds, R. Heidelbach Responds," *off our backs*, vol. 20 (October 1990): 24–25; Members of the Former NWSA Women of Color Caucus, "Institutionalized Racism and the National Women's Studies Association," *Sojourner: The Women's Forum*, vol. 15, no. 12 (August 1990): 8–9; "Time to Challenge Institutional Racism," *Sojourner: The Women's Forum*, vol. 16, no. 1 (September 1990): 6–7; "NWSA Responds to Charges of Racism," and Ann Froines, "Racism and NWSA—Uncovering More Questions," *Sojourner: The Women's Forum*, vol. 16, no. 2 (October 1990): 9–12; Trisha Franzen and Lois Rita Helmbold, "What Is to Be Done?" *Women's Review of Books*, vol. 8, no. 5 (February 1991): 29–30.

43. Musil describes an "organizational insight" that came to her at a meeting in 1991 when a member of the coordinating committee commented, "we don't have to pay any attention to bylaws, we're feminists." Author's interview with Caryn McTighe Musil, Washington, D.C., December 12, 1997.

44. Barbara Scott, "Speaking for Ourselves: From the Women of Color Association," *Women's Review of Books*, vol. VIII, no. 5 (February 1991): 29. Other contributors to this forum were Sondra O'Neale, Cynthia Tompkins, Chi-Kwan Ho, Sophie Liu, Andraea Smith, Bonnie Tu Smith, Ruby Sales, Jacqui Wade, Maria Lugones, and Rhoda Johnson. Two white women also contributed a discussion of NWSA's racism, celebrated the recent staff resignations as positive but insufficient, and called for NWSA "to apologize publicly." Trisha Franzen and Lois Rita Helmbold, "What Is to Be Done?" 29–30, quote on 30.

45. Christina Hoff Sommers attended the much diminished NWSA conference in 1993, in the aftermath of the Akron debacle. What she found was grist for her mill, and she described it with some glee in the *New Republic*: "The recent conference of the National Women's Studies Association (NWSA) in Austin, Texas, illustrated disturbing trends in the women's studies field. The reading of academic papers routinely takes a back seat to victim testimonials and New Age healing rituals at NWSA conferences; at the Austin conference, no more than 16 out of roughly 100 workshops and presentations could be called scholarly. On more and more campuses, the consciousness raisers are driving

out the scholars. Christina Hoff Sommers, "Sister Soldiers," *New Republic*, vol. 207 (October 5, 1992): 29–30ff., quote on 29.

46. See Linda Witt, Karen M. Paget, and Glenna Matthews, *Running as a Woman: Gender and Power in American Politics* (New York: Free Press, 1993), pp. 50–51; and Timothy M. Phelps and Helen Winternitz, *Capitol Games: Clarence Thomas, Anita Hill, and the Story of a Supreme Court Nomination* (New York: Hyperion, 1992), pp. 167–172, 236–244, 261–267, 295–298, 303, 432.

47. "Camille Paglia and Suzanne Gordon Meet Face to Face," 79.

48. "Sex and Power in the Office," *Wall Street Journal* (October 18, 1991): B1.

49. *New York Times* (July 13, 1992): 1.

50. Witt, Paget, and Matthews, *Running as a Woman*, p. 5.

51. Irwin N. Gertzog, *Congressional Women: Their Recruitment, Integration, and Behavior* (Westport, CT.: Praeger, 1995), p. 183.

52. Michael Specter, "Feminists Painfully Watching Holtzman and Ferraro Battle," *New York Times* (March 14, 1992, section 1): 1.

53. Ellen Malcolm, telephone interview with author, August 31, 2000.

54. See Faye Ginzburg, *Contested Lives: The Abortion Debate in an American Community* (Berkeley: University of California Press, 1989).

55. Alessandra Stanley, "Marilyn Quayle Says the 1960s Had a Flip Side," *New York Times* (August 20, 1992, A): 20.

56. Quoted in Maureen Dowd, "Hillary Clinton as Aspiring First Lady: Role Model or 'Hall Monitor' Type?" *New York Times* (May 18, 1992): A18.

57. *Cleveland Plain Dealer* (July 14, 1992): A4; and Anna Quindlen, *Thinking out Loud: On the Personal, the Political, the Public and the Private* (New York: Random House, 1993), pp. 197–198, quoted in Deborah L. Rhode, "Media Images, Feminist Issues," *Signs: Journal of Women in Culture and Society*, vol. 20, no. 3 (Spring 1995): 698.

58. See Laura Blumenfeld, "Ultimate Feminist, Hillary Rodham Clinton," *Cosmopolitan* (May 1994): 213.

59. See Kenneth T. Walsh, "How Hillary Clinton Plans a Bold Recasting of the Job Description for a President's Spouse," *U.S. News and World Report* (January 25, 1993): 46; Barbara Burrell, *Public Opinion, the First Ladyship, and Hillary Rodham Clinton* (New York and London: Garland Publishing, 1997); Joyce Milton, *The First Partner: Hillary Rodham Clinton* (New York: William Morrow, 1999); Gail Sheehy, *Hillary's Choice* (New York: Random House, 1999); and Bob Woodward, *The Agenda: Inside the Clinton White House* (New York: Simon & Schuster, 1994).

60. Rhode, *Media Images, Feminist Issues*, p. 699; Maurine Dowd, "Hillary Rodham Clinton Strikes a New Pose and Multiplies Her Images," *New York Times* (December 12, 1993): E3.

61. Rush H. Limbaugh, *See, I Told You So* (New York: Pocket Books, 1993).

62. Faulkner had been accepted to the Citadel until officials learned that she was female. That rejection prompted her suit. See Catherine S. Manegold, *In Glory's Shadow: Shannon Faulkner, the Citadel, and a Changing America* (New

York: Alfred A. Knopf, 2000); Laura Fairchild Brodie, *Breaking out: VMI and the Coming of Women* (New York: Pantheon Books, 2000); Susan Faludi, "The Naked Citadel," *New Yorker,* vol. 70, no. 27 (September 5, 1994): 62–81; and Elizabeth Fox-Genovese, "Save the Males?" *National Review,* vol. 46, no. 14 (August 1, 1994): 49–52.

63. Phyllis Schlafley, "Open Letter to VMI Alumni." *Eagle Forum,* Alton, Illinois (June 11, 1996).

64. Deborah L. Siegel, "Reading Between the Waves: Feminist Historiography in a 'Postfeminist' Moment," in Leslie Heywood and Jennifer Drake, eds., *Third Wave Agenda: Being Feminist, Doing Feminism* (Minneapolis: University of Minnesota Press, 1997), p. 62.

65. Leslie Heywood and Jennifer Drake, "We Learn America Like a Script: Activism in the Third Wave; or, Enough Phantoms of Nothing," in Heywood and Drake, eds., *Third Wave Agenda,* p. 48.

66. See Haywood and Drake, eds., *Third Wave Agenda,* especially Deborah L. Siegel, "Reading Between the Waves: Feminist Historiography in a 'Post-Feminist' Moment," pp. 55-82, and Carolyn Sorisio, "A Tale of Two Feminisms: Power and Victimization in Contemporary Feminist Debate," pp. 134-149.

67. E-mail message to Re-Imagining office, July 26, 2001.

68. Anita Shreve, *Women Together, Women Alone: The Legacy of the Consciousness-Raising Movement* (New York: Viking, 1989), p. 53.

69. Paula Kiamen, *Her Way,* chapter 5, quote on p. 117.

70. For example, John Tierney derided "Take Your Daughter to Work" day in an op-ed piece: "I'm sure there are guys out there pressuring their partners to become housewives, but I don't personally know any. I do, however, know men angry at their wives for not going off to work. One marriage ended largely because of the husband's fury at this wife's refusal to go back to her job as a lawyer once their kids were in school." "The Truth of the Myth About Mom," *New York Times* (April 26, 2002), B: 1.

71. See Deborah Rhode, *Speaking of Sex: The Denial of gender Inequality* (Cambridge: Harvard University Press, 1997), pp. 4-5, 146.

72. Rhode, *Speaking of Sex,* p. 240.

73. See http://www.wfnet.org/.

74. See the Center for Women's Global Leadership website at http://www.cwgl.rutgers.edu.

75. See the WEDO website: www.wedo.org.

76. Robin Morgan, "The NGO Forum: Good News and Bad," *Women's Studies Quarterly,* vol. 24, no. 1, 2 (Spring/Summer 1996): 49. See entire special issue: "Beijing and Beyond: Toward the Twenty-first Century of Women," *Women's Studies Quarterly,* vol. 24, no. 1, 2 (Spring/Summer 1996).

76. See, for example, Charlotte Bunch, with Peggy Antrobus, Samantha Frost, and Niamh Reilly, "International Networking for Women's Human Rights," in Michael Edwards and John Gaventa, eds., *Global Citizen Action* (Boulder: Lynne Rienner Publishers, 2001), pp. 217-229.

INDEX

ABOUT THE AUTHOR

Sara Evans is Distinguished McKnight University Professor of History at the University of Minnesota where she has taught women's history since 1976. She has served as the director of the Center for Advanced Feminist Studies, chair of the Department of History, on the Board of Editors of *Feminist Studies*, and on the national boards of the American Studies Association and the Organization of American Historians. Born in a Methodist parsonage in South Carolina, Evans was a student activist in the civil rights and anti-war movements and she has been an active feminist since 1967.

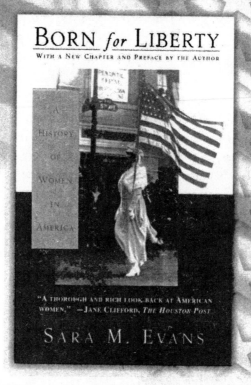

"A thorough and rich look back at American women."
—*The Houston Post*

From the indigenous women of the sixteenth-century wilderness to the dual-role career women and mothers of today, *Born for Liberty* brings American womanhood to center stage. In exploring the lives of pioneers and slaves, immigrants and factory workers, executives and homemakers, Sara M. Evans sheds light on their contributions to the shaping of America and transforms our notions about political participation and active citizenship.

"This chronicle of women in America is so interesting, informative and engagingly written that I found myself unable to put it down until I had completed it."
—*Greensboro News & Record*